The Pillar of Isis

22.11.92

The Pillar of Isis

A Practical Manual on the Mysteries
of the Goddess

Vivienne O'Regan

Aquarian/Thorsons
An Imprint of HarperCollins*Publishers*

Aquarian/Thorsons
An Imprint of HarperCollins*Publishers*
77–85 Fulham Palace Road,
Hammersmith, London W6 8JB

Published by The Aquarian Press 1992
1 3 5 7 9 10 8 6 4 2

A catalogue record for this book
is available from the British Library

ISBN 1 85538 236 9

Typeset by Harper Phototypesetters Limited,
Northampton, England
Printed in Great Britain by
Mackays of Chatham, Kent

Contents

To my beloved husband, Crys,

and

to the memory of Dion Fortune, Priestess of Isis

Acknowledgements

This book owes much to those many people whom I have worked alongside in the mysteries throughout the years. In addition I would like to give special thanks to:

The Reverends Olivia and Lawrence Durdin-Robertson, founders of the Fellowship of Isis, for years of inspiration and encouragement and wonderful rituals and exciting 'seminars' at Clonegal Castle. Also thanks to Sue and Simon for their hospitality and kindness during my visits to Ireland.

My past and present students who tried and tested these exercises and meditations. Also to the members and associates of the Lyceum of Isis-Sophia who taught me much about ritual work and positive group dynamics.

Brian Burgess for reading the manuscript, challenging me on certain points, and generally acting as 'mid-husband' for its birth, and to Cass for proof reading.

Elizabeth Taylor for her chapter illustrations which captured the spirit of my rough ideas and meditations as well as working to such a tight schedule. Thanks also to Philip Clayton-Gore for taking a sheet of scribbled notes and drawings and transforming them into the original design for the Pillar shown in Chapter 14 and for Elizabeth Taylor's last minute modifications to same. To my Aunt Gayle for additional diagrams for the text.

Tracy Hicks, whose search for the Goddess led her to ask me on our first meeting to write some lessons for her. This resulted in the course which inspired this book. And for the love and friendship which has endured between us.

Sunflower, for sharing ideas about solar Goddesses, suggesting references, wonderful postcards and being a terrific friend.

Felicity Wombwell, Naomi Ozaniec, and Caitlín Matthews for sisterly support and encouragement through all the stages of the book's growth, and John Matthews for always knowing the answers!

My teachers in the Western Mysteries: Steve Lomax, Dolores Ashcroft-Nowicki and Gareth Knight for instilling a sense of discipline and purpose as well as facilitating my quest. Also to Jean and Zac and the Companions of the Rainbow Bridge, for years of wonderful magic.

Janval Phagen and members of Owl-light coven for showing me the simple beauty of the Craft of the Wise.

My parents, for a million things, including raising me to question and to dream and to be my own person before it became fashionable.

Dion Fortune, whose works led me back to the Goddess, and who through the years has been a demanding yet wonderful source of magic and inspiration.

Diana Whitmore, Judith Firman and Kunderke Kevlin for being superb guides for my training in Psychosynthesis. To Patti Howe, Will Parfitt, Carole Madden and Elizabeth Rothenberger for stimulating conversations.

Finally, though not the least, to Crys for spiritual and physical nourishment and for being a dream come true.

Introduction

This is, first and foremost, a practical manual, although there will also be a degree of theoretical material. It is not my intention to attempt to chronicle in depth the forms of the ancient mysteries of the Goddess or to examine the forms of the current resurgence of the Goddess's mysteries in the present; these are in themselves vast subjects which have been adequately dealt with by other writers. However, I hope to present to my readers something of an overview of the forms that her mysteries have taken and are taking in the present and to refer them to the Bibliography for further reading to enable them to enhance their understanding of the subject.

The aim of this book is to provide a structured series of practical exercises based upon the Mysteries of the Goddess. This material was initially developed as a correspondence course for use within the Lyceum of Isis-Sophia of the Stars, a sister-centre of the international organisation devoted to the Goddess, the Fellowship of Isis.

Although the name of Isis is used, the Fellowship is not only concerned with the mysteries of the Egyptian pantheon but is also multi-traditional and multi-cultural. It was founded in 1976 by Olivia Durdin-Robertson, her brother Lawrence Durdin-Robertson and his wife Pamela, following many years of private worship. It quickly attracted women and men from many countries who were attuned to the Goddess. The Durdin-Robertsons cleared the basement of their castle which serves as the Foundation Centre in Clonegal, Ireland, and slowly transformed it into a temple to the Goddess in her myriad forms. At a very early stage the non-hierarchical structure of the Fellowship led to the founding of sister-centres of the Fellowship, called

Iseums, and the formation of a priesthood of the Goddess. The early ordinations were conducted by Olivia and Lawrence Durdin-Robertson, but as the network spread others were empowered to ordain in the Goddess's name.

In 1986 Olivia Durdin-Robertson was inspired to formulate the College of Isis within the structure of the Fellowship, and to invite a number of Iseums to change their focus. They became teaching centres, called lyceums, utilising the rituals written by Olivia over the years to form the core of those teachings. To those individuals she invited to take up this work, she granted a further initiation that they would function as Hierophants of the Fellowship, a title which, until that time, was held only by Olivia and her brother. I was the College's first Hierophant in Britain and Isis-Sophia was its first active Lyceum. The work undertaken by the Lyceum through both the correspondence course which is the basis for this manual and the active group work led to the ordination of many of its members and the eventual founding of their own Iseums and Lyceums.

Writing began on the course in 1986 to fulfil a need that had come to my attention after receiving numerous enquiries from people who wished to work actively with the mysteries of the Goddess but who had no access to a Centre of the Fellowship. They expressed the need for a degree of guidance in their studies and part of the aim of the course was to provide that guidance, to answer questions and generally to facilitate their process of exploring these mysteries under the aegis of the College of Isis.

My own work with the Goddess began long before my admission to the Fellowship in 1977. I cannot recall a time when she was not present in my life. As a child I was very interested in Greek and Egyptian mythology and through the influence of my Mother, herself a gifted psychic, always appreciated the hidden side of life. Much of this went 'underground' during my adolescence to emerge again in the early 1970s when I reconnected to my deep desire to explore the unknown through both the investigation of various esoteric traditions and the quest for self-knowledge that manifested through an on-going interest in psychology.

After a period of experiential work with various groups within the humanistic psychology movement, I formally trained as a therapist in Psychosynthesis. I was attracted to the rich symbolic content inherent within this trans-personal psychology. I believed then, as now, that a synthesis was possible between the teachings of the transpersonal psychologies and those mysteries of the Goddess held in trust by the native and hermetic tradition of the West.

I had found with working in various esoteric groups during the 70s and early 80s a tendency for people to focus on external results and on seeking to change the circumstances of their lives through occult means. This was, however, coupled with an unwillingness to focus within and to gain self-awareness. This tendency to shy away from the contents of one's own unconscious I attributed to the negative conditioning of our Western society. Therefore, as my work in the mysteries developed and I began to teach others, I incorporated material drawn from the various psychological systems I had worked with to encourage a gentle exploration of the self.

The key to the Goddess's mysteries has always been 'know thyself' and this awareness can only come from honest self-examination. Psychological health and balance are of prime importance to this work. Why? Because in coming to a better relationship with our own inner selves we come into a better relationship with those about us and with the world. This is the path of the Goddess, one of positive relationship on all levels including healing our relationship with the Earth herself.

This book is structured in two main sections. Part 1 covers various topics centred around the acquisition of basic skills with which to approach the later work. These include techniques of relaxation, rhythmic breathing, concen-tration, visualisation and meditation which provide the opportunity for the reader to develop or refine these skills and to strengthen and clarify the links between their conscious concrete mind and the more abstract levels of consciousness.

Certainly many people coming to this book will already have some experience of these basic skills. It is, however, quite important that the exercises be approached in a systematic manner as a manual and for the reader, through this, literally to 'tune in' to the pattern of energies being worked with. It is also important for each reader to develop an on-going relationship with the Inner Temple of the Goddess which has been the source of inspiration for the material in this book.

In order to derive maximum benefit, a high degree of discipline is required both in regularity of practice and in maintaining a daily journal record of the results of your practices along with relevant insights, dreams, etc. It is through consistent practice and the recording of experiences that the process of ordering thoughts and integrating insights gained in meditation into one's daily life is facilitated, along with the development and refinement of natural 'psychic' talents. Students of the original course with daily meditations took, on average, about 2 years to work through the exercises. Obviously my readers will set their own pace but for maximum benefit it is suggested that you take about a month of daily practice to work through the material of each chapter.

While it may be said that anyone interested enough in the subject of meditation and the mysteries of the Goddess is likely to already have some sense of awareness of inner levels of experience, the ability to work effectively with impressions, insights and information from such inner sources does not come easily. All too often, people will have these experiences randomly, and when they do occur they are unable satisfactorily to understand the relevance of such material. This can often lead to a degree of 'ungrounded-ness' which can manifest in a variety of ways including a sense of disconnection from physical reality and the inability to actualise these insights to enrich both their own life experience and the collective.

For others, the difficulty might be that these experiences occur very rarely and sporadically or that they feel blocked. While it must be said that the systematic following of such a course of practical work cannot guarantee positive results, it will provide a setting wherein the links between the conscious and unconscious mind may be enhanced. All too often it is the negative input from parents and the environment which suppresses natural psychic experience. Those centres closed down by the attitudes and pressures of 20th-century life and adulthood can be re-opened through gradual and sustained stimulation in a way which will enhance one's life.

In Part 2, the practitioner moves on from these basic exercises to the specific task of making individual contact with the Inner Temple of Isis which is a place of teaching and a repository of the love and wisdom of the Goddess Isis. Part of the process involves building within the aura (subtle body) of the practitioner the Pillar of Isis, which serves as an individual temple of the Goddess linked to the subtle energy centres of the body.

For many drawn to the mysteries of the Goddess, the quest for relationship to her goes hand in hand with the desire to give to others, whether they be human, plant or animal, or to the Earth as a whole. While it is beyond the scope of this book to include training in healing or counselling skills there is an emphasis on the sharing of the energies connected with through the meditations in the spirit of service.

Within the final two chapters guidelines are given for the reader to take work with the Goddess further. A pattern is laid out which allows for the established Pillar of Isis to be used as a base from which to work. The reader may either undertake work utilising the elemental, planetary and zodiacal correspondences given herein, or choose to employ the rituals of the Fellowship's Liturgy (which link to various manifestations of the Goddess as expressed through these correspondences) to explore these energies. While not everyone has the facilities (or the desire) to enact a ritual in a physical form it is possible, through reading, meditating and structured meditation, for the reader to gain the ritual's essence.

In the last chapter the theme of group work and vocation to the priesthood of the Goddess is explored. For those who might wish to enter into training for ordination, whether under the aegis of the Fellowship of Isis or elsewhere, guidance is given along with contact addresses of some individuals and groups offering such training.

Although the inspiration for this book comes from the College of Isis, I do not claim to be working with strictly Egyptian methods. My own training in this and previous lives has been eclectic and this, combined with the spirit of the Fellowship, has been incorporated herein. It must also be said that the views and meditations are my own and, although they form an integral part of my Lyceum's work, they should not be considered reflective of other Fellowship members' views.

Vivienne O'Regan
January 1992

Part 1

Chapter 1

Basic Principles

The primordial images that exist depicting our forebears' concept of Deity and the Creator are all female. Veneration of male deities came later and for a long time these were depicted in a dependent relationship to the Goddess as son/lover/consort. The usurpation of the Goddess came in some parts of the world with invasion and in other areas by a slower process whereby people came to experience the Goddess primarily in terms of her relationship to the Sky-Father, King of the Gods. With this came a general undermining of the role of women in society and their loss of rights.

While the pantheistic religions did retain the Goddess in a subjected form, the monotheistic religions which arose from the Middle East, although originally themselves worshippers of the Great Mother, began to identify the Goddess as their greatest spiritual enemy equating her worship with idolatry and evil. The pages of the Old Testament are filled with the battles against the followers of the Goddess.

Despite this there is little doubt that the ancient mysteries of the Goddess have had a formative effect upon the philosophical heritage of our Western culture. The Eleusinian Mysteries venerated the Greek Goddesses Demeter and Persephone and the mysteries of the cycle of life, death and rebirth. It is believed they were founded in about 1400 BC and managed to survive until around AD 400 when they were suppressed by Theodosius in his campaign to destroy all who did not accept the Christian faith. The mysteries of the Egyptian Goddess Isis also extended far beyond the bounds of ancient Egypt and flourished in the Graeco-Roman world.

Although recent years have seen a great resurgence of interest in the Goddess it is not true that in the intervening time she has been 'lost'. Her veneration and the teachings associated with her mysteries went 'underground' and have continued even within the patriarchal religions as secret traditions.

It is also important to keep in mind that the Goddess exists in her own terms and is not an anthropomorphic projection of human consciousness, matriarchal or otherwise, that has been overthrown with the coming of patriarchal consciousness. Deity is ultimately beyond gender and, as it has been said, 'God is God, not man; Goddess is Goddess, not woman'. This means that, although we may clothe the Goddess in the form of woman or the Earth, Moon or Sun, she is not these things. As Caitlín Matthews states in *Elements of the Goddess*, 'the Goddess is primarily a spiritual channel reaching down into our soul'.

The Qabalah, the mystical tradition of the Judaic religion, offers a structure for knowing the unknowable by formulating the concept that although the Creator is beyond our awareness, the process of Creation can be likened to a series of emanations which culminate in the physical universe we perceive about us. The polarity of Deity into the relative forms of God and Goddess occurs at a very abstract level of this process, yet it can be approached through these forms allowing that which lies behind form to be glimpsed. This is a controversial subject and I do appreciate that there are many readers who will have their own concepts of Deity which may be radically different from mine. But I hope that we still can meet on the common ground of veneration of the Divine Feminine.

Certainly the Goddess in her many forms is undergoing a resurgence in the West. I use the term 'West' very deliberately as this phenomenon is taking place primarily in Western Europe, North America and Australia. In much of the world the worship of the Goddess has continued for the most part unhindered by Christianity or the advent of scientific materialism. The Hindu and Buddhist pantheons are rich in Goddesses and those religions allow for her worship. The native tradition of Africa is also rich in Goddesses and in South and Central America (and areas of the Southern United States with a large Latin-American population) religions such as Voodoo, Santeria and Macumba give veneration to various Goddesses. These latter religions, although their mythology and pantheons are for the most part derived from African sources, have freely attributed their Goddesses to various popular Catholic Saints.

A variety of factors have attributed to the 'rediscovery' of the religion of the Goddess in the West. One cannot doubt the part played in this by the feminist movement as women began to seek to reconnect with their spirituality outside the framework of the male-dominated Judeo-Christian/Islamic religions. Women began to form study groups to investigate the religion of the Goddess and then began to express this connection by establishing women's mystery groups. Books began to appear written from both the historical and the experiential perspective, enabling women to connect to the Goddess as a symbol of women's emerging consciousness.

Many of these women's groups utilised some of the symbols and rituals of European witchcraft which itself had only recently re-emerged with the repeal of the Witchcraft Act in England in the early 1950s. These feminist covens differ from the mainstream Wiccan movement by their tendency to distance themselves from the Divine Masculine in any aspect. However, in a movement with as much energy as the Women's Spirituality Movement, little is static and many women, after gaining a sense of their own strength and relationship to the Goddess, are discovering that not all aspects of 'the God' are anti-Goddess or anti-woman.

Another important factor in the process of the Goddess's re-emergence is the ecology movement and the growing awareness of the plight of the Earth. This reverence for the Earth has also stirred the sleeping consciousness within humankind of the Earth as Mother. Here, with the appreciation of Earth as a living organism, a route back to the ancient reverence of Earth as Goddess has been made.

Also, although Sigmund Freud may seem an odd champion of the Goddess, there is little doubt that the development of psychoanalysis with its emphasis upon the 'unconscious' as the repository of all that is repressed/

dark/unknown once more gave voice to dreams which have always been a vehicle of the Goddess's mysteries. Following on from Freud are the works of Carl Jung and his successors which explored in depth many traditional symbols including the Divine Feminine principle. However, the shortcomings of the psychological worldview are many, not least their tendency to attempt to reduce spiritual philosophy and Deity to a creation of the human collective conscious in the form of 'archetypes'.

An interesting development emerging from the humanistic and transpersonal schools of psychology in recent years has been an awareness of the great value for both the individual and the collective of the use of 'sacred drama'. These are enacted as rites of passage and a way of healing the psyche which harks back to the mysteries of ancient Egypt and Greece for inspiration.

Survival of Goddess Worship in the West

The idea that awareness of the Goddess has been suppressed in the West until 'rediscovered' by the Jungians or the feminist and ecology movements is, however, a fallacy. While individuals within these movements are approaching the Goddess with great enthusiasm they are often totally unaware of the way in which her mysteries have been preserved throughout the centuries.

For there has always been a flame of her mysteries alight which has been held in trust by those who revered the Goddess in secret ways. These were (and are) the witches, magicians, mystics, Rosicrucians, visionaries, poets, musicians and artists whose Muse was the Goddess. These people have, each in their own way, continued to venerate her throughout the centuries secretly upon hearths and within glades, in temples of the magical arts, in the brushes of artists, in written and spoken word, and in music.

The Goddess even managed to survive within the Roman Catholic Church as the cult of the Virgin Mary which flourished throughout the Middle Ages, taking into itself many characteristics of the Isian Mysteries. This process was enhanced by the medieval troubadours who were influenced by the remnants of the Egyptian mystery schools they encountered in the Middle East during the Crusades.

Under the patronage of Queen Eleanor of Aquitaine during the 12th-century, there arose the cult of romantic love which served to idealise women as vehicles of the Divine Feminine. Thus, in a society where women were considered property, the tradition of priestesses as mediators of the Goddess continued.

In Europe the Goddess remained in the hearts of ordinary people even with the influence of the church. The early Church of Rome carried on in the tradition of the Roman Empire by not attempting to change the religious practices of conquered peoples. Instead, they absorbed them through tacking on their own deities. In the case of the Church they did not, for the most part, attempt to halt 'pagan' practices and festivals but found ways in which to assimilate them into the Church and then change their orientation towards Christ, the Virgin Mary and various saints. However, this was a double-edged sword for the Church as it served to keep alive the old traditions, albeit often in distorted forms.

There was a huge backlash against the remnants of Goddess worship in the form of the witchcraft persecutions which began in the late 15th century with the Pope's proclamation against witchcraft and the publication of *The Malleus Malleficarum* (The Witches Hammer). This kindled a hysteria which continued for nearly 300 years and resulted in the deaths of an estimated nine million women and men. It must be said that, although in the United States witches and Goddess followers have been able to gather together to worship with some openness, the memory of the 'burning times' is close to the surface in Britain and Europe, and fear still exists along with a subtle form of prejudice and persecution.

The Legacy of Dion Fortune

As I have stated above, the veneration of the Goddess continued within magical groups which had their foundation in the Renaissance and took their inspiration from the ancient mystery schools. In some temples of the magical arts earlier this century, a conscious and deliberate effort was made to revitalise the mysteries of the Goddess in the collective conscious of the West. One such operation was chronicled as fiction by the writer and magician Dion Fortune. Written in the 1930s, her novels *The Sea Priestess* and *Moon Magic* contain a fictionalised account of a series of magical workings undertaken by Dion Fortune and her inner circle of initiates within the Society of the Inner Light. The principle aim of these workings was to re-introduce the Goddess's mysteries and to revitalise the dynamic relationship between women and men. To this end, they employed the mysteries of the Goddess Isis.

My own relationship to Dion Fortune began in the early 1970s when I discovered her writings, which included her novels. Working with the images she provided I was able to make my way to the Temple of the Goddess Isis as it exists upon the inner realms of reality and made the connection which eventually resulted in the transmissions of the meditations which form the heart of the Pillar of Isis.

Dion Fortune died suddenly in 1946. After her death she communicated through the vehicle of automatic writing the fact that she had died with her work incomplete. She felt especially that she had neglected the task of training those of her own sex. 'I had not trained a successor. In the work of Isis that successor has to be a woman.' ('The Death of Vivien Le Fay Morgan', *Aspects of Occultism*). In answer to this her mentor and Inner Plane Guide, the Priest of the Moon, states: 'You have failed in part . . . Yet as the work has been good in standard, it will not die, but following seeming defeat will rise again in another manner.'

It is my personal view that there is a connection between Dion Fortune's sentiments and the visionary experiences (that by coincidence began in 1946) of a young Anglo-Irish visionary and writer, Olivia Durdin-Robertson, one of the co-founders of the Fellowship of Isis. Her mystical encounters with the Goddesses Isis and Dana (the Irish-Celtic Mother Goddess) provided her with the vision of a pattern of light raying out from the castle at Clonegal and with seeds which laid the groundwork 30 years later for the formal formation of the Fellowship of Isis. There is today a thriving network of members and 'sister-centres', an ordained priesthood of both women and men, and the ancient College of Isis has now been refounded under the aegis of the Fellowship, which could be perceived as one fulfilment of Dion Fortune's dream.

Basic Techniques

The remainder of this chapter will introduce basic exercises which will serve to build up the skills needed by the practitioner to approach the inner mysteries. Each meditation session should begin with a period of relaxation and rhythmic breathing. This will serve to centre you and prepare for the work ahead.

The benefits of relaxation have been widely reported and written about and I shall not reiterate them here except to say that stress and worry have a definite effect upon the physical body in the form of tensed muscles, and upon the emotions which, it is now considered, are at the root of much malaise and illness. When people are tense it serves to block the more subtle input and thus makes meditation difficult, if not impossible. Because the mind and body are not separate but a continuum, the relaxation of physical muscles also induces relaxation of the mind and emotions. Attaining a state of relaxation on a regular basis brings long-term positive effects for the body and mind. This period of time taken at the outset of each practice for relaxation and measured breathing allows you to effectively 'switch off' from everyday concerns and opens you to higher and deeper levels of consciousness.

Posture and Environment

It is important that you have privacy and freedom from distractions for your practice. Although it is possible to relax, meditate and visualise in very noisy surroundings, it is not advised that you do so. However, once you have gained proficiency you should be able to use these skills in any situation.

I would suggest that you do not lie down for your meditation as it is all too easy to fall asleep or into such a deeply relaxed state that you lose consciousness of the meditation. Yoga positions can be in themselves a strain if you are not used to them, so I suggest you adopt the position known as the 'god form' posture which is based on Egyptian statues. To do this, sit upright in a fairly firm chair making sure you keep your back straight. Avoid being too rigid as your spine has a natural curve and our intention is to decrease tension, not to put strain on your back. Your feet should be flat on the floor or, if this is uncomfortable because your chair is too high, then use a cushion or low footstool under your feet. Your knees should be fairly close together and your hands resting easily in your lap. Be careful not to cross either your legs or arms as this will disrupt certain subtle etheric currents. Once you are seated close your eyes.

Relaxation

There are various ways of reaching this state of poised relaxation. I will suggest three methods – two standard forms of progressive relaxation and one form based upon a basic self-hypnosis technique. You can experiment with each of these to find the one that suits you best. Many libraries carry books on relaxation and stress reduction which will suggest alternatives.

At first you can expect that it will take some time to relax but as you gain proficiency the time will reduce gradually. You may like to read out the meditations in this book onto an audio tape or to play soothing music in the background as an aid to relaxation.

1 Beginning with the feet, contract the muscles as strongly as you can for a few moments and then let go. Do this a couple of times, being aware that as you let go of the contraction your muscles are relaxing. Then move on to the muscles in your lower leg . . . upper legs . . . buttocks . . . abdomen . . . lower back . . . chest . . . upper back . . . shoulders . . . arms . . . hands . . . neck . . . face . . . scalp. As you complete the sequence sweep your attention back over your body and relax any part which still feels tense.

2 Begin by imagining that a feeling of being comfortably warm and heavy comes into your feet as a wave of relaxation rises up through them and then into your lower legs, knees, upper legs and thighs and continue the sequence as the wave of relaxation continues into your buttocks, abdomen, lower and upper back and chest, and continue as No 1 above, finishing with the

scalp. Again, conclude the sequence by being aware of your entire body and then focusing your attention on any part which is not relaxed.

3 Repeat to yourself or very softly aloud the following series of phrases. Remain aware of each part of your body as you mention it, and deliberately 'let go' of each muscle group in turn as you become relaxed.

I am now going to relax. I am going to relax my entire body. I am now beginning to relax. I am now relaxing the muscles in the top of my head . . . they are relaxed. I am now relaxing in my face – my forehead, eyes, cheeks, mouth and jaw. They are relaxed.

Continue this sequences as before, mentioning each part of the body and affirming that it is relaxed. Conclude with the affirmation that your entire body is relaxed.

Rhythmic Breathing

Changing the rate and depth of your breathing is a powerful way of inducing altered states of consciousness. There is a complete branch of yoga based on breathing called Pranayama. However, for our purposes we are avoiding the more complex and advanced techniques and instead use a method entitled the Fourfold Breath. This will set up a rhythm for a more complete cycle of breathing than usual which serves to deepen the relaxation of your body and mind and is a valuable aid in preparing for visualisation and meditation.

It is very important that you remember not to strain, force or over-breathe. On the in-breath allow your lungs to fill with air and your chest to expand. Then exhale as completely as possible.

As with the relaxation you will probably find that this method of breathing is a little strange but with practice it will come quite naturally. So with this breathing pattern you inhale to a count of 8, hold your breath to a count of 4 then exhale to a count of 8 and hold your breath out for a count of 4. If these lengths are too long then vary the count to suit yourself.

Meditation

There are many types of meditation, both structured and unstructured. These range from the deceptively simple counting of breath, emptying the mind of all thought, or concentration on a symbol, idea or object which can be as simple as a flower or as complex as the beautiful tankas of Tibetan Buddhism. Meditation is something which needs to be experienced rather than thought about. However, two basic and accessible guides to the history, effects and various meditation techniques are to be found in Naomi Humphrey's *Meditation: The Inner Way* (Aquarian 1987) and Lawrence LeShan's *How to Meditate* (Turnstone Press 1983).

Most of the meditation work we shall be doing will be through the creation of certain symbolic images, but in preparation for this it we shall explore types of meditation which require concentration.

The first type of meditation involves the holding in the mind a key idea and then following trains of thought associated with it. At first, you can expect to find yourself having thoughts based on material you have read or heard, but as you persevere you will get to deeper levels and your ideas will become realisations. You will find that an idea or awareness has become real for you, not merely an intellectual exercise. Such a realisation becomes a part of one's consciousness.

It is said that there is a pool of wisdom and knowledge that has been created through the years which the student can, with diligent practice, tap into and further contribute to. Insight and wisdom can thus be gained without reference to verbal or written instructions.

For this first phase you should select a key phrase from the following list (or select any phrase from inspirational writings/poetry which appeals to you and which conveys a theme of spiritual or transpersonal thought) and spend about 4 to 5 days on each phrase. This will allow you enough time to go beneath the surface of the phrase.

Suggestions for meditation:

All Goddesses are one Goddess . . . in whose nature all things are found.

I am everything that was, that is, that shall be . . . Nor has any mortal ever been able to discover what lies under my veil.

The Earth as Gaia – a living being.

The Goddess as Creator.

Zero: the mathematical symbol for the primary unborn nature of the feminine.

In these primary exercises you should aim to meditate daily for about an average of 15 to 20 minutes. As you progress through this manual there will be times when the nature of the meditation will demand longer periods, but even then a daily period of 30 to 40 minutes should suffice.

It is advisable to do your meditation practice at roughly the same time each day. This gets you into the habit of daily practice. Although doing meditation work in the morning before breakfast is often advised, this doesn't suit everyone. You have to find a time which suits your lifestyle. It is best, however, to meditate before eating a meal as the process of digestion tends to close down the psychic centres.

Opening and Closing

It is quite appropriate to mark the beginning and end of your meditation sessions with some form of ritual act or gesture. One way to do this is by lighting a candle as you sit down to begin, and then extinguishing it as you finish.

A simple ritual gesture which can be employed before you commence and end each meditation is the 'Opening and Closing of the Veil'. This is representative of the Veil of the Goddess or the veil between the outer and inner worlds. This is done by putting your hands together in front of you and then sweeping them open as if you were miming the opening of a pair of curtains. The closing sign is the opposite action.

As you finish, make sure you ground yourself and come completely back to normal waking consciousness. You can do this by taking a good look around you at the physical objects in the room. Eating and drinking something after the conclusion of the session is helpful in aiding the closing down process. Also, writing up notes of the experience will serve to earth the experience and this should be done before the memory fades.

THE DIARY RECORD

An important part of this work is keeping a written record of your meditation practices in the form of a personal journal. Besides keeping note of the formal session the journal is also a place to record significant dreams, insights and events in your inner and outer life.

It is advisable that you make a formal entry for each meditation session. Each should be headed with the date and include the time and length of the practice. It is also a good idea to make a brief commentary on how you feel at the outset of the session and note the environment you are meditating in. Be sure to note the subject of your meditation and follow with a brief report of the practice including any insights, realisations, images, etc. A specimen extract follows:

Tuesday September 23rd 1986 7.00 – 7.17 p.m. BST
  Self: a little tense following journey home but looking forward to session.
  Env: bedroom. Room slightly chilly but awareness of this passed.
  Med: The Goddess as Creator.
  After brief initial resistance found that the relaxation and breathing exercise went well. Thoughts did stray a bit but on the whole was able to stay with the subject. While meditating found myself aware of the depths of space being the womb wherein stars and planets are born continuously. Goddess as matrix. Aware that in the background of my mind early programming of seeing the Creator as male popping into my thoughts. Have a brief image of a spiral galaxy.
  Wednesday September 24th 7.10 – 7.26 p.m. BST
  Self: OK
  Env: as above
  Med: as above
  Lots of resistance to practice and as such felt quite dull and only managed to complete the relaxation and breathing.

Concentration

Once you have worked through the list of key phrases you should move on to the next section of this chapter which contains another very basic exercise – concentrating the mind upon a simple image, first externally and then transferring it to an internal image held in the 'mind's eye'. This type of exercise attempts to promote a state of one-pointedness which creates within the mind a focusing of consciousness with clarity, lucidity and potential energy. This is the result of inducing an altered state of consciousness wherein the separateness between the viewer and the object dissolves and the normal boundaries of time and space disappear. This practice is called Dharana within the Eastern tradition and is one of the eight 'limbs' of Yoga.

The creation of mental images is an activity that we are all engaged in throughout our daily lives, although we may not be aware of the process unless it is actually focused upon. As young children we learn to recognise different visual elements in our external environment and subsequently we internalise a vast catalogue of images. Later on these become connected in our minds with sounds in the form of speech and then as words in reading and writing. You may have memories of this learning process from your own childhood or have observed it in children. As we master language it distances us from the original image and the process becomes largely unconscious and very much speeded up. It certainly is possible to notice this image-making and connecting in action, for example, when we dream, daydream, evoke memories, read a novel or otherwise stimulate this function.

For some the ability to create mental images is so well developed that they need only shut their eyes to see quite clear pictures. Others do not exactly see the image or scene but have a strong sense of it and know what it looks like. If you feel you are unable to visualise, please do not be discouraged. Visualising is a skill which we all have, but, as with the psychic faculties mentioned in the introduction, this has often been suppressed by environmental factors. Practice and patience will develop the ability to visualise more clearly.

If you are lucky enough to be able to visualise at will this meditation should serve as an opportunity to enhance your ability to concentrate and sustain a mental image. Please do not be discouraged if you find it difficult to visualise an image as requested or even to hold your attention on the image externally. At times the holding of the mind for even a few seconds on a fixed image can be excruciating. The mind is often likened to a lively monkey, moving as it does so rapidly from thought to thought. Even with the earlier meditations in this chapter you probably experienced a taste of the mercurial nature of your mind when you focused your attention upon the relaxing and breathing exercises.

This flitting from one thing to another goes on subliminally all the time and this 'stream of consciousness' is further confused by the fact that we are constantly bombarded with visual and auditory stimuli in modern society. When we make the effort to switch off and open to our inner world these images often get replayed. A prime example is the tune that repeats itself over and over in our heads. When your thoughts do drift, don't use it as an excuse to beat yourself up; temper firmness of purpose with self love, and gently refocus on the exercise.

You will certainly encounter resistances and times when very little appears to be happening in your meditation sessions. These 'dry' periods are actually part of the process and an integral part of development. Being aware of these cycles can aid you in coming through these fallow periods. There is a potent formula within the Egyptian mysteries encoded within the 'word of power', IAO, which represents the initials of the Egyptian Deities Isis, Apophis and Osiris. It can, among other things, be contemplated as a formula for the process of meditation. To quote from Aleister Crowley, in his book *Magick in Theory and Practice*:

> In the beginning of a meditation practice, there is always a quiet pleasure, a natural gentle growth, one takes a lively interest in the work; it seems easy; one is quite pleased to have started. This phase represents Isis.

This pleasant Isian phase is sooner or later succeeded by the period of Apophis wherein resistances mount up, depression and even a detestation of the work arises. There are little or no insights gained and it is often at this point that people will give up on a particular practice or course of training. There is the temptation to begin something new in order to regain the comfortable energy of the Isian phase. The problem with this is that until one has gone completely through the Apophis stage, which is likened to a death experience, the rebirth phase cannot be entered. The final stage attributed to Isis's brother-husband Osiris, who as a vegetation god is continually reborn, is described thus:

> It is followed by the arising not of Isis, but of Osiris. The ancient condition is not restored, but a new condition is created, a condition only rendered possible by the process of death.

We grow spiritually through a series of death and rebirth experiences which can be viewed as the cycle of assimilating new material and experiences over the course of a month. For this we can use as a metaphor the cycle of the Moon's phases and the longer cycles of initiation into the mysteries of the Goddess which can span many years of our lives.

The Elements and the Tattvas

For this exercise in concentration, we shall focus upon very simple geometric shapes – the philosophical elements. These were formulated in ancient times as the basic substances of form comprising Earth, Air, Fire and Water. Later philosophers added the fifth element of Aether to represent the unseen realm of Spirit. It should be stated that these Elements are not to be confused with the elemental tables of chemistry but can rather be regarded as states of energy and being.

Within the Western Mystery Tradition the symbols of the Tattvas have been used as an aid to concentration since the late 19th century. The Tattvas are coloured geometric shapes that originated in the Hindu tradition and symbolise the philosophical elements of Earth, Air, Fire, Water and Aether/Spirit. They are Prithivi (Earth, a Yellow Square), Vayu (Air, a Blue Circle), Tejas (Fire, a Red Triangle), Apas

(Water, a Silver Crescent) and Akasha (Ether/Spirit, an Indigo or Black Oval).

These shapes and colours are merely a suggestion as it is perfectly allowable for you to use alternative symbols and colours to represent the elements. For example, the Platonic Solids, though requiring more visualising skill as they are three-dimensional, have long been associated with the five elements of Earth, Air, Water, Fire and Spirit (Aether). These mathematical solids, though ascribed to Plato, were 'borrowed' by him from the teachings of Pythagoras. It is not known whether Pythagoras developed these himself or wrote about symbols that were, until then, held as esoteric knowledge within the mystery schools. Esoteric tradition holds that sacred geometry and mathematics were part of the teachings of the Egyptian mystery schools and may well have been derived from Atlantean sources. However, it is these early philosophers who have left written records which have survived to modern day.

For the initial part of the exercise you will need to either cut out of coloured paper or paint the symbol to concentrate upon. In either case these should be put on a neutral coloured background. If you do choose to work with the Solids, you can find pictures of them through your local library. Alternatively, the dice used for the popular role-playing game 'Dungeons and Dragons' are in the form of these Platonic solids in miniature and can be obtained from games shops and painted in appropriate colours.

You will note in the following chart that the attributes to the elements are applicable to both systems. You will be working throughout the manual with various symbol systems and associations. Those readers with experience of astrology or the Tarot will already know how to make symbolic attributions, although this skill can be easily mastered with patience.

Element	Tattvic Image	Platonic Solid	P.S. Shape	Suggested P.S. Colour
Earth	Yellow square	Cube	6 square faces	Green
Air	Blue circle	Octohedron	8 triangular faces	Yellow
Water	Silver crescent	Isosohedron	20 triangular faces	Blue
Fire	Red triangular	Tetrahedron	4 triangular faces	Red
Spirit	Black oval	Dodecahedron	12 pentagonal faces	Multicoloured or neutral

Whether you work with one of the above symbols or devise your own geometric shape/colour/element, I suggest that you work with each symbol for about five to seven days. I would also suggest that you compile a table of the attributes and qualities of these elements drawn from your own background in reading and meditation work in order to enrich your understanding of their meaning.

It is also possible to use these symbols as 'doorways' into inner realities and we will be doing this type of exercise in the next chapter.

The technique of concentration is simple. Place at about eye-level the solid or card with your selected image on it. It is ideal to do this against a blank wall so that you are not overly distracted by the surroundings. You will need adequate light in the room – dim or muted light is better than glaring or bright light.

Sit as for meditation and, following your relaxation and rhythmic breathing exercises, focus your attention on the image. After a short time allow your eyes to close and you will find that you have an 'after-image' of the symbol which will continue for some seconds. You can then use this to create an inner image of the symbol which you should continue to concentrate upon. You will probably find that you have to alternate between opening your eyes and looking at the outer image and closing them to form the inner one.

For those with trouble visualising, one way of aiding the process is suggested by the writer Ernest Butler. This consists of using a paper or cardboard tube through which to gaze, using the right and left eyes alternately. As you hold the symbol in the field of vision, throw your eyes slightly out of focus, bringing the symbol within your head. This de-focusing is a psychological trick which allows you to bring a clear image into your mind. Once you have learnt this skill it is increasingly simple to bring the visual image inside, to the point where the image concerned is seen clearly with the eyes closed (Butler describes this as being analogous to the knack of learning to balance on a bicycle).

You may find that as you work with the elemental symbols other images and/or ideas will come to you which relate to the elements. These should be noted but not elaborated on at this point. Your task here is to focus your mind on the image. This is not an easy task and you will no doubt find that you often lose your concentration. When you notice this occurring, draw your attention back firmly but gently back to the image.

Concentrating in this way can feel quite intense, as though you are doing a mental 'press-up', and it is a good idea to conclude your session with a minute or so of relaxation. Write up your notes, including apparent failures.

Chapter 2

Worlds Within

Following on from the austerity of the last chapter's final practice, we now move into an area where your creative imagination will be brought into play as we create more natural visual images. It will still be necessary for you to use your powers of concentration in order to keep your attention upon the scene at hand. However, as these are more complex images and you will also be using multiple inner senses, it is bound to be easier to keep your interest engaged upon the task.

There are two basic approaches to this type of visualisation. For the first, you visualise a fairly detailed scene. The idea is to take in the images presented and elaborate on them. This type of visualisation is usual when doing guided meditations and 'path-workings'. You may well already have experience of this type of meditation. We shall also be using this type of visualisation to create the Inner Temple of the Goddess in the next section of the book.

The second approach is similar to the earlier meditation on phrases, bringing the personal imagination even more into play. A suggestion is given of a fairly broad subject, say a forest. Each person will use her or his own ideas, memories, fantasies, etc about forests to create that scene. These images arising from the personal and collective unconscious can be very powerful indications of inner emotional states, so images will change as one's moods change. The classic example is the sea which for most people will be symbolic of their emotions. This is not necessarily a conscious association but operates upon deeper levels of consciousness. Thus, if a spontaneous image of a very angry, rough sea comes into mind it is illustrative of emotional turmoil or unsettlement. The converse is true if a very calm sea is seen. These images are akin to those arising in the dream state and whole systems of psychology analyse such images as a major technique.

Taking this idea further, you can dispense completely with a suggested image and merely imagine before you a door marked with a particular symbol, word or phrase. Moving through this doorway you will enter into a symbolic landscape beyond it. This technique is known as 'skrying' and it is a powerful tool for inner exploration. Later in this chapter an exercise will be given that explores the skrying technique – your earlier visualisation work provides groundwork for this later exercise.

When you enter such an inner landscape it is very likely that you will encounter various beings and/or people. While these encounters are an important part of this type of visualisation work, I suggest that initially you do not consciously introduce beings with whom you could interact. What is suggested is that you concentrate at this point upon gaining skill with the creation of visualised scenes of clarity and depth. This process is known as the 'composition of place' and it is a vital building block for your future work. Feel free to bring animals into the scenes, in fact in many scenarios they are a vital part of the background. If people or beings do spontaneously appear in your visualisations at this point it is suggested that you merely observe them as if you were an invisible presence in the scene and not engage in conversation or interaction with them until after you have contacted your Inner Guide later in the chapter.

In the following list of suggested scenes you will find some from each of the categories mentioned above. Do work with each scene for a few days before moving on to another. This is done, as with the meditation symbols, so that you gain a deeper experience of each scene and enhance it.

Do be sure to make a note in your diary-record of what scene you are working with and record your success (or lack of it). Precede your work each time with a few minutes of relaxation and rhythmic breathing to ready yourself for the meditation.

SUGGESTED SCENES

1 You find yourself on a narrow but definite path winding through a forest on a bright summer's day. The sunlight doesn't reach you directly because of the trees and vegetation but there are areas where shafts of light penetrate and make beautiful patterns. You are aware of animal, bird and insect life all about you. You emerge into a clearing and find a small cottage obviously abandoned but inviting exploration. Beside the cottage is an old stone well.

2 A meadow with a stream running through it.

3 A mountain cave.

4 You find yourself in the room of a large house with French windows that open out onto a large, well-tended garden. There are many varieties of shrubs and flowers. There is an ornamental pond and a fountain. Although it is now sunny there has recently been a rain shower. The flowers and leaves are hung with raindrops which sparkle as the sunlight hits them. Looking up at the sky you see an arc of a rainbow. Explore this garden and be aware of the house as well.

5 Take a picture of a landscape – a postcard, painting or photograph. It may be realistic or fantastic. Recreate the scene in your mind's eye, enter and explore it.

6 Take a location from a written work of fiction and recreate it for yourself, enter and explore it.

7 Temple of Silence journey. You are walking along a path on a sunny spring morning. In front of you is a hill with a path leading to the top. On the top stands a Temple of Silence. Its shape and structure reflects your highest consciousness. Be aware of your body as you ascend the hill. Notice how you are dressed, the feeling of the ground beneath your feet, the breeze and sun on your cheeks. Look about you at the trees, bushes, grass and wildflowers.

 As you approach the top of the hill you are aware of an ageless silence pervading the atmosphere. As you move towards the temple's door you know that as you enter you will be surrounded by this silence. You open the door and enter the temple – feel the stillness and peace all about you. Look around. Moving inward you find a luminous dome through which comes not only the light of the sun but a light which seems to spring from within and is concentrated there.

You enter this area of luminous silence and allow it to pervade you, flowing through your being. Remain within the light for a few minutes. During this time listen to the silence which is a living quality not just the absence of sound.

Slowly leave the centre of radiance. Walk back through the temple and out of the portals. Outside, open yourself to the impact of nature. Descend the hill. (Adapted from *What We May Be*, Piero Ferrucci, Crucible.)

8 You are sailing a small boat around a tropical island. You come across a lagoon which you can sail into. You may explore, either by swimming in the clear blue waters or by landing on the beach.

9 You are walking on a bleak moorland and come across a circle of standing stones. Enter the circle and touch each stone. Let it tell you its story.

A couple of further points about this type of meditation practice. Using your auditory (hearing), kinesthetic (touch) and olfactory (smell) senses will markedly deepen the experience and your sense of 'being present' in the visualised scene. Remember with kinesthetic awareness that you should not only reach out to touch objects in the environment but also be aware of your sense of bodily movement and weight, the feel of the ground beneath you, etc.

You may also find as you visualise the scene that there is a tendency to drift off and begin to observe yourself rather than being present in it – i.e. looking through your own inner eyes. Again, whenever your attention wanders in these exercises, just bring it gently back to being inside your imagined body. You might like to employ the technique suggested by Carlos Castenada to help you. This is simply to look down at your hands in the experience. He originally meant this to be used to 'wake up' in a dream but it also serves to centre yourself in this type of visualisation exercise. I have also found that I can orient myself and bring my attention back by looking down at the ground and my feet. A sense of enjoyment and even adventure also brings you the cooperation of your unconscious mind.

When you complete the exercise, return to ordinary awareness and be sure to close down and earth your meditation. This is done by employing one of the gestures explained in Chapter 1. A drink of water, tea or other drink with a small bite to eat assists in this closing process, and so too does writing up the experience in your diary-record.

The Elemental Worlds

In this section you will be building upon the insights gained through the meditations upon the Tattvas and the 'composition of place' exercises. Here you will be visualising a doorway upon which the elemental tattvic shapes will be projected. Then you will pass in your 'mind's eye' into the landscape beyond the door which will be a symbolic representation of this element.

Before embarking upon the formal exercise I want first to explore some ideas about the elements themselves and the psychological theory connected with these related to the work of Carl G. Jung. A special meditation will follow, to precede your skrying work, that will serve to introduce you to an 'Inner Guide' who is to be a companion on all of these journeyings.

Carl Jung is not the only psychologist who has addressed himself to the exploration of spiritual realms, but he is certainly the best-known. Although transpersonal psychologies which have come to the fore in the past decade are, in many ways, more relevant to students of the mysteries, there is no doubt that Jung's work remains a milestone and has been the inspiration for these other psychologists' and writers' theories. We will be exploring more of Jungian theory in Chapter 5.

The four psychological types that Jung postulated are divided into the categories of 'Functions' and 'Attitudes'. The Functions are Thinking, Feeling, Intuition and Sensation and the Attitudes are Introversion and

Extroversion. The idea is that each of the functions could be experienced as either attitude within the personality of an individual. Thus the four basic types expand into eight. One can think of these functions as being ways in which we experience and deal with the things that we encounter in our lives. Jung believed that each of us had within our psychological make-ups all of these functions in some strength but one or two would tend to be dominant and greatly colour the personality.

The functions are arranged in polarised pairs. You can simply illustrate this by drawing a circle and then dividing it into four. Then place in the quadrants the four functions – thinking opposite to feeling and sensation opposite to intuitive.

An individual might, for example, have thinking as a 'dominant' function and so the feeling function will be their 'inferior' function. In most people the other two functions will probably also be quite rudimentary but not so much as the primary inferior function. Once you have grasped the idea you can add the complication of the introvert/extrovert attitudes to this formulation. These attitudes can also be viewed as polarities.

It is quite easy to make the attribution of these types to the elements and also to the 'humours or fluids of the blood' posed by the early physicians which were also linked to the philosophical elements that we explored in Chapter 1.

Element	Psychological Type	Humour
Earth	Sensation	Melancholic
Fire	Thinking (or Intuitive)	Choleric
Air	Intuitive (or Thinking)	Sanguine
Water	Feeling	Phlegmatic

As you will no doubt notice in the table, the thinking and intuitive functions may be attributed to either Air or Fire. Some authors have attributed thought to Air, while others make the attribution of thought to Fire. I tend to favour this latter view. My own work with the elements has led to my feeling that the activity of heat/fire altering, as it does, the structure of matter, suits the thinking function more than it does the intuitive function. Intuition, which acts in an invisible manner, is then attributed to the element of Air which is likewise a subtle and invisible medium. Also, as Fire/Water are already an accepted polarity it feels more symbolically right, for me, to match this with the polarity of thinking/feeling.

In these matters of attribution it is important to go with what feels correct in your own mind. Therefore, the actual linking of an element to any psychological type is only applicable if it seems right to you. The fact is that attributions of any kind are arbitrary. As you continue to work with symbol systems, either here or in another context, this will become more and more apparent.

For example, with the complex symbol systems of Astrology and the Tarot, many years of research and meditation by individuals have yielded data in the form of attributions and meanings for various symbols. This store of knowledge is always being refined and expanded in outer forms (books, etc) and on inner levels by pooled research meditation and personal and collective experience of the symbols. Readers coming to the subject for the first time may feel initially confused, especially as different authors give different interpretations of symbols. However, as you gain confidence you'll realise that it is more important that the information you receive through your own meditations or reflections is meaningful to you in the context of your life. Please keep this in mind as you work through this book.

Now let us begin to look a little closer at the types. If you wish for more in-depth information on this subject I would refer you to Jung's *Four Psychological Types* and Liz Greene's *Relating: an Astrological Guide to Living with Others on a Small Planet* which draws heavily on Jung's work and has a chapter on the types and elements. There are also available books which serve as introductions to Jung's ideas that will cover material on the types.

Thinking: This is a slightly unfortunate term because it is easy to equate what is essentially an attitude to thought with thinking itself. Obviously we all think – this label describes an approach to thought that is concerned with classifying, analysing, comparing and synthesizing experience; with taking an argument from premise to conclusion and tracing its reasons. The dominant thinking type may seem quite detached from the world approaching it more through ideas and favour 'rationality'. With a dominant thinking function it is feeling that is the inferior function and thus there is an unwillingness or difficulty in expressing emotions. *Star Trek*'s Mr Spock, with his devotion to 'logic', is a good example of the type. Indeed it is quite easy to spot the extremes of this type in the archetypal intellectual or scientist who seems to be alive only from the neck up.

Feeling: Again, as above, this is perhaps a misleading term as the word is synonymous with emotion. We all have emotions but our relationship to them varies. A feeling type is not necessarily 'emotional' in the negative sense of the word but will experience the world primarily via the emotions. The feeling type is not concerned with reasons but with values, not with logic but with worth. The feeling type is more concerned with wholes than with parts. For example, in describing music the thinking type will be concerned with the parts of the music and how it fits together but the feeling type will be concerned with the totality of the experience and judge the music as a whole. If the thinking type is head-centred we can consider the feeling type as heart-centred.

Sensation: This type is concerned with facts and perceives the way things are. Whereas both thinking and feeling types are concerned with making judgements and relationships between things, the sensation type is concerned with what is and isn't. They are usually comfortable with their own bodies and the physical plane in general. A result of this can often be an identification with the same and this type can be quite trapped in the material realm. Also their inferior intuitive function can leave them prey to superstition and irrational vague fears.

Intuitive: This type, like the sensation type, works by perception but in this case it is the perception of something beyond facts – the events beyond the horizon, the intangible possibilities, the shape of things to come. They will see the inner meanings and significance behind 'mere' facts and events. They can also have the knack of perceiving the undercurrents in a situation. Their intuitions are not always correct or accurate just as the awareness of the sensation type can be faulty.

Whereas the sensation type is rooted in the outer physical aspect of reality, the intuitive type is aware of inner realities, and intuition is in the main an unconscious process. They can be endowed with a strong imagination and often relate more easily to their inner worlds of fantasy than the outer 'real world'. This can mean that they function less well in the material world than the sensation type, yet they will be more comfortable with the complexities of existence even if they are out of step or feel alienated with the materialism of this day and age.

It is interesting to observe those around you in terms of the above types, noting their dominant functions as well as your own. There is a very useful exercise for linking the types with their related elements and achieving a balance of the elements in *The Magical Philosophy* (Volume 1) by Melita Denning and Osbourne Phillips.

Their suggestion is to keep a daily record of thoughts and actions for a period of time. At the end of this time take four pencils coloured red for Fire, blue for Water, green for Earth and yellow for Air and go through your record judging the elemental affinities of the material; underlining as you go in the separate colours. The idea is that at the end of the exercise it will be possible to judge whether one or more elements are dominant or perhaps even absent in the personality and then begin systematically to work at establishing a better balance.

It has long been known that one of the benefits of psycho-spiritual growth, whether through meditation or devotion, is that previously under-developed aspects of the personality are stimulated and enhanced. So although using a map such as Jung's types may show that a particular function is latent within you it does not mean that this cannot be enhanced through development.

One of the aims of the mysteries has always been the encouragement of what is known these days as 'wholeness'.

This concept of striving towards a psychological/spiritual completeness is not new though certainly in recent years it has become better known to the 'lay community'. For the priesthood an essential part of training for undertaking the channelling the energies of the Goddesses/Gods has always been the reaching of a high degree of self-knowledge and wholeness. When one is in communion with Deity or acting as a living channel and mediator for a spiritual force it is essential not to be overwhelmed by the contact. The ability to 'earth' the experience and clearly put it into perspective is very important not only for the health of the initiate but for the stability of the priesthood throughout the years.

This is why there is such an emphasis in all spiritual traditions upon basic work before embarking on the more advanced practices. If groundwork has not been done and energies contacted are not earthed properly, an inflation of the ego or an obsessional state can be the result. Although this can be a very seductive and powerful altered state of consciousness, it will not serve either the mediator or the Deity concerned. The priest/ess involved can be shattered by the experience or may become fanatical and distort the energies they are attempting to channel. History proves the amount of cruelty and devastation committed by either glamorised individuals or groups convinced of the supremacy of their chosen deity.

Organisations such as the Fellowship of Isis strive, through celebration of such a diversity of goddesses and gods, for the understanding of the principle that while individual cultures may have clothed goddess and gods in their own symbols, the eternal essence remains the same. We are very privileged in these times to be able to choose the pantheon with which we involve ourselves outside of the actual land where those god/desses had their initial worship. It is one of the benefits of the 'global village'.

However, it is important to keep in mind that although in essence two goddesses may embody the same principle they are not the same. For example, the Greek Goddess Aphrodite and the Egyptian Goddess Hathor are both 'Goddesses of Love' yet remain quite distinct entities. Each has her own qualities and is approached by a supplicant in a different manner.

Moving on to the practical work of this section, you should as usual begin every session with the preliminary exercises of relaxation and rhythmic breathing. It is an interesting exercise to observe whether this regular relaxation has yet had any effects upon your functioning in the outer world.

Inner Guide Meditation

When we begin to foray into the inner worlds it is important that we do it with someone who is experienced in this realm. The idea of an Inner Guide is an ancient one. The guide is found in myths, fairy tales and spiritual literature throughout the world. On a purely mundane level, when visiting somewhere new, the services of a guide in some form are used – maybe a map, a guidebook, or an actual human. Guides exist upon the inner levels and are well known within Spiritualist circles. In the following exercise you will be connecting to a special guide to assist you in the work ahead.

You may have already contacted an 'Inner Guide' spontaneously or through other meditation work. If so, there is no reason why this familiar guide figure shouldn't accompany you on these journeys. Or you may wish to use the following meditation to gain a guide specifically for your work with this manual. Your guide's function, no matter what method is used for contact, is to act as an intermediary and helpmate while interacting with the energies and beings you encounter through this skrying technique.

Some writers feel you should test your guide. Be assured that this meditation, along with all the others within this book, have their own built in 'safety feature'. This is the symbol of the Winged Isis. The guide who approaches you in this meditation will be a spirit working under the sign of the Goddess Isis and therefore will be friendly and willing to work for your growth.

1 Make yourself comfortable and perform your opening sequence of relaxation.

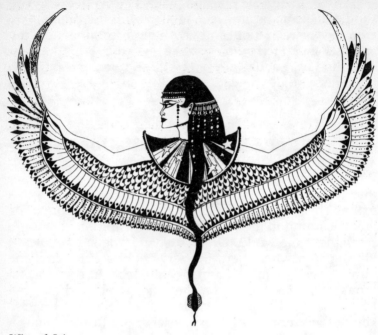

Winged Isis

2 Visualise before you an old wooden doorway. On its arch
  is carved the figure of the Goddess Isis in her winged
  aspect – kneeling, arms outstretched. On the doorway
  itself is carved a symbol special to yourself. Note this
  symbol for you will use it to make subsequent contact
  with your guide.

3 As you watch, a soft golden light begins to glow from the
  carved symbol and the door opens. Beyond the door you
  see the banks of a mighty river and upon it sails an
  Eygptian barge. As it comes towards you, say in your
  mind 'I call upon my Inner Guide to the mysteries of the
  Goddess'.

4 A figure disembarks from the barge and comes towards
  you standing just outside the open door. Be aware of the
  figure: their age and dress, and whether it is male or
  female. The figure stands awaiting your permission to
  enter. When ready, welcome your guide into your
  meditation space.

5 Take time to get acquainted – asking questions and receiving answers in your mind. Do ask your guide's name for when you call them again it will be by visualising the door only with your special symbol on it and calling your guide's name. The guide will then come to you through the doorway and you will together enter the inner landscape.

6 When you are ready, bid your guide goodbye for now. The figure will return through the doorway and the door will again close. Then bring yourself back to normal consciousness and close as usual.

Your guide will not only be your companion for the following set of meditations but will be involved with you throughout the work of this manual and even beyond. Many students find their relationship with the Inner Guides to be a source of great richness and the contact has remained even beyond the course. Certainly you may contact your guide in order to ask questions or receive guidance.

Entering the Tattvic/Elemental Worlds

After doing the Initial Guide Meditation, which you need only do once in full, you will again be working with the Tattva symbols encountered in the previous chapter. I suggest that you work with one symbol over 5 or 6 sessions before moving on to another and repeat the process. It is not necessary for you to make a journey into the symbolic world each day – in fact it might be more fruitful to do the full journey one day and on the next to meditate upon the landscape, symbols and any other experiences you have received. Then the next session make the journey in full again. You can determine your approach to the practices without feeling over-bound by a too rigid structure.

In the last chapter you worked with five tattvic symbols, although I have only been discussing the four elements in conjunction with the four psychological types. The fifth tattvic symbol, the black oval of Spirit, links not to any 'type' but to our essential spiritual nature.

1 Perform the opening sequences of relaxation and breathing.

2 Visualise before you the doorway bearing your special symbol and call on your Inner Guide. Once you have established contact visualise another door in front of you with the tattvic symbol you are working with this session. Hold the image for a few moments upon the door.

3 Move forward accompanied by your guide through the doorway into the landscape beyond. What you find there shall be representative of the symbolic world of this symbol/element.

4 Your guide will act as an intermediary for you when you encounter any beings or people in the elemental world and assist you in interpreting the experience.

5 When you have completed your exploration return through the doorway. Close it firmly behind you and take leave of your guide. Return to ordinary consciousness as usual. Write up your diary-record as soon as possible, noting what you have seen and your reactions to the experience.

Shrines

A shrine is a hallowed place which exists to focus the mind on the deity to whom the shrine is dedicated. This is an ancient practice dating back as far as humankind has been worshipping and is the preparing of the way to welcome the Goddess further into your life.

A shrine represents a place in which Deity can be present in our daily lives. Early shrines were caves and these were thought to represent the actual body of the Earth Mother. In time the caves became temples and later the idea of an enclosed sacred space became expressed in the magnificent temples of the ancient world, continuing today in churches, mosques and temples.

It is rare in these times for people to have a room set aside for religious purposes but often space can be found in a bedroom or study. A table, shelf or mantelpiece can function as a shrine. The keynote of any shrine is the bringing together of a series of linked symbols around a central image or images of the Goddess which will then function as a focal point for your meditation and devotional work; a place set aside.

The act of making a shrine is a very personal one. It is important to choose the space and cleanse it in any way you feel is suitable. Allow it to stand empty for a day or so and then begin to 'dress' it. A simple white cloth with a votive candle and perhaps some fresh flowers or a plant can be the first step until such time as you choose which aspect of the Goddess you will honour in the shrine.

The central image, whether it be a picture, photograph or statue, is important. There is probably at least one aspect of the Goddess which already appeals to you and it is relatively easy to obtain postcards and prints as well as statues. If you have any artistic skill yourself it is a good idea to make your own image. For some people who have a receptive family or live alone there is the opportunity to have more than one shrine.

I am beholden to my sister-priestess, Sunflower, whose creative use of small shrines revolutionised my own approach to shrines. Much of her work has been through shrines and as she states in 'The Path of the Solar Priestess' (*Voices of the Goddess*):

> One of the techniques I have used to focus my mind on a deity is to make it the centre of my home. Part of the path of Hestia and Hertha, Goddess of hearth and home, to me is the making and dedicating of shrines to welcome the Goddess in. If I am teaching a group, I also like to set up altars to consecrate the room. Shrines are an important act of magical intent as you are creating a space for the deity to live with you. On inner levels you enter the force field of the deity so you become linked and not separate.

She goes on to describe a series of shrines she has made in rich detail, and having visited her home I know that these are only a few of the temple-like settings she has created about her.

At the time of writing, I have four shrines set up on small tables and the mantelpiece of my bedroom; one in each elemental quarter dedicated to aspects of the Goddess I experience linked to that element. These have grown as I have over the years. The focal point of each shrine is a piece of original artwork which personally expressed the energies of that shrine/quarter. In some cases there is more than one image of the Goddess on a single shrine but they all reflect the theme of that quarter.

For example, in the South for Fire I have an image of Sulis Minerva and Athena. Around these pictures there is a cluster of owls and gathered bird feathers. Also I have a large crystal surmounted by a painted dragon of green and gold. The red candles with matching holders flank the central image, an incense burner stands to one side. There is also a collection of rose quartz crystals clustered together on a silver salver. Each of my shrines contains crystals and stones collected from significant places. In recent weeks I have obtained a small statue of a Cretan snake priestess which continues the fiery theme.

I find my shrines change as I do. Sometimes I will place cards or objects on them linked to special work I am undertaking. Objects are regularly cleaned and polished. It is important to keep a shrine active – neglecting the shrine will weaken the link between you and the deity on the inner and outer levels.

The theme of the shrine can be expanded by the colour of the cloth used, candles, and attendant symbols. Light is important and it is very effective to have two candles in holders flanking the main image of the shrine or a coloured or scented shrine candle. Plants and flowers make a focal point and are traditional gifts to the gods. So too are sea shells, pebbles from significant places, pictures of totem animals and birds. It is exciting to acquire new objects through coincidence or design.

I have on each of my shrines some form of holder for incense along with a receptacle for water in the form of a cup or bowl. In fact each of my shrines, though dedicated to a single element, contain each of the elements on them in some form. This wasn't done by planning but just grew naturally over the course of time. It is important to allow a shrine to grow. Precious gifts and tokens obtained or received are very important. Tarot cards which are significant can also be placed on the shrines.

The shrine should be aesthetically pleasing to you and you alone. If you have a family it might be possible to cover the shrine with a veil to keep it for special occasions – the last thing you want is someone putting a cigarette out in your incense burner or standing a coffee cup on the shrine. This is bound to happen at times, though, and the best thing to do is be good natured and, without making an undue fuss, explain that this is not an apt place to place such things.

It is rare to have a series of shrines; sometimes it is all one can do to have one in operation. Whatever is chosen it is important to feel happy with the result. Allow it to grow and reflect who you are.

The Temple of Isis at the Fellowship of Isis Foundation Centre in Ireland is made up of numerous shrines to different aspects of the goddess. I asked Olivia Durdin-Robertson to write something of her wide experience of working with shrines and she replied with the following:

A shrine is a meeting place for people and the invisible Deities. It is a hallowed spot, indoors or outdoors. The great holy places of earth need small personal shrines as antennae through which the rainbow network of deific radiations may be used for local interests. A shrine irradiates a room, a house, a garden and from there a whole area, a countryside, the world. We think of Stonehenge, Avebury, Newgrange, Jerusalem, Mecca, Lourdes. But holy places used by successive religions can be neglected, or worse, misused. This is where small private shrines, whether of individual people or groups, provide a re-awakening of spiritual power. A few small personal shrines to the Goddess can in time be as springs coming from the earth which, joining with others, become mighty rivers replenishing the land with water. Hence the mighty ruined temples of the ancient world are being revived not through archaeology, though this has helped with rebuilding, but through the personal devotion to the Ancient Deities offered in small shrines created in their honour.

It is extremely important now for followers of the Goddess to make shrines, whether in the corner of a room, in a wood, a garden, on waste land. Everything that is highly spiritual needs earthing if it is materially to save the earth from our own greed and ignorance. Unless we are very psychic we cannot always see the beautiful aura that surrounds a shrine, and the radiation that comes from a magnetised figure of a deity. But this animation of icons and figures is real and affects all open to its particular influence. Often followers of the Goddess, seeing mighty cathedrals and mosques exclusively dedicated to the Patriarchal Deity may sigh at the minute size of their own shrines – few of us can dedicate a whole house! Where are our spires, our great domes?

When a religion, however beneficent, is reaching a decline, its followers build immense edifices to assert their continuing power. At the time of Rome's decline her largest temples were erected. But the real power of the future lay with the small groups of Christians meeting in catacombs. Where Life is, vesture and manifestation are as simple and beautiful as Nature herself. Only when Life diminishes is a carapace of unwieldy masonry used to conceal a dying system of thought. We of the New Age of Isis are more like birds than tortoises. It was the small mammal that survived the Ice Age not the dinosaur! So let us make shrines with little figures, pictures, a shell, a crystal, incense sticks and a cup of water. The Goddess will use what we offer and make it a beacon of love, joy and harmony.

Consecration of a Shrine to the Goddess:

When you have brought together the image and other objects you may wish to do a small ceremony to consecrate this as a special shrine to the Goddess. Set the shrine up as you wish it, making sure that you include a vessel with some spring water, a candle, and an incense stick.

Bathe and put on a robe or clean clothes. Sit before the shrine, relax and centre yourself. When you are ready to begin light the candle and incense.

Take the incense and move it slowly over the objects on the shrine so that they are touched by the smoke. Say:

With this sweet smoke, I cleanse and consecrate this shrine to the Goddess . . . (insert name here) *and ask that She bless it.*

Take the water and flick drops of water upon the shrine and around it, saying:

With water, I cleanse and consecrate this shrine to the Goddess . . . and ask that She bless it.

Then address the Goddess in your own words asking for her blessing upon this shrine and upon your work. You may wish to follow this with a meditation.

Chapter 3

The Chakras and
the Goddess Kundalini

As stated in my introduction, Part 1 of this book is concentrating upon the building and improving of various basic skills and laying the groundwork for Part 2. You will probably have found that as the weeks pass the relaxation, rhythmic breathing and visualisation exercises have become progressively easier. We shall now begin to add a further dimension to the work which shall incorporate all of these skills – contacting the energy centres within the subtle body. This is vital work no matter what system of meditation one specialises in.

The most accessible terminology on the subject of these energy centres has been imported from India and indeed terms such as 'chakras' and the 'kundalini' have become well integrated into the language of the counter-culture. Part of the reason we use Sanskrit terminology is that within the culture of India, meditation has held a prominent and valued position and as such has been actively developed. In contrast, the mystery traditions of the West under the domination of Christianity have been actively suppressed with the result that invaluable knowledge has been lost or driven far underground.

There are indications that there has been, despite Christianity, a continuing hidden tradition in the West. The writings of Paracelsus contained references to what he described as 'star' centres in the body which could be activated to aid healing. Also the works of the Rosicrucians and alchemists hold much in coded form which may be interpreted along similar lines.

It is certain, though, that within the teachings of the Western Mysteries, Yoga and Tantric Buddhism, it is uniformly stated that within our bodies lies a vital key to the Mysteries. Writings of the ancient Greeks contained veiled references to 'hidden centres' within the human body and these teachings were most probably derived from Egyptian sources. Here, once again, are found indications of physical power centres which, when activated, allow ordinary human beings to enter into communion with non-physical states of consciousness and to commune with the gods.

The Sanskrit word 'chakra' means 'wheel' and indeed the chakras do spin like a wheel. They spin in relation to the degree of energy in the system of the individual. There are within Eastern texts beautiful images for each chakra, which are pictured as lotus flowers. Flowers are an evocative analogy for the chakras as they can be closed, in bud, open or blossoming depending on whether they are active or dormant.

It is important not to divorce the chakras from our physical bodies. Working with subtle energies is the basis for much alternative medicine including acupuncture, colour healing and homoeopathy. Chakras can be over-stimulated, under-stimulated, dormant or in balance. Physical illness will disrupt the chakras and such disruptions will often result in physical and psychosomatic symptoms. Our aim through the following exercises is gently to stimulate the chakras and bring them into balanced activity. If chakras are already stimulated this sort of exercise will also serve to restore a more balanced development of their energies. More details of these over-stimulations are covered later in the chapter when we discuss kundalini.

What follows is an outline of each chakra. For further books on the subject the reader is referred to the Bibliography. In this chapter the meditation material will involve energy exercises that vitalise these centres and prepare you for the meditation exercises in Part 2.

There is no overall agreement as to the number of energy centres – some systems consider 5, others 7, 10 or more. We shall examine the seven classical centres defined by yoga and the initial exercise will involve making contact with these vital centres and beginning to explore the energy relationships between them. The names of the chakras are initially given in Sanskrit and when referring to them

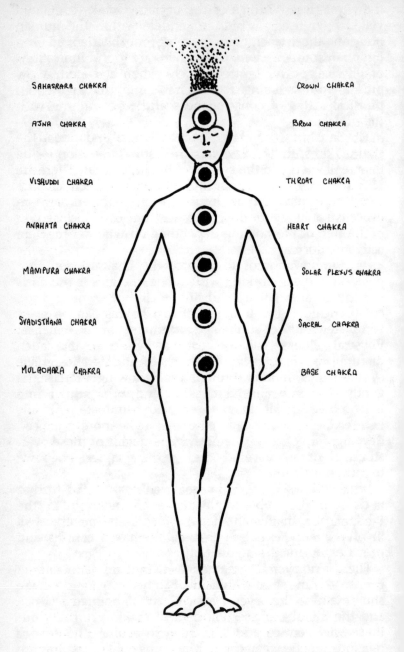

SAHASRARA CHAKRA — CROWN CHAKRA

AJNA CHAKRA — BROW CHAKRA

VISHUDDI CHAKRA — THROAT CHAKRA

ANAHATA CHAKRA — HEART CHAKRA

MANIPURA CHAKRA — SOLAR PLEXUS CHAKRA

SVADISTHANA CHAKRA — SACRAL CHAKRA

MULADHARA CHAKRA — BASE CHAKRA

The Chakras and the Human Body

individually we shall use either this or their commonly used Western keyword which identifies them through physical location. I emphasise again that it would be impossible to more than lightly introduce in these few pages such a complex system of spiritual development.

We begin with the muladhara (base) chakra which is located at the base of the spine. In the Qabalistic Middle Pillar sequence, referred to later in the chapter, this centre has been shifted to beneath the feet, which stresses further the relationship between this centre and the element of Earth. The tattva Prithivi (Yellow Square) and philosophical element of Earth are associated with this centre as are the sense of smell and the reproductive organs. It represents our deep connection to the physical world and is the seat of the sleeping kundalini energy and the libido (more than sexual energy alone but life energy in general). From the base chakra rise two currents of energy – the pingala (sun energy) and ida (moon energy) which terminate at the ajna chakra.

The next centre, the svadisthana (sacral) chakra, is located in the region just below the navel and associated with this centre are the element of Water and the tattva Apas (silver crescent) along with the very aesthetic sense of taste. In the martial arts much emphasis is placed on the 'hara' which is similar in location to this chakra. The hara is a prime place of body centredness and strength. The health of the organism is under the province of this chakra. This chakra shares with the muladhara a close affinity with the earth and underlines the importance of water in our bodies and to the planet.

We proceed to the manipura (solar plexus) chakra located at the solar plexus which is traditionally a centre of power. We see here the attribution of the element of Fire, the tattva Tejas (red triangle) and the sense of sight and development of inner visionary skills.

The anahata (heart) chakra is possibly the most important for Westerners. It is the centre of synthesis between the three higher centres which are concerned with transpersonal and transcendental states and the three body-orientated centres. It is the seat of compassion and is associated with the sense of touch – the medium through which we make contact with our environment. The element of Air and the tattva Vayu (blue circle) are attributed here. The heart centre shares an affinity with the solar plexus centre. Both are associated with the emotions – the solar plexus centre with the raw emotions which sweep through us and the heart centre with more subtle emotions such as altruism and unconditional love.

The vishuddha chakra is located at the throat and is associated with the sense of hearing, the Aether, the tattva Akasha (indigo/black oval) and the elusive 5th element of Spirit. It is the gateway to the subtle realms through which communication may be received and made to non-incarnate beings. It is the chakra through which 'channeling' comes.

The ajna (brow) chakra is the seat of the 'third eye'. All mental faculties are associated with this centre and it is also the place from which the subtle energies of non-physical realms are contacted and mediated. It is the place of telepathy and direct knowing. Here is found the termination of the solar (pingala) and lunar (ida) currents which began in the base chakra.

The sahasrara (crown) chakra is located just above the top of the head and is depicted as a thousand-petalled lotus which opens to the Divine. Attributed to it are intuition and the facility to perceive direct insight into the true nature of reality. It is the chakra wherein spiritual unity is experienced. However, it is ultimately beyond rational understanding.

The following summary chart illustrates a few more attributions of the chakras. The functions listed below are the traditional areas that the individual chakras are said to influence; likewise, there is thought to be some correlation between the subtle body chakras and the ductless glands of the endocrine system. The colours listed differ slightly from some other sources – those given were chosen because they relate to the visible spectrum, the rainbow which we will be working with in these and future exercises.

SUMMARY CHART

Centre	Location	Function	Colour	Planet/Element	Endocrine Influence
Muladhara	Base (of Spine)	Sex	Red	Saturn Earth	Gonads
Svadisthana	Sacral	Health	Orange	Jupiter Water	Spleen
Manipura	Solar Plexus	Power	Yellow	Mars Fire	Adrenal
Anahata	Heart	Compassion	Green	Venus Air	Thymus
Vishuddha	Throat	Creativity	Blue	Mercury Ether	Thyroid
Ajna	Brow	Paranormal	Indigo	Sun & Moon	Pituitary
Sahasrara	Above Crown of Head	Liberation	Violet	—	Pineal

RAINBOW CHAKRA EXERCISE

This chapter's first meditation may need to be approached slowly – hence you may spend the first two or three sessions establishing the first sphere then moving on to the crown centre and working with this for the next few sessions, then introducing the brow centre and continuing thus through the entire sequence. Do not be concerned if you fail to complete the entire sequence in the time period. Further energy exercises are given later in the chapter which are an integral part of future work, so it is important that you gain a good grasp of the technique.

1 Relax and begin your rhythmic breathing, continuing with this alone for somewhat longer than usual. To a degree throughout this exercise it is necessary to remain 'mindful' of your breathing. The coordination between this and the visualisation will come with practice.

2 With your eyes closed visualise well above the top of your head a sphere of brilliant white scintillating light/energy. Before proceeding further make sure you have a strong sense of this sphere's presence.

3 Once it is established imagine a ray of light emerging

from its bottom as a spectrum so there forms a rainbow band of light above your head. On an inbreath draw in from the rainbow the colour violet and visualise it becoming a sphere in the area of the crown chakra. On your next inbreath bring further energy/light into the violet sphere and continue this for about six inhalations. Following this just observe any sensations you may be having. If you need to you can draw in further energy from the source sphere.

4 Once this is well established, return your attention to the sphere and rainbow above your head and draw down a shaft of white light that will emerge from the crown centre. At the point of the brow chakra, visualise this becoming a sphere of indigo-coloured light/energy. Although your main concentration has shifted to the brow, do make sure you still are able to hold the image of the sphere at the crown chakra.

5 As you gain what you feel is a strong sense of this centre, again draw in a shaft of white light/energy which will blossom as a sphere of blue at the place of the throat chakra.

6 Proceed with this exercise in stages so that when you have a good sense of one chakra you move on to the next lower one using the rainbow colours in the sequence given in the summary chart. Do take note of any variations in the colours as you hold them and of any sensations or strong thoughts you encounter in the meditation. You may find that your thoughts wander. When this happens just gently draw your attention back to the task at hand.

7 At the completion of this stage of the sequence you will be holding a visualisation of the seven centres as spheres of coloured light/energy connected by a ray of white light along the line of the spine.

8 Once the seven are established we will begin to do the circulation of force exercise. Start this first by visualising a surge of energy coming from the glowing sphere above your head (the first visualised), pouring into and energising the crown chakra, then travelling down the

shaft of light to the brow, throat, heart, solar plexus, sacral and base chakras in turn. Do this at first very slowly to get the feel of it and then quicken your pace so that on a single inhalation you are pulling the energy from the crown through to the base chakra. At this stage, relax on the exhalation and allow the energy to wash through your body (including legs and feet) and be aware of any sensations you may experience.

9 Close the meditation sequence by visualising the centres as if the open flowers are now closing (apart from the crown centre which should be seen as open to the divine).

As any work with the chakras can have very powerful effects, do be especially aware of your reactions to it. Monitor yourself closely and do not overdo the exercises.

The Kundalini Experience

> The divine power,
> Kundalini shines
> like the stem of a young lotus;
> like a snake, coiled upon herself,
> she holds her tail in her mouth
> and lies resting half asleep
> at the base of the body.
> *Yoga Kundalini Upanishad* (1.82)

This section continues our exploration of the body's energy systems and specifically looks at the idea of the kundalini shakti. The word 'shakti' is one that crops up often within both Tantric and recent Western esoteric writings. It is a Sanskrit word which refers to the feminine aspect of the Divine in manifestation. It is creative power and activity inherent within reality.

This last phrase 'within reality' is a fundamental one. It is this awareness of Divinity being present within the physical world which is one of the major differences between Tantric yoga and the more well-known Hindu yogas. These are based upon a denial of the physical plane and the body itself, concentrating upon seeking bliss and enlightenment through the transcendence of physical limitations.

Tantric yoga teaches that enlightenment and bliss are possible through raising the quality of natural forces and refining the body's energy. In so doing one experiences enlightened states of consciousness within the body. Systems of thought, such as Tantric Buddhism, that have at their core the philosophy of 'immanence' – that is, the belief that the Creator (whether seen as the Goddess, God and Goddess, or pantheon) is not separate but active throughout Creation – have strong appeal to many initiates of the Western Mysteries, modern pagans and followers of the Goddess.

There is currently much material available in the West on both Hindu and Buddhist Tantras. It is such a rich and varied subject that again we can only briefly touch upon it here and the Bibliography includes books that will take you deeper into this subject. The Kundalini Shakti itself is a rich image of a Goddess in serpentine form lying at the base of the spine wrapped three and a half times round the spinal column. She is the Serpent Fire, the Universal Life-Force, deep within. She lies sleeping, though at times she stirs in that sleep. Such a 'stirring' of the kundalini can be a very ecstatic or traumatic event – sometimes the most profound visions and states of consciousness can result, though in the early stages these are often accompanied by unsettling or terrifying dreams or visions and quite unpleasant mental and physical side effects.

The possibility of trauma exists because of the inherent non-refinement of and blockages within the physical/etheric body. Therefore, when working with kundalini yoga, whether within the framework of formal teaching or in adapted form, attention is always placed upon this very refinement – working on cleansing and clearing the subtle centres through meditation, breathing, gentle energy work and right action and thoughts. Any direct work upon the rousing of the Kundalini herself is left for advanced stages of the work – it is much better not to attempt such work at all, since if it is meant to rise it usually will. Forcing the issue can often lead to some unpleasant side effects.

I am spending some time on this subject, not to alarm you but to alert you. The spontaneous stirring of the kundalini is a fairly common experience and can be open to misinterpretation. It can be one of the 'traps on the path' just because of its powerful side effects.

After reading of the 'symptoms' of a stirring you may well realise that you have experienced one at some point in the past. The kundalini is said to stir during periods of physical growth and so is obviously likely to be active throughout childhood and adolescence. Indeed, it may have some links with the vivid dreams, nightmares and 'night terrors' that often accompany these years. However, in most adults, once this period of growth is completed the Kundalini Shakti settles down and will sleep soundly unless the person begins to grow again – though this time it will be psychological and spiritual growth which brings about the stimulation.

Very often spontaneous stirrings will occur just after falling asleep and are accompanied by high pitched noises (like whistles or loud tinnitus), a feeling of paralysis – especially the back may feel rigid – sensations of light, great heat or cold. These may climax with a further intensifying of the experience with even greater noises and at this point one may either awaken or have a so-called 'false awakening', unusually intense dreams, even an out-of-body experience. A dream may precede the experience itself and this sort of dream usually has a high degree of lucidity and subject matter – often a strongly erotic, visceral or excretory content.

The following example is very much a typical experience which has been taken from the diary of a woman who had been meditating for approximately six months:

> I was aware during the two days before the experience of severe back pains and feeling like a tight band about my head. Just after I fell asleep I was dreaming of driving my car and suddenly the car went out of control, the brakes failing. I brought the car to a stop at a petrol station and shaking, got out and went into the toilet. Was aware of unpleasant smells and I began to feel very hot and nauseous. I thought I might vomit but fought against it feeling quite confused as to where I was. I suddenly became lucid – awake in the dream – and looked up into the mirror over the wash-basin. My hair and eyes looked wild and I barely recognised myself. As I looked I became aware of a high-pitched whistling noise that grew and grew and a

noise like a baby crying. I realised the sound was coming from me!

I then woke up but the heat and noise I had experienced in the dream was still with me – my body was in a totally catatonic state incapable of moving. The noise increased and increased until it seemed as though I was standing in the stream of a jet-engine. I began to see shooting colours especially white light behind my eyes. I began to wonder how long could I tolerate this when there seemed to be a climax of energy like a wave starting low in my body and travelling like an orgasmic wave through me. After that things quieted down and I could move again. It took some time before I was able to return to sleep and when I woke in the morning the sun streaming down through the window felt like I was being bathed in heavenly light – I went around in a state of heightened awareness and euphoria for the next 48 hours that gradually slipped away.

Following this the subject had a number of similar episodes and a frequent pattern of these was the preceding of the experience by acute bodily sensations. During this time she was under the tutelage of an experienced meditation teacher who assisted her in the process of understanding and channeling the powerful energies aroused.

This experience is a very typical one. Other symptoms of the kundalini syndrome can be both physical and emotional and can include numbness, especially in the lower legs, that is unrelated to any physical cause; strong tingling sensations; feelings of heat and cold; back pains and headaches; depression and elation and increase in emotional response and sexuality. Obviously any or a combination of these occurring in an individual do not automatically point to kundalini disturbance, but when someone does report any of these along with powerful or unusual dreams or meditation practices it is usual to monitor more closely to see if this is the beginning of such a stirring.

Naturally, it is the intention of the individual which is important in these matters. Casualties of what has come to be called the 'physio-kundalini syndrome', are usually people who are meditating without some form of inner or outer guidance or who are using it as a panacea to avoid reality, the way some use alcohol or drugs. It can also result from the mixing of drugs with occult techniques. The most usual outcome of such an occurrence is that the person gives up their meditation practices and life returns to normal.

Meditation and related practices have a subtle but definite effect upon the nervous system which involves long-term stimulation. This results in what may be most aptly described as an evolution of that system. These type of practices can sooner or later result in a stirring of the sleeping kundalini with the resultant release of energy. What actually happens here is a mystery – certainly no one can give a definite answer – but it can be said that, according to many people who have experienced these states of consciousness, something quite important is occuring. It allows for an acceleration of development within the individual and this brings positive benefits such as new perspectives on solving problems.

So what of those who have the right intention and yet find themselves distressed by the experiences? The very process of initiation and rebirth is often painful as one experiences the death of the old self which precedes it. The answer does, of course, differ from individual to individual, but the most common advice is to cut back on meditation work, while not stopping completely. The stirring of the Kundalini Shakti is an important sign and should be honoured as such. Continuing gently with the practices allows the natural process of re-adjustment and refinement of the body's energy system to continue so that manifestations of the kundalini can be experienced without distress.

It should also be stressed that these stirrings, as powerful as they may feel, are not the 'raising of the kundalini'. They may be a prelude to it but again it is better not to seek this experience directly. It will come in its own time and is not in itself a sign of greater spiritual stature or progress. Some people have highly developed and sensitive nervous systems that quite readily respond to esoteric practices in this manner. One of my first teachers remarked that some individuals could hang upside down for a week and do all manner of intense meditation work and never have a flicker of kundalini energy and yet others merely had to do a few bouts of pranayama (rhythmic breathing) to set off intense experiences. It may well be a sign of training in the Mysteries from a previous life or of inherent abilities. This kind of experience can be a huge trap if one becomes glamorised or addicted to it or is rendered so sensitive that it becomes ineffective! Before going on to detail the next exercise I would like to quote from the Oracle of the Goddess Kundalini from Olivia Robertson's ritual, 'The Mystical Awakening of Kundalini and Scorpio' (from *Sophia: Cosmic Consciousness of the Goddess*). It contains much to contemplate and meditate upon with regard to this primal power which we call Kundalini Shakti.

Divine Kundalini, the World's Mother, Hidden Fire, Mystic Life Force, Devi, Shakti, arise within us and bring us eternal life! . . .

Seek Me throughout all the realms of Being with selfishness, and you shall never find Me! You acknowledge that from Me proceed the vital flames of the Cosmic Life Force. But why do you seek my Power? Do you love Me, your Mother? Do you desire to bring to birth, to care for others, as I do? Or rather do you seek My energy that you may increase your importance without regard for your fellows? A planet savaged by power-hungry humans is left a wasteland, devoid of all living things, pock-marked with craters. And as with a planet, so with my children, both human and beast. For My Fire either creates or it destroys. It will never for long lie inactive . . .

My occult Power may be still more misused both by the foolish and the wicked. But know that a severe penalty is paid by the ill-doer for each act that misuses My Force . . . If you truly seek My creative energy with good intention, find Me in the Heart of Love. Feel Me through parenthood, through caring for all existences. Then your noble ideals, your great projects, will come easily into manifestation with ever increasing effectiveness. Take heed to balance force with gentleness.

CHAKRA CLEANSING AND BALANCING EXERCISE

Once you have completed the sequence as suggested in the first part of this chapter you will be holding the visualisation of the seven centres/chakras. It is perhaps a good idea at this point to take some time to be aware of the present state of your chakras. It is inevitable that some of these will be over-energised, others under-energised. You may find on investigation that you have congestion or blockages in one or more of your centres.

It may be worthwhile to work with the cleansing exercises as described below for a few days then return to the earlier exercise of establishing the pillar of light. Working on the same exercise day after day can become a little tedious, so introducing a little variety can help.

1 Before continuing with the moving of the energy in the vital centres some time should be spent upon attuning to the quality of the energy in each chakra – this can be considered as a 'cleansing' of the centres. This is done by focusing upon the normal colour of each centre in turn and introducing – through rhythmic breathing and visualisation of the essence of the colour as it would be in ideal conditions – a clear and true reflection of the rainbow spectrum light.

2 Allow yourself to be aware of each centre in turn, working with one at a time (though in any one session you might work with more than one centre in total). Be aware not only of the natural colour of the centre but of the quality of that energy. Any emotions, thoughts or images that come to you should also be noted here.

3 Following this, focus upon the essence of the colour from the sphere of light you have visualised above your head. With an inhalation, bring the pure colour into the chosen chakra. Observe the colour of the chakra following this for a few moments and then inhale again. Do three inhalations in sequence and then stop and observe for a longer period. Also examine your feelings and perhaps any emotions, recurring thoughts or images that arise for you.

4 You are aiming to experience within the centre a clear, well-balanced colour and energy. Do not force this colour but allow it to be there. If you are having muddied or different colours do record the results carefully and perhaps pay a little more attention to that centre when you work again with the meditation.

5 Repeat the cycle of three inhalations either until you are aware of a very clear colour in the chakra or until you have completed three breathing cycles. Then you can move on to another centre. For example, when focusing upon the base chakra, it's colour should be a clear, vital red yet this may on inspection be cloudy or tend towards orange, dirty red, etc. The same follows for all the centres as you work with them. Keep in mind what we have discussed and monitor your experiences. If you do get some unusual phenomena, do make sure you keep a record and merely do as suggested in the text above – cut back on your meditation work – just do the relaxation and breathing as previously and perhaps take a meditation subject or do some gentle visualisation work.

The Chakras and the Qabalah

In the West the subject of subtle energy systems came to prominence in the late 1800s with the emergence of the Theosophical Society, the Society of the Golden Dawn, and various Yogic and Buddhist groups. Indeed one of the major techniques taught by the Golden Dawn was a western version of kundalini yoga – the Middle Pillar technique. For those unfamiliar with the practical Qabalah, the Judaic mystical system which has for many years been adopted by practitioners of the magical arts in the West, and the terms associated with it, I will attempt to give a thumbnail sketch of this system. As with the chakras it is a complex subject and many texts have been written on the subject. The Bibliography contains titles which I consider to be the most useful.

The word 'qabalah' means 'from mouth to ear' and implies the oral tradition of the Hebrews. Since the time of Cornelius Agrippa in the early 1500s Western occultists

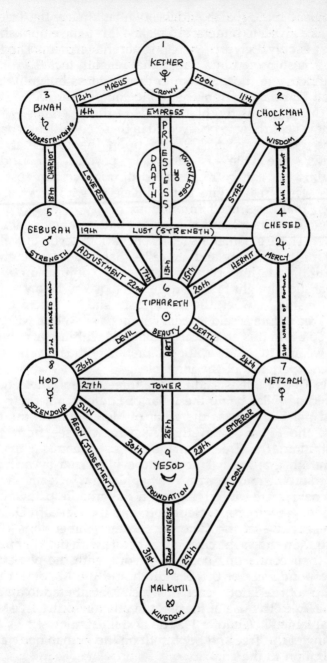

The Tree of Life

have used the Qabalah and its attendant image the Tree of Life as a glyph to understand reality. It is to be emphasized that it is only a glyph – a map is not the territory. The fact that it is so rooted in a patriarchal religion makes it often unattractive to those drawn to the Goddess but to be fair to the Qabalah a strong feminine component has always run through it as the hidden side of the teachings which are now beginning to be revealed in these enlightened days.

The Qabalah is itself based upon the idea that the Creator – the One – is ultimately beyond our understanding but can be represented through certain abstract ideas. The Tree of Life is the image of withdrawn light which manifests itself throughout reality in the form of 'emanations' or spheres in a zig-zag pattern of descent into matter. These emanations represent various levels of reality and spiritual energy and are called Sephiroth (as singular Sephira). An important principle in conjunction with Qabalistic thought is the adage 'as above so below' – the relationship between the macrocosm and the microcosm. The Tree of Life is said to exist within us as well as without and so again it is emphasised that it is within our natures that we find the gateway for exploration of the universe and direct experience of the ineffable.

The Tree of Life is said to have three 'pillars', the central or middle pillar being the Pillar of Equilibrium, the right hand pillar known as the Pillar of Mercy and on the left hand the Pillar of Severity. As you will see from our illustration, the Tree is made up of dynamic pairs of Sephiroth that are balanced and synthesized by a third, placed on the middle way. The Sephiroth which align with the chakras are those lying upon this middle pathway.

There are ten proper Sephiroth and the eleventh Daath, representative of the Gateway to other dimensions. The illustration shows the classic Tree of Life with the Sephiroth and their connecting pathways, along with the planetary correspondences of the Sephiroth and the Major Arcana trumps of the Tarot – each of which is attributed to a path of the Tree. The use of the Tarot in relation to the Tree will be explained in Chapter 14. The next illustration shows the placing of the Tree and Sephiroth on the human body and attribution to the chakras.

The first Sephira is the highest sphere, Kether, meaning

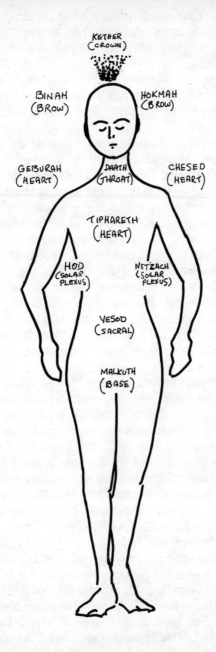

The Chakras and Tree of Life in Relation to the Human Body

crown. It equates with the beginning of Creation and can
be considered a point of omniscience and omnipotence – a
fountainhead for the manifestation to come. Kether equates
to the crown chakra.

The energy of Kether descends and becomes the
Sephiroth Chokmah, meaning Wisdom, which stands at
the head of the Pillar of Mercy. It is the power of Kether in
dynamic action.

The third Sephira is Binah which means Understanding,
and it stands at the head of the Pillar of Severity. It is known
as the Great Sea and the Great Mother and is the Womb
of creation. Likewise Chokmah is seen as the Great Father.
They are archetypal Form and Force respectively. These are
portrayed in terms of the male and female but it is to be
remembered that the physical form of these is but a dim
reflection of the spiritual reality. Chokmah and Binah
together are expressed in the brow chakra.

Below these three Supernal Sephiroth lies the Abyss.
Within the Abyss is the eleventh Sephiroth Daath. It is
known as the 'hidden' Sephira and is essentially a bridge
over the Abyss which separates the Divine from 'that which
is not quite divine'. The Abyss can be crossed by means of
Daath which means Knowledge – the knowledge of
experience. Daath equates to the throat chakra.

The fourth and fifth sephiroth are Chesed and Geburah
representing Mercy/Compassion and Severity/Justice
respectively. It is also possible to link the archetypal
energies of Love and Will to these spheres. Chesed can be
seen as being the place of the building up of forms and is
anabiotic, while Geburah breaks down forms and is
catabolic in nature. The mundane spheres (i.e. planets) of
Jupiter and Mars are attributed to Chesed and Geburah and
many of the qualities of these planets can be seen in the
nature of these sephiroth.

Their balancing point is Tiphareth which links to the
heart centre in the body. The name means Beauty and it
is a sphere of Harmony and Perfect Balance. As mentioned
previously, the chakra which is located here also has this
attribution – Tiphareth is seen to be the place of balance for
all the energies of the Tree. It combines the benevolence of
Chesed and the vital ferocity of Geburah. The Sun which
is capable of nurturing or destroying by its heat is attributed

here. These three Sephiroth are expressed in the heart chakra.

The next two are again a dynamic pair Netzach (Victory) and Hod (Glory). Hod is the sphere of the Intellect, logic and insight. It governs the hermetic path and ceremonial magic as well as science. Netzach is the sphere of the Emotions, the senses and passions. It is concerned with the elements and nature and the sheer thrill of living. The planets Mercury and Venus are attributed to these spheres and they are expressed in the solar plexus chakra.

Their balancing sephira upon the Middle Pillar is Yesod which means Foundation. It relates to the underlying foundation of material life – the Astral Plane – and in our personalities relates to our unconscious. The Moon is the planet attributed here and the chakra is the sacral.

Finally there is Malkuth, the Kingdom – the physical world. By this we do not mean only our Earth but the entire manifest Universe. Malkuth is the final sphere and is attributed to the base chakra. It absorbs the qualities of the others giving physical form to less material forces.

One way to approach the Tree of Life and the energy of the kundalini is through the Middle Pillar technique. It is probably the best example of a safe and sure method of working with this powerful energy. Unlike the kundalini yoga practised in the East it does not seek to work directly on the physical body but aims to have an effect upon the subtle astral-etheric body which indirectly effects the physical. It is also notable that it works with the energy from the top down, not raising the power from the base chakra upward. When devising the Rainbow Chakra exercise earlier in this chapter, I drew on my experience of the Middle Pillar.

In working with this technique it is found that the infusion of energy it brings into the chakras will begin gently to stimulate the kundalini into waking. There are very sound reasons for this approach. The average Western practitioner, due to cultural conditioning, is less sophisticated in spiritual matters than her/his Eastern counterparts and, in general, his/her consciousness is more centred in the material plane. More care is therefore needed in order not to rouse these energies prematurely.

We can view the planes of existence as being of a similar

nature to the Qabalistic emanations moving from the subtle spiritual levels to the density of matter in successive stages. This is not to say that the physical world is evil, only that its vibratory nature is more dense and thereby more open to distortion. Why this should be so is the subject of much speculation and indeed it may be our very thinking that aids in the creation of this solidity. A very interesting exploration on the subject of our 'co-creation' of physical reality can be found in the records of Jane Robert's Seth Material. Her channelled writings contain concepts that jerk the mind of the reader out of its usual rut and makes fascinating if demanding reading.

The aim of the Middle Pillar technique is to make a connection with the energies of the Sephiroth by drawing on the energies of the highest Sephira, Kether, and bringing these down Sephira by Sephira, charging them with the appropriate name of God and using visualisation and breathing techniques. Once the energy in Malkuth is grounded, the energies are circulated throughout the body. I will not be reproducing the Middle Pillar exercise in this manual for drawing upon Hebrew 'god-names' is not really appropriate to the subject matter. However, I have adapted the basic technique in the closing exercise of this chapter to work with a similar circulation of force.

CIRCULATING THE ENERGY

Begin this exercise with the usual relaxation and breathing. As feels appropriate use either of the earlier exercises to establish an awareness of your chakras and to energise them.

Experience this for a few minutes and then go on to become aware of the energy that is available all around you, especially through the elements and the Earth herself. See this as a vast reservoir that, as you become aware of it, forms into a pool all about your feet. Using a gentle but steady inhalation draw that energy through the soles of your feet, then up through your body. Imagine it flowing out of the top of your head to fall all about you as if you were a living fountain of radiant light and energy.

Do this a number of times, then stop get a sense of the experience and continue again through a number of cycles.

Then, either taking a pre-chosen theme or just attuning to what feels right at the moment, meditate for a few minutes. Complete the session as always by writing up your notes.

Chapter 4

Ritual and Sacred Drama

This chapter concludes Part 1 and the initial phase of your work. We will, in the course of this chapter, be looking at the subject of ritual as well as touching upon two classic stories of initiation into the mysteries of the Goddess. We will conclude with two rituals, the first a simple ritual to create a sacred space dedicated to the Egyptian pantheon and the second a rite of self-initiation into the mysteries of the Goddess. Although this is a solo ritual there will be added notes with which to expand it for a small group allowing each of the members to assist, on separate occasions, in the process of initiation.

In preparation for this ritual and to mark the end of Part 1 you may wish to write a summary of your ideas, thoughts, feelings and insights about the time that you have been working with this book. This will allow you to evaluate the progress you have made with the exercises and, more importantly, how this has reflected in your life. Place this in your diary-record before undergoing the initiation ritual and going on to Part 2.

Ritual is an evocative word for it conjures up images in the imagination of clouds of incense and people in robes making strange gestures by candlelight. But what does the word mean? A ritual is a series of actions which are done with intention. That intention depends on the person or persons doing the ritual. Rituals can be religious, magical or mundane.

We all do rituals on the mundane level. These need not be linked to any religious beliefs but can be our routine formulas for doing things such as getting up in the morning, coming in from work, cooking and eating meals, preparing for bed, which make us feel comfortable. This is a process learnt in childhood where such routines become our habits in later life. Man is a creature that ritualises. In Japan, for example, there are beautiful and elaborate ceremonies wherein tea is prepared or flowers are arranged in a ritual manner. However, if you examine your own life you will probably find examples of how you and others about you are already working some form of ritualised or ceremonial behaviour.

I mention this partly to dispel the mystique that ritual is only done within secret societies, magical groups, covens or pagan gatherings. One very accessible example of rituals which happen daily are in the religious ceremonies around the world including those church/synagogue/mosque services which we take for granted including rites of passage such as christenings, bar mitzvahs, weddings, funerals. There are even more mundane festive rituals connected with Christmas, Thanksgiving (Harvest Festivals), Halloween, Bonfire Night and birthday celebrations. Even the act of saying a short prayer or grace over a meal is a small ritual which is observed quite unconsciously.

Take a few moments to contemplate your experience of the use of ritual in the mundane world in your diary-record and write too of your reaction to the rituals you have taken part in so far in your life. Did you feel comfortable or alienated by them? Do you resist these sort of routines in your life which border on ritual or do you seek them out? What is it that attracts or repels you by this.

Murry Hope, in her book, *The Psychology of Ritual*, gives in her opening chapter a comprehensive list of the various types of ritual worldwide in both esoteric and exoteric settings which I include here with her kind permission:

1 Recollective ceremonies – the remnants of earlier, more advanced civilisations, the true meanings of which have become obscured.

2 The worship or acknowledgment of cosmological or celestial influences – the sun, moon, stars, or natural phenomena such as thunder, lightning, and so on.

3 Pantheistic, Pagan or Animistic Rites . . . in which due reverence is paid to the spirits of nature. Seasonal rituals would come under this category, also Rites of Sympathetic Magic.

4 Placatory or Propitiatory Rites – performed with a view to keeping the gods or spirits happy . . .

5 Ancestral Rites – which involve making contact with, and securing the good offices of, those of the tribe who have passed on.

6 Self-Exploratory Rites – including those self-analysis techniques which project the participant back into his or her own inner resources.

7 Fertility Rites – involving the multiplication principle which, as much as it may surprise some, is not limited to the human reproductive system.

8 Social Rites – including those rites which greet us when we first enter life, Maturation or Puberty Rites which are designed to prepare young people of the tribe for the step into adult life, and the Last Rites administered at the approach of death.

9 Sacrificial or Expiatory Rites – which make their appearance in both religion and magic to this day.

10 Initiatory Rites – including Rites of Submission, many of which originally involved physical mortification or deprivation. In this day and age, however, as with many other rites which originated in more primitive times, these are usually enacted symbolically.

11 Supplicatory Rites – including general unspecified collective prayer offerings and invocations which may or may not involve energy exchanges (gifts). These can be purely devotional, or may include specific pleas for bounty or guidance.

12 Rites of Protection, Purification, Banishing, Cleansing and Healing – which naturally vary in intention according to the persuasion of the users.

She goes on to reflect that most rituals are layered, in that they contain a blend of these categories. Within the mysteries of the Goddesses most rituals are of a devotional nature, mark a Rite of Passage (Hope's No 8) or are initiatory.

Within the category of devotional rituals, i.e. those which seek union with deity, these can take one of three forms. The first is purely devotional wherein union is sought through love, devotion and service. This is the path of the Mystic. The second is by means of ceremonial magic where the goddess/god are approached by use of magical methods such as invocation and again there can be an aspect of service to this. This is the path of the Magician. The third way is thought to be the finest because it combines the techniques of both of the above and adds a further dimension of mediation, which is the channelling of divine force. This is the sacred drama where participants act out a myth taking the parts of the gods and goddesses and other participants in the tale. This is the path of the Priestess and Priest.

Ritual can be merely empty actions or they can be imbued with life, energy and meaning. Much depends on the consciousness of the person or persons who are doing the ritual.

Two rituals are given in the course of this chapter. The first is a combination of the first two ways given above in that invocations are used with devotional actions to create a sacred space for you to meditate in or do other type of work. The example given uses Egyptian Goddesses but with a little imagination you may change the emphasis to another pantheon. The second ritual also creates a sacred place but in this case it is one in which you will enact the sacred drama of initiation.

First, let us look at our initial two examples of initiations into the mysteries. The first is written as a novel, yet lays out the process of initiation, albeit with deliberate 'blinds', so that the author would not break his oaths of secrecy. This tale relates to the Mysteries of Isis and Osiris. The second is the mythic drama of Ishtar's descent to the Underworld. As you progress through the second part of the Pillar of Isis you will find scattered throughout a number of examples of this type of mystery drama. Both traditionally and within the Fellowship of Isis these are used as initiatory rituals which span a number of traditions. It is also true that there are many, many more stories than these and in Chapter 12 we look at utilising contemporary stories in a similar way.

The Goddess Within The Golden Ass

The first tale we shall examine is related in the pages of *The Golden Ass* by Apuleius (translated by Robert Graves, Penguin Classics). The proper title is *The Transformations of Lucius* and it is an evocative account of the adventures of a prospective initiate to the Mysteries of Isis written in the 2nd century AD by a man who we know to have been an initiate of the Isian Mysteries. It is believed that genuine keys and teachings from those times have been encoded within the text. As Gareth Knight writes in his commentary on *The Golden Ass* within his *The Rose-Cross and the Goddess*:

> Just as the wisdom of the Tarot was preserved because it was put in form of a common card game, so with The Golden Ass. It is at base simply an elaboration of an ancient Greek dirty joke and has come down the ages as a comic erotic novel. Human nature being what it is we find that complete texts of Apuleius's other books have not survived . . . whereas the Golden Ass has not only survived, but is freely available in cheap paperback form to this day.

Knight goes on to point out that Apuleius drops a number of hints to his readers in the preface in the form of apologies that qualify it as:

> a form of literature known in later Rosicrucian days as a ludibrium, a fantastic tale embodying great truths of which another example is *The Chemical Marriage of Christian Rosencreutz*. The narrative uses the tale of Lucius's transformation into an ass to illustrate the Neo-Platonic idea of the spirit falling into physical incarnation, i.e. a semi-animal condition and that his adventures 'are thus parallel to the initiations of the Mysteries, that lead from the material world to the condition of unfallen spirit'.

The text is full of stories within stories and layered meanings which have the effect of taking the reader through a series of sacred dramas. The protagonist, Lucius, is a noble-minded young man who is visiting the land of Thessaly and, despite many a warning against the 'witchcraft' practised thereabouts, yearns after the magical secrets of the wife of the man he is lodging with and conspires with her maid to steal the magical ointment which will change him into an owl, the bird sacred to the Goddess of Wisdom, Athena. However, as luck would have it, they take the wrong jar and when he applies the ointment, Lucius is transformed into an ass. The ass was the sacred animal of Set, the brother of the god Osiris who engineered his murder and dismemberment. Thus, rather than approaching the mysteries of Isis aligned to the Wisdom Goddess, he is transformed into the beast which is 'most hateful to her of all beasts in existence'.

The antidote to change Lucius back to a man is that he must eat roses, the flower that is sacred to the Goddess, but before he can do this simple act, he is stolen by thieves and thus begins his adventures that last for a year and a day. This is symbolic of the period of probation into the mysteries where one is tried and tested and hopefully found worthy of initiation.

At the end of his wanderings, Lucius finds himself by the sea-shore and awakes to find the full Moon rising over the sea. 'It is at this secret hour that the Moon-goddess, sole sovereign of mankind, is possessed of her greatest power and majesty.' He directs an empassioned prayer to the Great Goddess begging her to transform him back to human form or to grant him the gift of death.

After the prayer he is overcome by sleep and as he is about to close his eyes, 'an apparition of a woman began to rise from the middle of the sea with so lovely a face the gods would have fallen down in adoration of it'. He goes on to describe in poetic imagery this transcendent vision.

> Her long thick hair fell in tapering ringlets on her lovely neck, and was crowned with an intricate chaplet in which was woven every kind of flower. Just above her brow shone a round disc, like a mirror, or like the bright face of the moon, which told me who she was. Vipers rising from the left hand and right hand supported this disc, with ears of corn bristling beside them. Her many coloured robe was of finest linen . . . but what caught and held my eye more than anything else was the deep black lustre of her mantle . . . it was embroidered with glittering stars on the hem and

everywhere else, and in the middle beamed a full and fiery moon. In her right hand she held a bronze rattle.

The Goddess addresses Lucius in an exquisite declaration of her Nature.

> You see me here, Lucius, in answer to your prayer. I am Nature, the universal Mother, mistress of all the elements, primordial child of time, sovereign of all things, queen of the dead, queen also of the immortals, the single manifestation of all gods and goddesses that are . . . Though I am worshipped in many aspects, known by countless names, and propitiated with all manner of different rites, yet the whole round earth venerates me. The primeval Phrygians call me the Mother of the gods; the Athenians call me Cecropian Athena; for the islanders of Cyprus I am Paphian Aphrodite; for the archers of Crete I am Dictyanna Diana, for the trilingual Sicilians, Stygian Proserpine; and for the Eleusians their ancient Mother of the Corn, Demeter.
>
> Some know me as Juno, some as Bellona of the Battles; others as Hecate, others again as Rhamnubia, but both races of Ethiopians, whose lands the morning sun first shines upon, and the Egyptians who excel in ancient learning, worship me with ceremonies proper to my godhead, call me by my true name, Queen Isis.

Isis then instructs Lucius to attend a public ceremony held in her honour where the High Priest, acting on a vision she will send to him that night, will be carrying a garland of roses. However, she states that from this day to the end of his days he will be dedicated to her service as it was only right that he should devote his life to the Goddess who has made him a man once more.

This he does and in due course is initiated into the mysteries of Isis and later Osiris, both of which he says little about as he is bound by oaths of secrecy. Much can be gleaned by the reader by careful reading and meditation on the entire story, especially the story of Psyche and Cupid encapsulated in the heart of the tale. We will return to this particular story in Chapter 12. The writer Apuleius was not only an initiate of the mysteries of Isis and Osiris but later became also a Priest of Asclepios, the Greek god of medicine, and was also a historian and poet. None of his other works have survived but this ribald tale containing high initiatory secrets has survived for well over 1,800 years.

The Descent of the Goddess

The second story illustrates a type of initiatory ritual traditional to many societies; that of a symbolic descent into the labyrinthine realm of the Earth Mother and subsequent ascent, reborn from the experience. The archetypal tale of this is contained in the mythology of the Sumerian Goddess Inanna, who was known to the later Assyrians and Babylonians as Ishtar. She was a goddess of many forms, embracing both the light and dark aspects of the Goddess and was especially associated with the Moon and Venus, ruling fertility on many levels. Over time the myths associated with each of the forms of this goddess have become somewhat blurred but there is a difference.

Both Goddesses enter the Underworld realms, but in the later myth of Ishtar's descent, the focus is upon the theme of the dying and resurrecting vegetation god. Ishtar is seeking the return of her son/lover Tammuz from the Underworld regions after he is killed by a wild boar. In order to do this she enters this realm ruled over by Her sister, Ereshkigal, and passes through the seven gates of the Underworld. At each gate she is challenged to surrender one of her ornaments until she stands naked before the Queen of the Underworld. However Ereshkigal does not release Tammuz but rather imprisons Ishtar, only releasing them when pressure is brought to bear by the other gods. On their return to the Upper World Ishtar regains those garments and ornaments that she had surrendered and the Earth which had grown barren with her absence is once more fertile.

This myth forms the basis for the Fellowship of Isis's formal initiation ritual entitled The Rite of Rebirth. This recreates as a mystery drama the descent of the Goddess and her surrendering of her powers, using it as an exploration of the theme of Spirit choosing incarnation into the world of matter, wherein it surrenders its powers, only regaining them upon initiation. In this version of the tale, which I have incorporated into the adaptation which concludes this chapter and section of the book, the Dark Goddess of the Underworld, Ereshkigal, although imprisoning Ishtar and Tammuz, is in fact their initiator and not an adversary.

In the original story of Inanna's descent, her journey to the underworld is motivated not by loss but by the desire to know. Inanna is the Queen of Heaven and the Upper Earth but of the Underworld realms, ruled by Her older sister, she is ignorant. In order to gain understanding of the 'Great Below' (the inference is to understand the process of death and rebirth), she must herself undertake this journey. She does so, leaving behind her worldly strongholds. However, before the journey she instructs her servant, Ninshubar, that if she does not return within a certain period of time Ninshubar is to seek the aid of the other gods to aid her to return. In this mythic cycle Ereshkigal again can be considered the 'shadow' side of Inanna, for descriptions of her as infertile, insatiable and without loving relationship with parent, sibling or lover, ruling a dark and dry realm are in stark contrast to Inanna, appearing at the first Gate of the Underworld in her glory and light as Goddess of Love. Ereshkigal is enraged and instructs her gatekeeper to set aside Inanna's symbolic ornaments of her roles of queen, priestess and woman. This she does and standing vulnerable before Ereshkigal, she is struck and killed. 'Inanna was turned into a corpse, a piece of rotting meat, and was hung from a hook on the wall.'

After Inanna has been absent for three days and three nights, her servant seeks out Enlil, the Sumerian sky-god, Nanna, god of the Moon, and Inanna's father, but each refuses to interfere in the politics of the Underworld. Finally, Enki, god of the waters and a god of wisdom, appreciates the plight of the Earth with Inanna's absence from it, and sends two magic creatures to Ereshkigal who is suffering labour pains. These pains are linked to her having killed her sister and somehow now giving birth to her. The creatures assist Ereshkigal and in gratitude she allows Inanna to return to life and to leave the Underworld. However, she can only do this if a substitute is found to take her place there.

Inanna returns, taking up her ornaments and powers

once more, and is greeted by her servants and two sons. Each of her sons offers to take her place but she declines to send them. However, upon returning to her palace she finds her consort, Dumuzi, has ascended the throne in her absence and quite enjoyed the power he was holding. In anger Inanna declares that Dumuzi will take her place and he, after some struggle and long pursuit, is carried off to the underworld by Ereshkigal's demons.

Inanna does mourn Dumuzi and when his sister, Gestinanna, herself a daughter of Enki, comes to Inanna to plead for his life and offers to take his place in the Underworld, she relents and releases her former curse. Although Dumuzi has to dwell in the underworld for half of the year, his sister will take his place there during the second half of the year when he will return to Inanna. Certainly each of the protagonists has at the end of the story undergone a process of death and rebirth and through such has gained in self-knowledge and wisdom.

I have tried to simplify in a few paragraphs a myth which has many levels of meaning with respect to the often painful process of self-knowledge leading to a direct experience of the Goddess and initiation in Her mysteries.

AN EGYPTIAN OPENING AND CLOSING RITUAL

This first ritual is a simple opening and closing rite in which the elemental quarters are opened and the Goddesses are invoked in the Quarters, Above and Below the Place of Working, both as Guardians and as a Source of Inspiration. You may wish to read further in the text or elsewhere to get a sense of the attributions of the Goddesses.

This ritual can be used in its own right to have an experience of these Goddesses, or before the ritual of self-initiation or any other form of ritual or special meditation work. You can use it as often as you like and combine it with other exercises such as the relaxation and chakra exercises of the previous chapter. It is a variation on a ritual used by the Lyceum of Isis-Sophia of the Stars to open and close each meeting and prepare the celebrants for the main ritual or working to be done. Thus its function is the same as the 'casting of circle' done in Wicca.

You will need some undisturbed time for this ritual as indeed you need for all such work. If you are living with others you will probably need to alert them that you are unavailable for a time though hopefully this will be understood. Make sure the phone will be off the hook or unlikely to intrude. You will need to have available a table or stand to serve as a central altar, a candle, an incense stick or charcoal and loose incense, a bowl of spring water, an object to represent Earth (such as a crystal, stone, flowers), a vial of oil and a small bell to ring. If you wish you can also use appropriate coloured candles or 'quarter-lights' to designate the elemental quarters which should be lit during the initial section as the Guardians of the Quarters are called. You may also wish to utilise suitable music to play in the background during the ritual. Although written here for a solo ritual it can easily be adapted for a group.

As the invocations of the Goddesses are recited the appropriate forms of these should be visualised. You will probably find for a time you will need this script to read the rite but as you become familiar with the text you will be able to dispense with this and recite from memory, releasing more of your attention for visualising.

Opening
The bell is rung. Move to each quarter and raise your hand in a gesture of greeting. If you wish light the candle in that quarter and say:

East: *Hail to Thee, Guardians of the East, Powers of Air, quarter of all beginnings and of discrimination. Hail to the Goddesses Astarte, Aurora, Ushas of the Dawn; Sylphs, eagles, crows and all birds, spirits of the air. Come and be present at this sacred place and witness this rite.*

South: *Hail to Thee, Guardians of the South, Powers of Fire, quarter of great passion and will. Hail to the Goddesses Selket, Vesta and Bridgid, to Salamanders, sparks and spirits of fire. Come and be present at this sacred place and witness this rite.*

West: *Hail to Thee, Guardians of the West, Powers of Water, quarter of lore and understanding. Hail to the Goddesses Aphrodite, born from the foam, and Isis, bringer-in of the waters of life; Undines, dolphins, fishes – all spirits of the waters. Come and be present at this sacred place and witness this rite.*

North: *Hail to Thee, Guardians of the North, Powers of Earth, quarter of mystery and the unseen. Hail to the Goddesses Ceres, Demeter and Persephone, Earth Mothers and the Fates; Gnomes and spirits of caves, burrows and the earth. Come and be present at this sacred place and witness this rite.*

Centre: *In the Centre, I invoke the Element of Spirit and the Goddess of Infinite Space and the Infinite Stars therein. Pour your Divine Blessing into this sacred place.*

East (Light coal and place incense upon it or light stick. Hold the burner/stick aloft facing East): *In the East I invoke the Goddess Hathor. Sweet Hathor, Queen of Beauty, Gentle Mother of all creatures be present here. May your Light and Purity shine forth nourishing me as they do all Life that I may bring these virtues onto my own path and likewise nourish all about me.*

This incense is offered to the Goddess Hathor. (Walk slowly sunwise around the room with the incense creating a circle, finally replacing the burner on altar or stick in holder. If there are space restrictions in the room you are using – you may have to adapt these movements accordingly.)

South (Light candle on the central altar and holding it, face South): *In the South I invoke the Goddess Bast, Lady of Joy and Bounty, Protectress of the Sun who slew the Serpent Apet. Be present here. Grant me the joy of song and dance and the power of healing that I may send this out to the Earth and All Life. This eternal flame is offered to Bast.* (Holding the flame walk slowly sunwise about the room and then return candle to central altar.)

West (Take bowl of clear water and holding it, face West): *In the West I invoke the Goddess Isis – Oh Goddess of Ten Thousand Names, Mistress of Magic, Celestial Queen, Star of the West! I ask for your Grace and Blessing. You who taught many skills to humankind, be my teacher now that I may grow in wisdom and love and truly count myself your child. Aid me in my work and grant through this blessed water, offered to Isis, True Vision.* (The bowl is carried sunwise about the room and, returning it to the altar, draw a circle upon your brow as a blessing.)

North (Take the object being used to designate the North and hold it aloft while facing North): *In the North I invoke the Goddess Nephthys, Dark Lady, Ruler of the Night and Death. It is through you that we come to know these Mysteries and encounter the darkness within and without. Your hidden face confronts our fears and draws us into contemplation of the Unknown. I would ask for your protection and that you be my Guide as I journey inward. This . . . is offered to Nephthys.* (Again walk about the room holding the object and return with it to the central altar.)

Centre (Raising arms above head): *I raise my eyes to the Heavens and invoke Thee, Blessed Nuit – Mother of the Universe and the Gods. Your starry body bends in naked splendour over the Earth. Be as a veil about me and my place of working. May your Divine Milk run forth as a Blessing that I may be filled with the Glory of the Stars.* (Move arms to indicate the floor.) *Below and all about me is the Earth. May my work this day enrich the Earth even as my spirit is touched by the Eternity of the Stars.* (Vial of oil is taken from the central altar and held aloft.) *This sacred oil is offered to Nuit.* (The celebrant anoints brow with oil, saying): *In the Name of Nuit, may my soul awaken to the Mysteries.*

Take a few moments of silence, then proceed with further work – ritual, meditation, etc – the bell may be rung here to signal the change of mood.

Closing

After the meditation or other piece of work you may wish to do a formal closing. You may wish to say more to each Goddess in way of thanks, and should allow your heart to be your guide in this:

I now send forth rays of blessing and healing to all beings and existences. (If you wish to make a dedication of healing for energy to be sent to a specific person, place or event, this can be done now. A short silence while energy is sent forth)

East: *I give thanks to the Guardians of the East and to the Goddess Hathor for that which She has granted me this day.*

South: *I give thanks to the Guardians of the South and to the Goddess Bast for the gifts She has granted me this day.*

West: *I give thanks to the Guardians of the West and to the Goddess Isis for the love She has given me this day.*

North: *I give thanks to the Guardians of the North and to the Goddess Nephthys for the protection and guidance She has given me this day.*

Centre: *I give thanks to the Goddess Nuit for the Blessing of the Stars.*

Final bell is rung and, if appropriate, notes are written up.

RITUAL OF DEDICATION TO THE MYSTERIES OF THE GODDESS

My own experience of the descent of Ishtar took place in 1982 when I was formally initiated by the Fellowship of Isis's *Rite of Rebirth* (Ceseara Publications, Clonegal). That particular ritual continues to be used within the Fellowship of Isis as one of the myriad ways to gain initiation into the mysteries of the Goddess. It is considered that the actual ritual, although published and available from Clonegal on request, is rightly reserved for members of the Fellowship. The version that follows has been freely adapted from that source and others. Of course, there are many ways of doing such a self-initiation/dedication However, this formula, inspired by the Mysteries of Ishtar and Tammuz, has proven over the years to be a highly effective one.

It is a ritual that can be utilised by men as well as women. At the core of the ritual the celebrant walks the same route as the Goddess, surrendering in actuality or mime the items required at each of the seven gates of the Underworld. This is not a direct identification with the Goddess, she is experienced as walking with you. If the ritual is done in a group an attendant priestess would take the part of Ishtar, another man or woman the part of the Guardian and yet another woman the part of the Goddess of the Underworld.

While it is obviously of great advantage to go through an initiation ceremony conducted by a Priestess and group, this adaptation, done alone, does allow for a deep experience of the Goddess. Of course, initiation can only occur when someone is ready for that experience of rebirth and this ultimately takes place within one's own being. A ritual such as this can either be used as an outward confirmation of something that has already taken place or it can serve as a catalyst to begin an inner process that may eventually manifest itself in some form of spontaneous initiatory experience, dream or out-of-body journey.

PREPARATION

A certain amount of work beforehand is required for this ritual – both in inner preparation and collecting together various items. You will need to have some familiarity with the story of Ishtar and Tammuz, at least from reading the text of the ritual and the material given previously in this chapter. In the days leading up to the Rite of Ishtar take this study further and actually meditate upon the text. Make sure you feel comfortable about what you are doing on the day. You may wish to copy out on small cards the words you will be speaking so that you do not have to carry the book about with you.

On the day itself, you will need seven small candles, placed on a small table in the Centre of a room (this will be referred to as the central altar/shrine), and another small candle or lamp placed in each of the four quarters of the room. The elemental opening will ward your space and prepare your mood.

Prepare yourself with a ritual bath. This is simply a bath in which, as you wash your body, you mentally feel yourself being cleansed and prepared. Wear a robe if you have one; if not, then you should change into something clean and comfortable. You will need a piece of gauzy material or a scarf to act as a veil. This can be worn as a head-covering while you are reading, then pulled forward at the appropriate time to cover your eyes, and finally removed at the conclusion of the Rite as symbolic of your birth into a new life.

You will also need a vial of oil, a bowl of water and some corn kernels in a small dish. These should be placed on the central altar. If you would like to wear some jewellry or something else to symbolise those items mentioned in the text, please do so – however, the ritual is just as effective if you visualise these things and mime taking them off and surrendering them. As with any working, choose a time when you will not be disturbed and make sure the telephone is off the hook.

THE RITUAL

Prepare your place of working either using the Elemental opening provided or just taking some time to sit quietly. Make sure that you have lit the candles on the central shrine and in the four quarters.

Declaration: This is unscripted – you will need to make a statement of intent about the ritual you are about to do. Basically, you declare yourself an aspirant to the Mysteries of the Goddess and ask for Her Blessing on this Rite of Dedication and Self-Initiation. Remember:

> None may choose Rebirth for another. Nor may the soul demand entry into the Other Sphere without Divine Authority. Know that the awakening into eternal life comes through Deity and no one may declare that moment nor that hour. Yet the keys of the Spheres are in the hands of the Goddess Ishtar and through the witnessing of her Mysteries, may you choose thus to throw off the veil of division.

You may wish to use the following invocation or something similar to open your rite and then follow it with your personal dedication:

Hail Ishtar! Giver of Revelation, Queen of Heaven, the Goddess with the beautiful voice. Inspire me this day as I enact thy Mystery.

Extinguish all candles apart from the seven upon the central altar and the quarter light in the North. (This represents the 'dark altar' in the Rite.) Read from the text as follows:

Now as I speak of the Epic of Ishtar and Tammuz as was performed in the great Temples of Babylon, let my soul hearken to this divine drama, that new life shall be born within me.

Continue building in your mind's eye the images you have

been preparing. As you speak the words of the Rite visualise the unfolding of the story.

Long ago in time immemorial Tammuz, the Shepherd husband of the Goddess Ishtar, was mortally wounded by a wild boar and he sank into the Underworld, domain of the Dark Goddess, Ereshkigal.

For Ishtar, Queen of Heaven, grief was great for She had lost he who is dearer to Her than life. She wept long in her heavenly palace. In Her lamentations She resolved to enter the realm of the Underworld, to descend through the spheres and humble Herself before the Queen of the Underworld, Ereshkigal, her dark sister.

Thus I, child of earth and heaven, seek the way to the Dark Kingdom, wherein I might be reunited with my lost soul and follow in the footsteps of the Goddess as She is confronted at the seven gates of the Underworld.

Rise from your chair and slowly circumambulate the central shrine, repeating the walk of Ishtar – two steps forward, one back. As you do so be aware that the Goddess walks with you and together you will be challenged and will respond to the Guardian's demands. Stop before the first candle and hear within your mind the Voice of the Guardian who challenges you.

Why come you to the first gate of the Underworld?

You answer: *I come seeking that which is lost to me.*

The Guardian replies that you must surrender your bright Crown of Spirit as did Great Ishtar when she faced the first gateway. Thus surrender either your own crown or emulate this gesture saying:

Thus too, did my spirit enter this world, in blindness separate from the Divine Light.

Extinguish the first flame on the central altar and again circumambulate the altar and stop before the second candle. Again you are challenged and asked by the Guardian why you have come to the second gate of the Underworld. You may reply as above or whatever feels appropriate at the time. Again you will be asked to surrender something precious to you at the second gate. This will be that with which you are able to hear the words of the Inner levels. This can be depicted as an earring or a crystal or other small object upon a ribbon looped over the ear:

Thus, too, did my soul enter this world, having lost the power of hearing the voice of the Divine.

Extinguish the second flame.

You will continue this process of circling the central altar, being challenged at each gateway by the Guardian, speaking from your heart at each challenge and surrendering the item required and extinguishing the flame of that candle symbolising you have passed that Gate. Each Gate also symbolises the closing of a psychic centre (the chakras – beginning with the crown) as the soul enters into physical incarnation. You may use these words or adapt your own.

At the Third Gate, surrendering a jewel worn over your heart:

Thus, too, did I surrender my heart's warmth.

At the Fourth Gate surrendering a cord/magical girdle:

Thus, too, did I surrender my magic.

At the Fifth Gate, surrendering a ring:

Thus, too, did I surrender the awareness of my True Will as I entered this world.

At the Sixth Gate, surrendering magical sandals:

Thus, too, did I lose the ability to move between the worlds and awoke only to the limitations of a physical form.

At the Seventh Gate, surrendering a veil:

Here, too, I surrendered my innocence – my veil.

The Room is now in darkness – apart from the single light upon the Northern shrine. Return to your seat. It will be too dark to read but with your preparatory reading you can now imagine what takes place. Ishtar has come to the depths of the Underworld and, stripped of her royal robes and magical jewels, lies before the dark altar. Here Tammuz who, as a shade in the Underworld with no recollection of his former life, finds her and loves her. She arises at his words of love as he declares:

For would I choose to be in a dark underworld with this woman than dwell in the Upper World. What care I for Her name, when I know not my own. Where love is – that is Heaven.

Ishtar, who likewise has forgotten her divine origins, also declares as she sees Tammuz:

Praise be to the Goddess Ereshkigal! Blessed is this place and all within it! Gladly would I dwell here with this man!'

See then the dark Goddess Ereshkigal, clothed in black, approach the couple speaking her words of blessing:

Blessed are they who love my dark earth. Blessed are they who love my children who wear skins and scales and feathers. Wise are they who fear me not. Beneath my black veil of dreams is my True Being, the Primordial Mother.

At this point just be open to what happens. It is likely Ereshkigal will reveal Herself to you. When this is complete see the Divine couple as they awaken to the Knowledge of their True Selves, Ishtar, Queen of Heaven, sister to Ereshkigal and her husband Tammuz, the Shepherd-King, protector and guardian of the land.

If you have music to play at this point do so (gentle flute would be appropriate) – visualise the couple ascending the seven levels and as they do so move about the central shrine seven times yourself and each time relight a candle. At each gate recover any object you have surrendered in actuality or in mime and acknowledge the chakra point beginning with the base chakra and ending with the crown chakra – making again the connection in your mind that these chakras are the gateways. With each circumambulation remind yourself that you are reclaiming those gifts and abilities (albeit in latent form) once more.

Finish this section with the words:

Thus as Tammuz was held in the Underworld in dreams, so was he brought to life by the love and courage of his wife. So does each soul awaken when the time of Rebirth is nigh. Thus may I receive of the gifts of the Goddess so that, as a butterfly draws forth from its chrysalis when it is ready, so may my soul awaken to the Eternal life.

Light the other candles in the quarters and come to the central altar. Take up water and anoint your brow with the words:

With the Blessing of the Goddess of Spring – may I receive the Water of Life that I may always see with True Vision.

Take the corn in your hand and say:

With the Blessing of the Goddess of the Harvest may my imagination and creativity be awakened.

Place incense on charcoal or light a stick and allow its smoke to play about you, saying:

In the Name of the Goddess of Winter and the Starry Darkness may my soul receive this incense – that the Fire of Spirit will bring strength in this hour of initiation. Ishtar, holder of the Keys of the Spheres, awaken me to Eternal Life.

Now wait until it feels appropriate to remove your veil. You may well receive a personal message from the Goddess or have some other form of experience. Just be open to what happens.

Then take the oil from the central altar and anoint your brow with it, giving an acknowledgement of your having become an Initiate:

I anoint my brow with the sign of the Eight-pointed Star of the Goddess. Thus in this hour of awakening and initiation into the Mysteries of the Goddess, may I bring others with me into glory.

Close by giving thanks to the Goddesses Ishtar and Ereshkigal and the God Tammuz. Then leave the room for a minute or two with the nightlights burning on the central shrine. Return and extinguish them.

Write up your experience during the ritual including any sensations or messages which have come to you. You may be inspired to write a poem or draw a picture depicting the experience.

Part 2

Chapter 5

An Inner Room

One of the main premises of this book is to encourage a gentle process of self-exploration utilising some of the tools of psychology. The meditations in Part 1 were the initial stages of this. By working through them you will have gained skills in self-observation; the prime tool to assist you with the process of self-awareness. Further exercises within Part 2 continue this aspect of the work supplemented by some theory related to various schools of psychology.

There are many 'self-help' books on the market promoting self-awareness. One way in which this book differs from them is in linking these exercises with the process of connecting with the Goddess. Why do this at all? Why not just focus on an appreciation of the Goddess for herself? The simple answer is that this book seeks to facilitate a course of development which brings the practitioner to an experience of the Goddess: not only externally but an appreciation of her within their own souls.

As I have mentioned previously, the key to the mystery traditions has always been 'Know Thyself'. It is through self-knowledge that we have the opportunity to be whole people and thus, connected to our true purpose, can more effectively 'reflect our Mother's glory'.

Being prepared to observe oneself also assists in the process of assimilating the powerful spiritual energies contacted by this sort of esoteric work. It is all too easy for these energies to create an imbalance within the individual working with them. Indeed it is almost impossible to avoid some form of imbalance as the psyche is infused with the transcendental energies of these inner realms. This is not a reason to avoid these sorts of meditations or practices and, in being conscious of what is going on, it is possible to regain an inner equilibrium which has been enriched by the experience.

Two possible 'spiritual pathologies' that can take place are those of 'inflation' and 'deflation'. With inflation the individual's sense of power and place in the scheme of things grows to the point wherein they consider themselves superior to 'lesser mortals'. This can grow to the point of confusing their own identity with that of Deity or setting themselves up as a 'guru' or 'teacher'. In short a spiritual 'ego-trip'.

Deflation is the opposite to this in that following a strong spiritual experience and the return to normal consciousness, the contrast between what has been experienced and the conditions returned to feels so pronounced that a sense of sadness and depression ensues. Certainly, gaining self-knowledge is a painful path as we realise our shortcomings, but this is only part of the process. It also involves recognising our true strengths.

In Part 2 we shall be working more directly with the Mysteries of the Goddess. The most significant part of this work is the establishment of a Temple of the Goddess which I have called the Pillar of Isis within your aura. This will function upon the various levels explored in your work with the elements and chakras in Part 1, opening you to the possibility of deeper access to the inner worlds represented by those centres.

This process cannot be hurried or rushed through, though obviously each student will set his or her own pace to work through the exercises and main meditation sequences at the end of every chapter. It is important to follow the sequence as set out and to get to know each section of the Temple and Pillar slowly so that it becomes well established within your mind and 'subtle body' and is easily accessible to you.

Later in this chapter the scene shall be set for a meditative journey to the Inner Temple of Isis through the establishment of an Inner Room. This shall serve as a staging-post for further exploration in the chapters to come. This Inner Room can also be approached as a place where you are able to 'go inside' and find relaxation and peace. It will be a deeper experience of relaxation to that gained through the exercises in Chapter 1. The supplementary exercises given throughout each chapter can be done as 'one-offs' or however often feels appropriate. In their own way they encourage an inner journey of self-knowledge.

In this chapter I want to introduce some theories about the nature of the unconscious mind as expounded in the works of Sigmund Freud, Carl Jung and Wilhelm Reich. The reason for this emphasis on theory is to inform my readers, giving them the opportunity, if they so wish, to explore the subject in greater depth. The majority of theoretical books on psychology are dry tomes which give little practical application to the lay reader. By contrast books, promoting self-exploration, where exercise follows exercise, often convey little sense of the philosophy behind them.

This theoretical material can only be an overview. Those cited have each founded major schools within the movement of psychology and psychoanalysis and their collected ideas fill many volumes. However, for the lay reader an overview should suffice and for those who wish to investigate these ideas in more depth there are plenty of books readily available.

The concept of an area of the mind which is unknown or relatively inaccessible to our normal waking consciousness was known to the ancients and has been encoded into both the written and oral teachings of the Mysteries. These include the journey into the underworld, the cave wherein can be found great treasure, the value of dreams and the vision-quest. Many of the trials of the would-be initiate were and are generated by this journeying within to the dark, unconscious realms. Hence the significance of the story of Ishtar's descent into the Underworld as a mystery drama in the ritual of Chapter 4. The myth itself has many levels, such as the symbolism of our spirit's incarnation and willing embrace of the limitations of matter, and the turning within of our conscious mind to understand the nature of the unconscious.

This knowledge of the unconscious was pretty much lost during the Dark Ages though still found some expression in esoteric teachings. It was only with the birth of modern psychoanalysis at the beginning of this century that the theory of the unconscious saw the light of day once more.

It was during the late 18th and early part of the 19th century that doctors such as Sigmund Freud and Carl Jung sought to explain the neurotic illnesses of their patients. Through these investigations they came to believe that much early experiences and feelings were still held in an individual's mind but were outside of everyday conscious recall. Yet it seemed that these memories were still capable of having a powerful effect on the personality and colouring the individual's perceptions of the world. This created, for many, a sense of dis-ease, tension and anxiety leading often to neurosis and/or psychosomatic illnesses.

It was found that once this repressed material was made conscious, through a process of recall, analysis, catharsis and mature understanding, a key would be provided to make possible an easing of the emotional and physical problems. In realising that the mind was capable of greatly influencing the body they were the forerunners of the movement towards holistic thinking.

For the moment, I shall look at some of the theories of Freud, Jung and Reich, then move on in the next chapter to incorporate those of humanistic and transpersonal psychology. In some ways each theory can be considered to be a development and further refinement of the previous one.

However, by no means do all psychologists or schools of psychology believe in the existence of this unconscious part of the mind. In fact, in the psychology courses offered by most schools and colleges, the emphasis is still upon behavioural and cognitive psychology which fit the criteria of scientific materialism and also allow for repeatable experimental assignments. Those promoting these disciplines are often extremely dismissive of ideas found within psychoanalysis and humanistic psychology. The general reductionist world-view of these 'rats and mazes' psychologists with their often unequivocal disbelief in the sublime makes their work of limited appeal to students of the esoteric, for it is psychology without a soul.

The legacy of Freud and Jung and their attempts to understand the structure of the mind and to map it, have had a profound effect upon our culture. As these ideas have gradually percolated into popular culture, often through the arts, they have altered our perceptions of ourselves and opened a rich symbolic world. For example, the surrealist movement in art and film took its initial inspiration from the work of Freud, and films such as the *Star Wars* trilogy drew strongly on Jungian symbolism.

Also each man, in his own way, was profoundly affected by esoteric teachings. Freud was very drawn to the tradition of the Hebrew Qabalah though he kept this interest secret. Jung explored in depth many spiritual and esoteric traditions taking much inspiration for his writings from them. He is usually considered the champion of such subjects, though there is no doubt that even his work tended to psychologise the ineffable. Reich, as we shall see later, walked the fringes in a number of areas. Roberto Assagioli, the founder of Psychosynthesis, was familiar with esoteric teachings and incorporated these into his theories and exercises. His wife was a member of the Theosophical Society and both were closely associated with Alice Bailey, a famous Theosophist whose writings and organisation, The Lucius Trust, have functioned as influential forerunners of the New Age movement.

Freud (1856–1939)

Living most of his life in Vienna, Freud, besides being the 'Father of psychoanalysis', carried out major research in the field of local anesthetic and studies of cerebral palsy. His name is perhaps most closely associated with his discovery of the link between sexual tension and neurosis. This may not seem so shocking in today's climate of acceptance of human sexuality, but Freud was writing at a time of extreme social abhorrence of sexuality.

However, it is not Freud's theory of sexuality or sexual development I want to examine, but that of the unconscious mind which developed from his early work with hypnosis. He postulated that within each of us, below the threshold of our conscious minds, resided a level of pure instinctual, primitive drives of a mainly sexual/violent nature. This he called the id. The id's powerful energies are directed towards the immediate gratification of its needs. One only needs to be around a small child for a short period of time to see the id in action!

Freud postulated that because of a child's dependency and relative weakness in respect of their environment these drives are soon tempered by an internalisation of what is right and wrong via parental and environmental mores. These become the basis of the superego or Conscience. However, these primitive feelings, as well as early traumatic experiences (real or imagined), become unacceptable to the conscious mind and so are 'forgotten' through the process of repression and suppression becoming subconscious. Yet these are still capable of exerting a powerful influence upon the personality.

So, according to Freudian developmental theory, the child's personality forms and the ego develops and is directed by the superego. The ego's task within the personality is to modify the drives of the id and to sublimate them in ways acceptable to their environment and culture. A metaphor often used is of an iceberg with the ego represented by the visible tip and the id and superego (including personal memories) forming the part below the waterline.

The 1950s science-fiction film classic *Forbidden Planet*, based on Shakespeare's *The Tempest*, used this basic idea of the id in its storyline to create a ferocious 'mind monster' which was unleashed when the normally controlled and intellectual Dr Morbeous slept. It sought to maim and murder those who trespassed upon the territory Morbeous subconsciously considered his. In the film these same energies were cited as being the destroyers of the previous alien civilisation upon the planet who had developed their intellects to an extremely high degree but who had forgotten about the 'monsters of the id'.

The 'popularity' within films of psychopathic killers such as Hannibal Lecter (*Silence of the Lambs*) and 'Bob' (*Twin Peaks*) externalise the nightmarish image of the id. However, the picture painted by Freud of the nature of the subconscious is very two-dimensional and, one might say, a crude attempt at trying to understand the nature of the psyche. It has its uses and applications despite this.

In 1899 Freud published his first book, *The Interpretation of Dreams*. In this he wrote of his belief that dreams were a major key to accessing the contents of the subconscious mind. He postulated that within the dream state the id could express itself through symbolism. His insistence that the majority of dream symbolism was sexual in its meaning again stimulated controversy. These ideas have influenced many dream dictionaries where almost every reference is to disguised genitalia or intercourse.

Jung (1875–1961)

Jung worked at a Swiss mental hospital and in 1907 published a pioneering book on the subject of schizophrenia which led to his forming a close association with Freud. This lasted until 1913 when the nature of Jung's work caused him to break away and found his own system of psychoanalysis. Jung was widely read in both philosophy and theology and these, along with his own mystical experiences, led him to postulate a very different 'map of the mind' to Freud's.

Jung recognised, as had Freud, that our conscious minds did repress a great deal of the early experience that was unacceptable to it. However, he did not agree with Freud that the basic 'stuff' of the psyche was driven purely by the Pleasure Principle and the selfish desire for gratification of pleasure and power. Jung was by nature more philosophical than Freud and less pessimistic in his approach. Thus his maps are more universal and include not only the drive to pleasure but the more sublime desires for knowledge, altruistic love, service and the spiritual quest.

Jung postulated the existence of a personal unconscious (a term I prefer to use because it doesn't imply 'beneath' the conscious mind – as in subconscious – but that which is 'not conscious') wherein memories and experiences are stored. A useful analogy, along the lines of the iceberg, likens the unconscious part of our minds to an untidy library or filing cabinet with no order or system for retrieval – things pop up at random. One of the benefits derived from therapy and regular meditation work is that more and more of the unconscious becomes more ordered and available to the conscious.

Jung also proposed that each of us also has contact with a Collective Unconscious, shared with all other humans and perhaps all life. He described this as consisting of building blocks of primordial images, symbols and mythological motifs to which he gave the name 'archetype'. In Jungian theory, the characters of myth and legend are representative of basic archetypes. Thus we have the archetype of the Great Mother, the Magician, the Warrior, the Fool, and so on.

This, though liberating from the 'all is sex' attitude of Freud, is still rather limiting as it postulates these archetypes are only elements of human thought and not in themselves independent entities. Of course there is truth in this view, as humankind has throughout time clothed the ineffable in forms that are recognisable to us. Therefore we have imagined the gods and goddesses of various pantheons as anthropomorphic personifications. However, this does not mean that they are only products of our collective imagination. They have their own separate consciousness, life and reality.

Jung's other theories of the make-up of the conscious and unconscious mind of the individual include the persona, shadow and anima/animus.

The persona, a Greek word meaning the mask worn by an actor, refers to the aspects of our personality that we show to others and society. Although formed by unconscious factors it is the acceptable side of ourselves which our egos feel comfortable identifying with. In astrology this can be represented in the birth chart by the Ascendant.

By contrast, the shadow is the aspect of the personality which is denied expression. Jung writes 'the shadow personifies all that the subject refuses to acknowledge about themselves and yet is always thrusting itself upon them directly or indirectly'. The shadow is the unwanted part of our nature and is often experienced by the ego as evil, though this is not necessarily so. Because of this, the shadow is repressed, though it can express itself in nightmarish dreams. The shadow is often projected outwards onto other people or things that seem to embody these unacceptable qualities. This can be a collective as well as individual process as, for example, the archetype of the Devil or the irrational prejudice levelled towards certain individuals, races and cultures.

In films and books, the shadow is the adversary which

the protagonist must overcome. In the more psychologically sophisticated of these there is usually a bond between them, a point where the hero or heroine reluctantly recognises themselves in their enemy. In Jungian terms the shadow manifests with the same gender identity as the individual. The shadow does not just exist as an adversary; part of the process of becoming whole is to integrate the shadow into the total personality. In the *Star Wars* trilogy, the figure of Darth Vadar represents a powerful symbol of the hero's shadow and yet, true to its Jungian inspiration, rather than being defeated he was redeemed, eventually joining Luke Skywalker's other inner world allies.

In Jungian terms, we are psychologically androgynous. The anima/animus, or soul-image, usually, though not always, is personified in the unconscious of a man as a woman, and in the unconscious of a woman as a man. The attributes of the anima and animus are determined by a variety of factors including archetypal material, environmental conditioning and actual experiences with men and women. They are often experienced as dual, with the bright anima/animus embodying those contra-sexual qualities considered positive and 'ideal' to the individual and the dark anima/animus embodying perceived negative and destructive qualities. In dreams they can manifest as strong symbolic characters to whom we are drawn.

The anima and animus are often projected outwards onto others who are perceived in terms of their fitting an internal 'identi-kit'. Anima and animus projections often are directed at unattainable public figures, such as film and music personalities who are perceived again as ideal representatives. Again these qualities are perceived as 'out there' and not as part of ourselves. As with the shadow, ultimately the anima/animus has to be integrated within the psyche for the quest for wholeness to be fulfilled.

The following exercise returns to a setting explored in Chapter 2 and will serve to give you some material to consider about both your conscious and unconscious minds.

THE HOUSE OF THE PERSONALITY

Return to your notes from Chapter 2 in which you explored various inner landscapes. Return to one of these – either the cottage in the forest or the house (if you did not use either of these scenarios, please do so now in preparation for this exercise).

Look at these experiences from the exercise using the framework that the cottage/house symbolically represents the totality of your personality, or rather how your unconscious mind views your personality. For most people the ground floor of a building visualised in this manner will represent their conscious personality; the basement their subconscious and the upper floors/attic area abstract, spiritual and collective consciousness.

After considering the earlier experiences, return in your imagination to the house/cottage and explore the various rooms and levels. Do not attempt to make things happen, merely be open to what you see there. While you are visualising don't attempt to analyse the experience. Treat it like a waking dream.

Return to ordinary consciousness and write up the experience taking time to consider what these images are telling you about your perception of yourself. Is the house large or small? Are there many rooms or few? Is the way to the upper and lower levels clear or blocked? What are the furnishings like? Does it remind you of a place you have lived in or dreamed of? What associations have these to you? What ambience does the house have for you? What message does this image give to you?

This exercise need only be done once or twice in order to obtain some material for you to consider.

Wilhelm Reich

Now we will briefly look at the work of Wilhelm Reich and his successors and focus upon the emotional life of 'the body'.

Wilhelm Reich lived and worked in Austria in the early 20th century and became one of Freud's most promising young associates. However, his theories on sexuality, politics and energy were controversial, to say the least, and even Freud eventually disclaimed him. Freud found Reich's assertion that sexuality needed to be openly expressed unacceptable; for it was Freud's belief that society needed the repression and sublimation of sexuality in order to flourish. Reich's response to this was that although society needed this repression of the natural instincts it was only so that people would remain docile and blindly responsive to authority.

We now take it for granted that the release of tension and deep relaxation gained through sexual orgasm is a positive goal. It was Reich's research in this area and publication of his book, *The Function of the Orgasm*, in 1927 which broached this previously taboo subject. Reich maintained that orgasm was more than a 'climax' or ejaculation but an involuntary response of the total body, manifested in rhythmic, convulsive movements.

His writings on politics analysed social and political events. These were mainly ignored during his life and disclaimed after his death by his devotees. However, his guidelines for efficient and humane left-wing politics have often been an unacknowledged source of inspiration for modern left-wing political thought. His principle writing on this subject was *The Mass Psychology of Fascism* (1934).

He struggled throughout his life to bring about a more healthy regard for sexuality and contraception and yet, like many pioneers in this field, he was the subject of controversy and harassment. He was hounded by the authorities in Europe and was exiled from country after country, finally settling in the USA. There things were not much better; his books were banned and burned by both the Nazis and officials of the US Government. He was eventually imprisoned for two years in America and died in prison in 1957.

Reading of his life and works, one is aware of a man of great genius and vision who slowly but surely withdrew further into himself. Eventually he succumbed through stress and loneliness to delusions and paranoia. His peculiar beliefs and anti-social behaviour towards the end of his life led to his being labelled as mad.

Yet what were these theories? Were they that outrageous or was he the victim of the general paranoia rampant throughout the United States during the 1950s? He postulated that there was a living and vital energy field present throughout the physical world which he dubbed 'orgone'. He stated that orgone energy was present everywhere and through it function electromagnetism, light and gravity. He speculated that it could be measured by sensitive instruments and accumulated in specially constructed boxes and blankets for the acceleration of both physical and psychological healing. It was his refusal to withdraw 'orgone accumulators' from sale that led to his imprisonment.

Of course, anyone who is at all physically open will have had some sense of this same energy, though maybe under another name. What in *Star Wars* was termed 'The Force' and in various spiritual traditions is called 'chi', the tao, etheric/astral energies of the aura, is that energy which Reich claimed was the energy from which the Universe of matter was created.

Reich, however, was no occultist. He was a scientist and a doctor and had not the theoretical framework to contain his experiences. In speaking so openly he came under scrutiny and censor by the society of his day. His ideas were certainly not all that different to those now accepted by a whole alternative society resulting from a general liberation of thought in the 1960s.

Reich also worked with the unconscious, but concentrated on how these processes of repressed emotions and experiences affected the body. He believed these were literally locked into the musculature of the body creating what he described as 'body armour'. This armouring is caused by deep patterns of tension resulting in various emotional problems, psychosomatic illnesses and sexual dysfunction. His primary way of working was directly with the body; what he termed vegetotherapy, deep massage that would loosen the tensions held in the body allowing for an emotional catharsis and an eventual clearing of the blockages.

From this pioneering work have come, after Reich's death, a variety of Neo-Reichian systems of 'bodywork' including various techniques of therapeutic massage. These have tended to concentrate upon Reich's work with emotion held in the body and 'character analysis', and dropped his more controversial ideas about orgone energy, UFO phenomena and conspiracy theory.

These therapies also primarily use massage and exercises to free up areas of the body's frozen muscles. This can result in a release of powerful memories, emotions and energy, eventually bringing about an integration of these. It is very much a system of holistic psychotherapy. One of this century's leading occult teachers, Dr Israel Regardie, was himself a Reichian therapist and strongly advocated the need for psychological health and balance, favouring the use of such body therapies to balance the often over-intellectual approach of those working in the mysteries.

David Boadella, who has written extensively on Reich, began his own work with bioenergetics (named so because it works with the energy systems of the body), though he has taken these ideas forward and developed his own system which he has called biosynthesis. He writes in his introduction to *Lifestreams*:

> The capacity of emotion to mobilise or paralyse the body is well known. Furthermore it can be said fairly generally that every neurotic (or psychotic) person has lost part of the full range of human emotional expression. Such a person has lost, or never developed, the full range of movement possibilities of which any healthy child is capable. In some degree or another *mobility* is disturbed. A neurosis then is equivalent to a system of blockages which prevent the free flow of feelings through the body. The aim of bio-energetic therapy is, therefore, to overcome the blockages and restore free flow.

Though starting off working with the body alone, Reich's successors such as Alexander Lowen, John Pierrakos (bioenergetics) and David Boadella eventually began to explore material on meditation, healing, the aura, chakras and even the teachings of Huna, the indigenous Hawaiian magical tradition which we will explore in Chapter 6. They integrated these aspects into their work, thus slowly aligning Reich's more controversial theories into a framework where they become accessible to a greater audience.

For example, Reich identified seven body segments or

rings of tension – the first including the scalp, forehead, eyes; the second the mouth and jaw; the third the neck and throat; the fourth the thoracic – heart, lungs and arms; the fifth the diaphragm and solar plexus; the sixth the abdominal and lower back; the seventh the pelvis, sexual organs and legs. There is an obvious correlation here with the seven chakras. As Boadella writes that, although Reich and the originators of the chakras 'were arbitrarily fascinated with the mystical number seven, it is important to recognise that the anatomy of the spine naturally generates seven nodes corresponding to the chakras.'

This point about the continuum between the actual physical body and esoteric teachings has been much commented on of late and perhaps constitutes one of the major revelations of the mysteries in our times. The works of Maxwell Cade and others have opened up the whole area of biofeedback where meditational states can be monitored and enhanced through awareness of and from the body. Part of the process, which has been encouraged throughout this book, is the ability to deeply relax. Through this we seek to move towards an integrated sense of wholeness in body, feelings and mind rather than the robotic state that modern living so often produces.

Our goal is quite similar to that of Reich's – to free the individual from the conditioning of the past, to wake them up, and to give them back that freedom and aliveness that was lost or never known in childhood. For as that aliveness is regained, what is also reclaimed is the sense of wonder, innocence and a reconnection to Deity.

At some point during your work with this chapter's material it would be a good idea to set aside a few sessions just to explore your relationship with your own body. This can be done by noting a number of things: the degree of tension or absence of feeling in various parts; the colour and texture of your skin; general feelings connected with your body (does it feel comfortable or do you experience a sense of unease or even disgust associated with your body or parts of it?). You may also wish to allow images to arise in your mind's eye to illustrate the various parts and your body as a whole and these can be looked at as messages from your body to your conscious self.

We recommend that you do the following exercise which

is a variation on a standard one used by body therapists to gain a greater awareness of one's body. Rather than work through this sequence from memory it would be more effective for you to read this exercise into a cassette tape, placing short pauses after each body part mentioned to allow for your awareness, and then play it back to yourself.

BODY AWARENESS

Sit or lie in a comfortable position and close your eyes. Become aware of which parts of your body are in contact with the chair, floor or bed. Allow yourself to relax into their support and become aware of your breathing, in and out. Don't attempt to change it, just notice how you are breathing – whether it is deep or shallow, slow or rapid. Notice what parts of your body move as you breathe. Now begin to focus your attention on various parts of your body working through them step by step, gaining a sense of how you feel about it and allowing with each exhalation of breath all bodily tension to leave you.

First your forehead. Is it smooth or frowning? Are you aware of your scalp at all, is there a sense of tightness there? Your eyelids, are they closed or fluttering? Your eyeballs – still or moving? Are you experiencing any after-images? Be aware of your cheeks – are they relaxed or smiling? Your nose – does it feel congested or clear inside? Your lips – are they dry or moist? Are they closed or parted? Is your tongue lying still or is it touching the roof of your mouth? Your teeth – do they feel clean and is there any feeling of pressure or other discomfort? Be aware of your face as a whole and whether it is relaxed or held in some form of expression.

Now allow your attention to move to your neck. This is an area where tension can be easily held. How does it feel, is there a sense of tiredness or is it relaxed? Become aware of your spine and your vertebrae – all of them from the large ones just under your skull to the coccyx at the end of your spine. Be aware of the muscles connected to your spine. Is your back tense or relaxed? Be aware of your shoulders – are they raised up or do they hang loose? Be aware in turn of your upper and lower arms, elbows, wrists, hands and fingers. Note how they are lying – is there any tension here?

Now move inside your body, which is a place we are often unconscious of. Be aware of the rhythm of your heartbeat, but do not try to count its beats. Listen to the echo of this rhythm in other parts of your body as pulses – at your temples, wrists, groin, ankles. Be aware of your breath again, following it down through your nose, trachea, and into your lungs. Be aware of your lungs expanding and deflating. Now swallow and be aware of your oesophagus which leads to your stomach. Do you have any sense of feeling there? Does your stomach feel hungry or full? Do you have any sense of other internal organs? Does your abdomen have any sensation? How about your intestines – is there any sense of activity? Your rectum and bladder can often be quite sensitive – is there any sense of pressure here? Your anus – is it held tightly or relaxed?

Be aware of your sexual organs both internal and external. What sensations do you have here. If you are a woman, do you have any sensations about your ovaries and womb and the phase of your menstrual cycle? Become aware of your pelvis and those bones which cradle these internal organs. Is it tilted? Is there any sense of muscle tension linked to your lower back? Gently rock your pelvis and be aware of how this feels. Be aware, too, of your buttocks. This is an area where deep tension is often held – do you have any sensations here?

Now move your awareness into your hip sockets and your thighs. This is another area where there is often a strong lack of feeling due to deeply-held tension. What temperature are they? Are they warmer or colder or the same as the rest of your legs? Are the muscles here developed or flaccid? Move your attention down to your knees – do they have any sense of strain or tension? Your calves – is there any tension in the back of them? Your ankles and feet – what degree of movement do you have in them? Your feet and toes – are you aware of the tiny bones and muscles within them? Do they feel cramped from shoes or socks/stockings?

Now take a journey back up your body from your toes to the top of your head. Compare your left side to the right. See if it is the same or if it feels different. See if you can be aware of your body all the way up. Or are there any holes in your awareness? Get a sense of how you feel about your body not just physically but emotionally. Do you have a positive experience of it or are there things about it you wish to change? Try not to judge it on this occasion but just to accept it as it is. Remember to breathe and stay connected with your body as you consider this.

Now take a moment to experience your body as an integrated whole. Say 'This is me, this is (say your name). This is where I live, this is the temple of my spiritual being'.

Now take a deep breath, stretch and slowly get up. Now as usual ground yourself and write up your notes of your experience.

We will now move straight into the final exercise of this chapter, the building of the Inner Room.

AN INNER ROOM*

This exercise is quite simple and follows on from the earlier visualisation exercises in Part 1. The exercise should be done daily over a period of weeks. You may be tempted to move on quickly to further exploration of the Temple but it is important that this Inner Room is firmly constructed within your mind first.

As usual begin your practice with relaxation and some rhythmic breathing and do one of the energising exercises worked with in Part 1. Build the images as described, enhancing them each day:

In front of you is a large, old, wooden wardrobe. This is an object you remember from your childhood. Sometimes when you were just falling asleep you would be aware that there was a doorway in the back of this wardrobe. However, when in the morning you looked it wasn't there. But now, as you look within, you will find the doorway. Allow the door to open for you.

You see before you a secret passageway in the form of a flight of stone steps spiralling down and around out of sight. It is well lit and you can descend quite easily without fear. Observe how the passage is lit with torches or lamps. Feel the stone beneath your feet; what is its temperature, its texture? Smell the air – is it fresh or stale, warm or cool.

What do you see or hear as you descend? After a number of steps you come to a landing. Stop and see, recessed into the wall, a door. Be aware of the door – of what it is made of and also of any designs upon it.

This is the doorway to your own personal sanctuary. It is locked, but around your neck you have the key. Open it and enter. You may find your room already lit or you may need to kindle a lamp from the light in the passage. Close the door behind you and be aware of the room. It may be furnished already or you may need to furnish it with your imagination. Whatever, you can take the time to further decorate it.

Sit down, relax and just be aware. Each day build the room, keeping things constant within it. As you become familiar with it you may find a number of special items that will be of assistance later. Somewhere in the room you will find (or place) a small shrine table upon which is a candle and perhaps an image of the Goddess. This may mirror the physical shrine you have or be the ideal shrine you would like to meditate in front of.

The building of this Inner Room should become quite easy with regular work – so that you can visualise yourself going to it and then sit there before your shrine to meditate before closing down and returning to normal waking consciousness. You will need to close down from this meditation as previously advised. It is also a good idea to write up notes of your experience as soon as possible. You may wish to include a drawing of this special room in your diary-record.

* Adapted from *Mind Games*, R.E.L. Masters and Jean Houston, Turnstone Press (1972), with thanks to Jean Morton-Williams for permission to adapt her 'Pagan Pathfinders' variation of this meditation.

Chapter 6

Journey to the Temple of Isis

Having looked briefly at 'maps of the mind' and body, postulated by Freud, Jung and Reich, we will now move on to consider the relevance to our studies of the works of humanistic and transpersonal psychologies. Of prime interest to us is the attitude of these systems towards the psyche, along with the way these have developed to incorporate esoteric teachings into their philosophies.

The works of psychoanalysts in the early 20th century were mainly focused upon people with severe problems.

They also held the attitude, similar to that of the behavioural psychologists, that our experience of the world and the contents of conscious and unconscious minds were shaped by external stimuli and instincts. This continued to promote a mechanistic world-view.

Humanistic psychology developed from the ideas of existential philosophers such as Nietzsche and Sartre as a reaction to those aspects of our technological society which sought to reduce us to just machines. It emphasised particularly the quality of 'free will' as well as postulating a natural drive in the individual towards growth and 'self-actualisation'. Humanistic psychology promotes the idea that people who are fundamentally healthy might wish to understand their own psychological experiences and seek self-knowledge. It focused on the 'here and now' quality of life as well as subjective personal experience. Although it developed in the 1950s it is perhaps not surprising that it saw its flowering in the 1960s when there was such an emphasis upon various types of 'consciousness expansion' and mystical experiences.

Humanistic psychology favoured 'client-centred' therapy in which it was considered that the client had both the motivation and the ability to change and that the therapist's task was to facilitate progress towards this change. While in psychoanalysis the therapist 'analysed' the patient's history in the context of whatever theory they favoured, the assumption of non-directive therapy is that the therapist acts as a sounding board for the client's own exploration of problems. The concept that people are capable of finding their own solutions to problems is the basis for self-help books on psychology.

The term self-actualisation refers to a basic tenet of humanistic psychology: the belief that there is a basic force within each of us that has a tendency towards fulfilment and development with all parts of the personality in harmony. Abraham Maslow, a leader in the development of humanistic psychology, formulated a classification of human motives in the form of a pyramid. These are in ascending order: the physiological needs for satisfaction of hunger, thirst and warmth; the safety needs of feeling secure and safe, free of danger; the need for a sense of belonging and love; needs related to self-esteem, gaining approval and recognition; the need to know, understand and explore; aesthetic needs in the appreciation of order and beauty; and finally self-actualisation needs: to find self-fulfilment and realise one's potential. He postulated that only when the basic needs are met can there be time for intellectual and aesthetic interests.

An obvious amendment to this list, which cuts across its structure, is the need for a spiritual connection which is capable of finding expression even when the needs of the body are threatened.

Maslow formed his theories about self-actualisation by observing the qualities expressed by men and women who were themselves 'self-actualised'. These were not necessarily 'perfect' people but those who made use of their talents and capabilities in a balanced way. Some of the characteristics he identified were the ability to perceive reality efficiently and to cope with uncertainty; accept themselves and others for what they were; be spontaneous in thought and behaviour; have a good sense of humour; be highly creative; have a concern for the welfare of humanity and the planet as a whole; be capable of a deep appreciation of the basic experience of life; establish deep, satisfying relationships, and look at life from an objective viewpoint.

He also identified behaviour indicating that people were on the road to self-actualisation. These are: the ability to experience life as a child does, with concentration and spontaneity; willingness to try something new rather than sticking to secure and safe ways; ability to listen to and trust one's own feelings in evaluating experiences rather than the voice of authority or the majority; honesty and freedom from pretences and 'game playing'; the willingness to be unpopular if their views don't coincide with those of the majority; the ability to resume responsibility for one's own life, and to work hard at whatever they decide to do. You may, in reading through these lists, see in which ways you are either self-actualised or on the road to it, as well as identify areas you are weak in.

Maslow's other research was into a phenomenon experienced by many people, often only momentarily in their lives, of a state of extreme happiness and fulfilment, a sense of wholeness and perfection. These he called 'peak experiences'. In these experiences the sense of self is transcended and an awareness of the eternal soul experienced.

Here once more we have a link to the various classical and living traditions of mysticism and magic as a goal of many practices is the cultivation of such 'alternate states of consciousness'. While a peak experience could conceivably occur in any circumstances, such practices as meditation, contemplation, devotion and ritual heightened the probability of such an event.

During the period when humanistic psychology began to come to the fore there was a great drive in the West towards self-knowledge and a movement away from the conventional structures of Christianity. The popularity in the 1960s of psychoactive drugs such as cannabis and LSD served for many as a gateway experience to glimpse inner realms. Whereas for some this became an end in itself, for others it was the start of a quest that would incorporate both a psychological and mystical component.

Before it was declared illegal, LSD was utilised in a number of research projects as a form of psychotherapy, being especially effective in the treatment of alcoholics and people suffering from neurotic disorders. The drug stimulated self-awareness as well as mystical experiences. Many people spontaneously experienced initiatory journeys and meetings with Deities, mythological characters and other-worldly beings as well as experiencing feelings of oneness with the universe. Approached as a developmental tool rather than for recreation these drugs served to bring lasting changes into the lives of those participating in these experiments.

For example, research by Robert Masters and Jean Houston into the varieties of psychedelic experience led them to look for ways in which to re-create these experiences without the use of drugs. They turned to classical and living traditions for the magical and mystical practices that were the keys to the inner worlds. In 1972 they published *Mind Games: The Guide to Inner Space* wherein visualisation was used 'to penetrate the obstinate barrier between the conscious and unconscious mind'.

Jean Houston has continued to research and teach 'sacred psychology' throughout the world. In 1981 she founded The Mystery School in the United States, which seeks to recreate the initiatory mysteries of the ancient world. Her own on-going relationship with the Goddess has been expressed in this context. Likewise in 1988 her husband, Robert Masters, revealed in print that since the early 1960s his life and work had been inspired by his intense relationship with the Egyptian Goddess Sekhmet to whom he had dedicated his life in service.

Transpersonal psychology has been a development of humanistic psychology as well as linking inherent psychology to various mystical and magical traditions. It began to make its presence felt as people wanted to integrate the spiritual dimensions of existence so often ignored in ordinary psychotherapy.

Psychosynthesis is probably the foremost of all transpersonal psychologies. Roberto Assagioli was unique in that he developed his theories in the early part of the 20th century, contemporary with Freud, Jung and Reich (his first conception of psychosynthesis was presented in his doctoral thesis in 1910), and was still involved in the development and refinement of psychosynthesis up to the time of his death in 1974. He had an active association with Abraham Maslow and others, enabling psychosynthesis to take account of ideas arising from the humanistic psychology movement during the 1960s and early 1970s. Also incorporated was material emerging out of research by people such as Masters and Houston, Charles Tart and Stanislav Grof into biofeedback and altered states of consciousness.

Assagioli had a life-long interest in esoteric matters and had contact with others working in this field including Dion Fortune, herself a lay analyst who had studied both Freudian and Jungian systems. This connection between Assagioli and Fortune is not, to my knowledge, formally documented but was related to me by one of Fortune's associates who had also been an early student of Assagioli's. This connection is not that surprising given Fortune's keen interest in psychology and Assagioli's in the mysteries. It is fairly obvious looking at some of the basic exercises within psychosynthesis and those of the western mystery schools descended from Fortune's Society of the Inner Light that there has been a degree of cross-fertilisation of ideas and exercises somewhere along the line.

Psychosynthesis takes the view that the 'Greater Self' of an individual is involved in this process and that the work of the therapist, called in psychosynthesis the Guide, is to facilitate this by whatever means feels appropriate. While similar to the client-centred approach of humanistic psychology it takes a further step towards acknowledging the spiritual dimension of the therapeutic process. Thus before beginning, a Guide will meditate, holding in their consciousness the session to come and will also begin by sharing a few moments of silence with the client to allow for inspiration and inner guidance to emerge from both parties. This is a very different attitude to most therapies as it allows and nurtures whatever needs to happen.

In contrast to psychoanalysis where an attempt is made to break down and analyse the contents of the conscious and unconscious mind, psychosynthesis attempts to find emerging patterns in a totally non-judgemental way and to allow the spontaneous emergence of meaningful and coherent fields within the psyche.

In the opening chapter of *What We May Be*, Piero Ferrucci writes:

The process of synthesis is visible everywhere in the natural as well as the strictly human world: cells assemble to form an organism . . . musical notes combine to form a melody . . .

The Italian psychologist, Roberto Assagioli, noticed several years ago that a great deal of psychological pain, imbalance, and meaninglessness are felt when our diverse inner elements exist unconnected side by side or clash with one another. But he also observed that when they merge in successfully greater wholes, we experience a release of energy, a sense of well-being, and a greater depth for meaning in our lives.

Assagioli believed that there was a natural growth within that tended to be seeking synthesis and balance, though this was often countered by inertia and blockages. His whole range of techniques was aimed at facilitating this process. There is no one set of exercises that 'are psychosynthesis'; it is fundamentally an attitude not a technique.

It is this same attitude which I have striven to incorporate into these pages, under the guidance of the Goddess; for while I call upon the tools of psychosynthesis, this manual is aimed at the mystery teachings of the Goddess and not meant to replace those manuals which are purely psychosynthetic.

Let us move on to examine Assagioli's primary 'map of the psyche'.

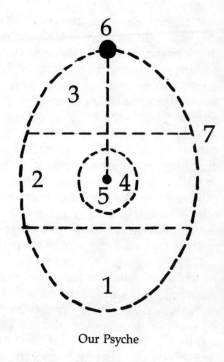

1. "Lower" unconscious
2. Middle unconscious
3. Superconscious
4. Field of consciousness
5. Personal Self, or "I"
6. Transpersonal Self
7. Collective unconscious

Our Psyche

Psychosynthetic 'Egg' Diagram

The 'Egg' diagram is the basic psychosynthetic model of the Psyche – the foundation of the whole system. Simply, 1 represents the *lower unconscious* which is seen mainly as the repository of our personal psychological past – memories and repressed complexes; 2 is the *middle unconscious* which contains material such as skills and memories which are can be brought into our *field of consciousness* (4), with relative ease. This field is quite limited at any one moment – it is what you are consciously aware of but it still has easy access to quite an array of material at will.

The *superconscious* (3) is, according to Assagioli, the region from which 'we receive our higher intuitions and inspirations – artistic, philosophical or scientific, ethical "imperatives" and urges to humanitarian and heroic action. It is the source of the higher feelings, such as altruistic love; of genius and the states of contemplation, illumination and ecstasy.'

Within the superconscious resides the *transpersonal self* (6), our true essence which is in a sense beyond verbal description, though mystics and inner explorers have sought to express the ineffable through writings, images, music, poetry, etc. However, it is also seen from this map that within the field of consciousness we have the *personal self* or *I* (5) which is a reflection or 'outpost' of the transpersonal self in our everyday lives. This is an extremely important idea and is quite a few steps further along the road from Freud's concept of the ego. Even Jung, for all his sophistication with religious symbols was, at least publicly, evasive over the question of reincarnation or life-after-death. He believed that the self was something that developed through the process of individuation and did not exist as an entity in its own right.

This is possibly the most fundamental difference between psychosynthesis and Jung's School of Analytic Psychology. Assagioli, perhaps because of his own personality or his culture, had less difficulty expressing these ideas. Certainly he was able to state that the self existed not as a possibility but as a living actuality for each of us, which is very close to esoteric thought and teachings throughout the ages.

Finally, outside the field of the 'egg' is the sea of what Jung called the *collective unconscious* (7). Notice in the diagram that all the lines are dotted 'to signify that no rigid compartments impede interplay among all levels'.

Looking back to the material in Chapter 3 on the Qabalistic Tree of Life, we can relate the psychosynthetic model to the teaching of the mystery schools such as Dion Fortune's. We can fit the Egg diagram neatly onto the Tree – identifying the transpersonal self with Kether, the superconscious with the supernals – Chokmah and

Binah – and the 'I' with Tiphareth.

Further meditations on these ideas should prove fruitful.

Subpersonalities

A unique feature of psychosynthesis is the theory of subpersonalities. What is a subpersonality? In a sense it is exactly as you would expect it to be as defined by the word, a 'sub-section' of your overall personality. A cluster of various ideas, beliefs and behaviour that have formed some sort of whole within the personality yet is not the totality of our personalities.

One of the most accessible ways of approaching subpersonalities is to consider them as the various roles we adopt in the world. This means that we will all at times be different people. This can sometimes be perplexing to ourselves and others. It is usually easy to see how people will adopt different personas when they encounter their parents and often another with partners, friends of the same sex, yet another to their children, and different again when dealing with strangers. Some subpersonalities will form in childhood and adolescence, others in response to our adult world.

This inner inconsistency can be a confusing experience, but once we understand that this is the normal way in which our personalities have developed, we can begin to gain a sense of centre amid the conflict. Piero Ferrucci simply defines subpersonalities as 'psychological satellites, coexisting as a multitude of lives within the overall medium of our personality . . . Each of us is a crowd. There can be the rebel and the intellectual, the seducer and the housewife, the saboteur and the aesthete, the organizer and the bon vivant.'

We could extend this list indefinitely. Yet how can we begin to explore this 'multiplicity within'? The first step is, quite simply, to identify your own subpersonalities and to begin to work with them.

Identification of Subpersonalities 1

This is an active method for examining your major attitudes, traits, etc. Closing your eyes, become aware of this part of you – allow an image to emerge spontaneously to represent it, be it man, woman, animal, monster, imaginary being or object. Also be aware of any feelings connected with that image. Let the image talk in your imagination and express itself to you. Find out what it's needs are. You may find that some of your subpersonalities have been characters in your dreams. Then record the image you have received and the message. You may wish to read ahead to Chapter 8 on dreamwork to access techniques for dialoguing given there.

Give this subpersonality a name – one that fits it through description and allows you to identify it in the future. This naming function is very crucial, and while a literal description is fine (such as Boss, Mother, Father, Careerwoman/man, Victim, Child, Clown, Complainer, Artist, Mystic, Feminist, Witch, Flirt, Sceptic) it is much more useful to give personal names which in themselves are descriptive statements.

For example, I expressed my 'Mystic' subpersonality as 'The Blue Nun'. Her attitudes were extremely conservative and repressive and were at odds with the more care-free and vivacious subpersonality whom I named 'Esmeralda' after the gypsy girl in *The Hunchback of Notre Dame*. Another subpersonality I named 'Old Salt' and he manifested in my imagination as a crusty old sailor who swore, drank everyone under the table, told tall tales and joked, generally living it up. I found he most often manifested when I had had a drink or two. 'Old Salt' had a strong sense of adventure and courage which endeared him to me though was often a problem and in conflict with my Blue Nun!

Some of these subpersonalities embody parts of what, in Jung's terms, would be considered our shadow and anima/animus. 'Old Salt' held some of the qualities of my animus and an extremely unpleasant subpersonality which I named 'Jaws and Claws' was very shadow-like. It is certainly possible to have subpersonalities of the opposite gender to our own, thus a woman can have some male subpersonalities and a man female ones. It can be a very liberating process to acknowledge these.

One you've identified and named a subpersonality you can go on to write about it – when you first noticed its appearance in your life, where and when it pops up. Perhaps you dress differently when you are strongly identified with it? Make an attempt to draw it (technical skill is not the important thing) – allowing a spontaneous drawing which can convey much meaning.

Identification of Subpersonalities 2

This method is more passive than that given above. A situation is set up in the form of a symbolic scenario in which you can encounter a number of subpersonalities.

1 Imagine that you are walking down a country road. A bus is coming down the road and comes to a stop in front of you. A number of people get off the bus. You are drawn to two or three of these and go up and introduce yourself. These are some of your subpersonalities. Proceed as suggested above and get to know them, talk to them and eventually record the experience.

2 Make a return visit to the house/cottage in which you worked in Chapters 2 and 5. You will find a number of people living there. These will be subpersonalities. Introduce yourself and proceed to get to know them as suggested above.

It should be stressed that subpersonalities are not spirit guides, channelled entities, or in any way all-knowing. They are merely fragments of our totality. The attribution of this sort of power to subpersonalities is a trap I have found many of my students falling into, which comes from a slight misunderstanding of the principle.

Having had the opportunity to identify a number of subpersonalities the following three exercises will deepen your experience of them. You will need to do the previous exercises until you have identified and named four of your subpersonalities. If you discover more than this number then choose those four which seem to be most relevant to where you are in your life at present. By now you will hopefully begin to understand how these operate within the larger whole of your personality.

Inner Essence of Subpersonalities

We have so far looked at subpersonalities as bits of ourselves, in most cases disconnected from one another, and now we shall look at the underlying qualities beyond the surface aspects. In order to do this, as Piero Ferrucci states:

> . . . we have to learn to look at them as degraded expressions of the archetypes of higher qualities.
>
> Any content of our psyche can be degraded (literally 'stepped down from its higher state'). Compassion can become self-pity, joy can become mania, peace can become inertia, humour can become sarcasm, intelligence can become cunning, and so on. But the converse is also true: contents of consciousness can be elevated; self-pity becomes compassion, and so on.

An illuminating picture of the transpersonal self (see Figure 7) is to imagine that the contents of the superconscious which are archetypal qualities such as 'Energy', 'Will', 'Love' and 'Compassion' are, upon incarnation, projected into the personality just as the transpersonal self projects itself to become reflected as the personal self. However, these archetypal qualities are thereafter affected by a variety of influences including karmic, genetic, hereditary, and environmental factors in home and school. These have an undeniable effect upon the developing personality. Thus in time these pure qualities become distorted and crystallise in the form of subpersonalities. That the quality may be degraded out of all recognition does not alter the fact that it remains at its heart.

So if we consider that subpersonalities, too, 'are degradations or distortions of timeless qualities existing in the higher levels of the psyche', and keep this in mind as we begin to work with them we begin to see that these are more than 'a bunch of nonsensical patterns'. They begin to reveal their hidden potential. When we view them as degraded expressions of the archetypes of higher qualities, they are transformed.

As we become aware of the dynamic nature of them they can change and reveal hidden potentials, allowing us to reconnect to the archetypal energy at the core of the subpersonality. My previously mentioned 'Blue Nun' subpersonality was, when I initially contacted her, a rather sad lady, very uptight and prone to prudishness. However, working with her I discovered she contained a deep sense of innocence and strong mystical traits. How easy it would have been for my more dominant, fun-loving sub-personalities to have the 'Blue Nun' regulated to the dust-heap, but what a loss to my overall personality if this had been so.

It is important to be aware of their dynamic nature. They can change and reveal hidden potentials and allow us to reconnect to the archetypal energy at their core. There are various ways to discover the quality at the core of a subpersonality. One way is to undertake a visualisation with the theme of ascent. This can be the climbing of a tall hill or mountain which is symbolic of moving to 'higher levels'.

In Chapter 2 you climbed a mountainside in order to enter the Temple of Silence. Now undertake a similar visual-isation in the company of one of your subpersonalities. On each occasion you do this exercise only travel with one subpersonality.

As usual bring in as many of your senses as possible as you visualise. Note how easy or difficult the climbing is. Also, very importantly, keep in contact with your subpersonality and note if it changes in any way. When you reach the top of the mountain let the sun shine on the two of you, allowing it to reveal the inner essence of your subpersonality. As this occurs, let your subpersonality express itself and communicate with you.

After this is complete go back down the mountain. Your subpersonality may revert to its old form or remain somewhat changed by the experience. Write up the exercise and in the days and weeks that follow observe any changes in the way in which that subpersonality functions or in your perception of it.

A Wheel of the Elements

With the four subpersonalities you have chosen to work with, divide a piece of paper into four parts and write in each section one subpersonality name along with a brief description of their qualities. On another piece of paper draw a circle and divide it into four parts. Let each section be allocated to a specific direction and element (East/Air; South/Fire, West/Water, North/Earth). Use the information given in Chapters 1 and 2 along with your own ideas about the elements to fill this with associated ideas.

Now place your two sheets beside one another and allocate one of your subpersonalities to each section of your elemental wheel. This may be very obvious or take some time to discover. Enter the subpersonalities' names within your elemental wheel.

You may wish to write the names in pencil and then look at it again after a few days. If, at the end of your work on this exercise, it seems that you cannot assign one to each then allow them to be bunched up.

CONFERENCE TIME

Having explored these four subpersonalities and related them to the elemental wheel, you can now explore them in concert. Visualise a room and within it a table. See your four subpersonalities enter the room and place themselves around the table. Now imagine yourself, accompanied if you wish by your Inner Guide, sitting at the head of the table. Now you will chair a discussion. The topic of the discussion will be determined by your needs at this time. It may be along the lines of 'how can we all get on with one another' or about seeking their opinions about an aspect of your shared life – work, health, relationships, even your esoteric studies. Listen to what each subpersonality has to say.

This exercise does not need to be done often, although it is a handy way to see how these various sides of your personality are relating to one another.

JOURNEY TO THE TEMPLE OF ISIS

Our journey continues. As usual begin with some relaxation, breathing, and one of the energising exercises. Journey to and build your Inner Room as at the end of the last chapter. In your room sit before your shrine and light the candle. You may also wish to have an actual candle before you to light at the start of your session.

This is a long sequence of images and should be built up in progressive stages. Also, though regular practice is encouraged, it need not be done every day but can be varied with other exercises or simple relaxation, breathing and general meditation.

Draw about your seated body and the shrine a circle of cool, blue flame. This will guard and protect your body as you journey even deeper. If at any point you feel the need to return swiftly to consciousness, just think of the room, the circle of blue flame and the candle/shrine and you will return to it.

Now imagine yourself stepping away from your body in the inner room (you are transferring consciousness to an even more subtle body than that in which you have travelled so far). Move out of the room and back into the stairwell. Continue your downward journey as before – noting the different sensations. Soon, as you walk down and around, you come to the end of the stairway and find yourself in virtual darkness upon a stone quay with water lapping gently nearby. As your eyes adjust to the dim light of the place you become aware of a small boat moored nearby. In the boat are cushions and a light blanket. Enter the boat and cast off the rope.

The current carries you towards a distant spot of light which grows larger and larger. You realise that you are on an underground river and your boat is travelling towards a cave entrance. Quite quickly you emerge into a glorious summer's day. Your boat continues to float and you pass by freshly mowed fields. You now see animals, trees and bushes on either side. You hear the song of birds, the hum of insects and feel the warmth of the sun upon your face and body. Lean over and feel the coolness of the water and watch fish play in the clear depths. You see before you a low mist upon the water. It is cool and damp as your boat enters it. As it envelops you, become aware of the sound of a clock chiming the time. Seven times it chimes and as the seventh note fades the mist clears and you find yourself on a very different river . . .

The land on either side has changed to that of the ancient Egyptian desert and the river you travel on is the inner Nile.

Observe many sights as you travel down its course. Your destination comes into view – a large island in the centre of the mighty river. From this distance you can see the outline of many temples and the green lushness of gardens and trees. Your boat, as if with a will of its own, glides into dock by a pathway flanked with numerous stone statues and pillars adorned with the sacred lotus. It is early morning and the temple is quiet . . .

A person awaits your arrival. This person, clad in a simple white robe, assists you in mooring your boat and helps you to shore. With a short greeting you are told you are expected and are led around to the side of the temple complex. Here are found the residences of the novice priests and priestesses. Your aspiration has led to your being accepted as a student in the mysteries of Isis and this is the first stage of that inner training . . .

Much will take place within this temple. For now, follow your guide who escorts you into the gardens of the temple and to the side of a large pool upon which float many lotus flowers. Your guide assists you silently in disrobing and you enter the waters to bathe and purify yourself. Take some time to experience this. The morning sun glistens on the water, the air is filled with music and distant laughter . . .

As you complete your bath, your temple guide assists you from the lotus pool and wraps a linen sheet around you so that you may dry yourself. Holding this about you, you now follow your guide through to a courtyard with a number of long, low buildings around it. There are many doorways, some open, others curtained. These buildings contain the individual rooms wherein the novices live during their training. You are led to one of the empty rooms. This shall be your own room. Notice where the room lies in relation to the other rooms, note that above the door is carved a symbol or image. This designates it as your own.

You are led inside by your guide. The room is small and nearly bare, containing only a small couch and a plain wooden chest. Along one of the walls is a recessed niche; another wall contains a window that looks out on the gardens. Lying upon the couch is a plain white robe similar to the one worn by your guide. You are left alone and given time to put this on.

Your guide returns and tells you that for now you should remain close to this courtyard and room. Your subsequent journeys for now will be to this room – where you will meditate and prepare yourself for further work. It will also be your task to make sure this room remains clean. Your guide shows you where to find palm leaves and rushes with which stray sand may be swept out into the courtyard, and the well and washpool nearby where the linens and robes may be washed.

Once these practical instructions are over, your guide leaves you for now. Sit and meditate for a few moments. Then, lying down on the couch, think of your body back in the Inner Room within the circle of blue flame. There is a light mist all about you and as you open your inner eyes you find yourself seated once more before the candle flame. When you feel ready to return to normal, waking consciousness allow the circle of blue flame to die down and leave as you came in, returning up the steps and back out of the wardrobe.

Obviously this is quite a long journey and *thus should be built up slowly in stages*. At any point along the way you can will yourself back into the Inner Room and quickly return to ordinary waking consciousness. Close down thoroughly and write up your notes on the meditation journey soon after each session.

Chapter 7

The Gardens of the Temple

In my own exploration of the relationship between the conscious and unconscious minds I encountered the Huna tradition, the magical system of the indigenous people of the Hawaiian islands. It has powerful techniques to assist in the establishment of a better relationship with our personal unconscious. Like many native traditions it was largely ignored by the white settlers, or considered mere superstition. However, in the early 1900s, two men working as curators of a museum in Hawaii became fascinated by the local native tradition and the incredible healing and other psychic powers attributed to the practitioners of Huna, their magical system.

They laboured to discover the secret behind these abilities of the Kahunas – feeling instinctively that the language of the Hawaiian people held the key. However, despite forming strong bonds with practitioners and experiencing firsthand their abilities, the secret eluded them. When the elder man died, the younger, Max Freedom Long, laboured on. It wasn't until 1934, after he had returned to the mainland and given up on the search, that he managed to break the code.

In the meanwhile, Long had become interested in the works of Freud and his ideas about the conscious and unconscious minds. With this knowledge he returned once more to the language of the Hawaiians and indeed discovered a key to their system. Soon afterwards he formed the Huna Research Associates, a society devoted to the study and development of Huna techniques. At this time he wrote his first and most famous work: *The Secret Science Behind Miracles* (1948).

The Huna system, though it has similarities with Freud's and Jung's ideas, has much wider implications. As Enid Hoffman writes in *Huna: A Beginner's Guide*:

> All Huna practices are based on a very simple, logical concept. Briefly, it states: A human being consists of three selves living in a physical body: High, Middle, and Low (Long's names for them); Aumakua, Uhane, and Unihipili in Hawaiian; and in modern psychology, Superconscious, Conscious, and Subconscious.

Hoffman goes on to explain that Long's use of the terms high, middle and low referred to the area of the physical body each self occupied. Thus the higher self has its centre in the right hemisphere of the brain (origin of intuition and inspiration); the middle has its centre in the left hemisphere of the brain (powers of logical thought, speech); and the lower has its centre in the solar plexus/gut area.

It is the low self/unihipili (literally meaning 'spirit that is secret' or 'servant spirit' in Hawaiian) that is in control of the functioning of the physical body and also sorts out incoming stimuli. It is the organising principle within our personal unconscious. Our waking minds would ordinarily have little access to this level.

Among the qualities given for the low self/unihipili are: that it is passive and receptive; it does not have the faculty of choice or self-determination; it is capable only of deductive reasoning and literal thinking; it is fixed and conditioned by its experience; it is mute but expresses itself through feelings, images and symbols; it expands with warm emotions and contracts with cold ones, and it is the self which cries.

In contrast, the middle self/uhane (meaning 'spirit that talks') is active and capable of change; it has free will and is capable of both inductive and deductive reasoning; it is capable of literal and non-literal thinking; it will repress crying and other emotions and is aggressive. The uhane thinks of itself as the I.

The high self/aumakua (meaning Great Parent or Great Mother-Father spirit) is evolutionarily beyond the other two selves. In terms of the original native tradition they are considered three separate 'souls' for they can operate independently of each other. This is very similar to the Egyptian classification of separate soul bodies and at their root may be a common tradition, possibly Atlantean.

There can be great conflict between respective wills of the low and middle selves and this can cause of much strife. A common example of this occurs when the middle self decides to go on a diet but the willpower can be overcome by what can seem quite irrational cravings emanating from the lower self. This is why successful hypnosis and other techniques of positive affirmation will address the lower self/unihipili and seek to positively reprogram it.

I would like to move away from the term low self for, like Enid Hoffman, I find the word tends to denote inferiority by association. She thus uses the term 'junior' to describe the lower self/unihipili. One of her correspondences for the lower self was to refer to it as the 'moon self' and to the uhane/middle self as the sun self. Perhaps because of my background in the mysteries, I felt happier with this term and began to use the phrase 'lunar self' for the unihipili and likewise for the uhane the phrase 'solar self'. The aumakua had no designation but I felt it could be termed the 'stellar self'. These are the terms I shall use throughout this book.

I have found over the years that the Huna teachings have been a major thread running through my work both personally and in teaching others. The reason for this is that they are highly effective and, whether one is working with any sort of psychic development or training in the mysteries, it is so very important that the energies of the lunar self are in alliance with the solar self. For not only is that relationship important for psychological reasons but it is through the channel of the lunar self that the energies of the stellar self flow.

Connecting to the Lunar Self

This chapter's supplementary exercises are designed to assist you in getting better acquainted with your lunar self and to begin to understand its needs.

As was said above one of the main qualities of the lunar self is that it takes things literally and is thus extremely open to conditioning. Once conditioned it will remain fixated, for it has learned to function in the world by internalising various attitudes, ideas, skills and habits, and lacks the capability to discriminate. In this it fits much of Freud's model of the Id, though it is more complex. In the Huna model the lunar self looks to the solar self for that discrimination, although with most people this quality is lacking. For the most part, we also condition our lunar selves through our words. Unfortunately this is usually via self-deprecation which adds to the often strong sense of worthlessness and poor self-image that lies at the heart of most lunar selves in our present society.

The most essential part of the process of getting to know your lunar self is merely to begin to listen to it. You may already do this to some degree, but perhaps not in such a formal manner. Once you are open to it, it can communicate its thoughts, feelings, attitudes, etc. Then begins a process of dissolving unwanted conditioning and taking a more active role as the solar self in monitoring incoming information to the lunar self.

This idea of three-in-one sounds like a subtle form of schizophrenia, but it most definitely is not. We need always to keep in mind that although our various parts tend to act independently of one another, they are parts within a whole. That whole is the totality of you and no part is in actual isolation.

So, how to begin this work of getting to know your lunar self? As Hoffman writes:

> Everyone should talk directly to his own Low Self, but always in a kind, courteous, and considerate manner. Treat your Low Self as someone you do not want to hurt, for it is sensitive and will flinch at anything unkind. It recoils from insults and retracts from the chill of disapproval.

She also warns against talking about yourself in a deriding or demeaning manner because this feeds straight to your lunar self and conditions it to believe it is unlovable, stupid, worthless. Once you become aware of your own words, you will probably find yourself becoming aware of how other people talk about themselves. It is easy to see where negative conditioning comes from! We are also constantly bombarded by images and sounds which seek to condition us. One of the major ploys of advertising is to try and convince us that if we buy this or that product, we shall be attractive, successful. Advertisers know that this doesn't have to be a message to our conscious minds, because we shall take it in on a subliminal level and our naive lunar selves responds to it.

It is surprising how, when one becomes more conscious, such hooks begin to have less and less effect. As we establish a better relationship with our lunar selves, it is much easier to shrug off other people's negativities or attempts to 'get under your skin' through disapproval or remarks.

A primary phase of this work with your lunar self is to name it so that it will not be confused about whom you are addressing when you work with it. This doesn't need to be elaborate but should be a name which you associate with dignity and self-worth. It should also be clearly different from any subpersonality name. After you have selected one, do pause to see what reaction you get from your lunar self. If you get a feeling that it isn't right, select another. If after a number of names you still haven't had the 'thumbs up' – then ask it to 'pop' one it would prefer into your conscious mind. Lunar self names should remain private between the two of you.

Thereafter take a few minutes of quiet time each day just to open up and ask your lunar self to 'send up' into your conscious awareness any reminders, problems, etc that it feels you should clear up. You may have noticed at times when you sit down to meditate and relax that often it is these type of thoughts that will pop into your mind. So often we are so involved in our outer worlds that we tune out these vital messages. You may well find that your lunar self does, in its own fashion, begin to answer you back in some non-verbal way – through images, feelings or even physical sounds and sensations.

It is a good idea to keep a small notebook to record this unfinished business so that you can act on it. After a time, once the relationship becomes better established, this whole process can become quite subliminal. However, for now a little work and formalisation of the relationship will aid you in becoming more aware of what is going on. This is especially important as we move into the realm of dreams in the next chapter, which is the province of the lunar self.

COMMUNICATING WITH THE LUNAR SELF

A useful tool for communicating with the lunar self is the pendulum.

This is a very simple technique and should come fairly easily to you even if you have not worked with a pendulum before. First, choose a suitable pendulum. This can be almost anything really; it should weigh about 2 ozs and be suspended from a length of thread or chain of about 7 to 10 inches. The string is held between the thumb and index finger very lightly so that the pendulum hangs freely. When working with it, you may wish to support your elbow on a solid surface so that your arm does not tire.

The first part of the work involves setting up a code that your lunar self can use to communicate its answers to you via the pendulum. To keep it simple, the code for Yes can be like an affirmative nod of the head – swinging away from your body and back again. In order to teach the code, swing it that way manually, telling your lunar self that this is the code for 'yes'. Then stop the swing, saying 'stop' as you do so. Repeat this process until you feel that your lunar self is ready to try moving the pendulum by itself. Holding the pendulum still, watch for any movements.

Above all, be patient as this is a new skill and the first few times the movement may be quite tentative until your lunar self gets the hang of it. Encourage and praise its efforts, and soon your lunar self will be merrily swinging the pendulum! Having taught it to swing 'yes' and to stop on a verbal command, you now can go on to 'no' which is like a sideways shake of the head. Again, at first move it with your hands, and stop it with your free hand as you utter the word 'stop'. Keep this up until you feel your lunar self would like to try it.

When this has been assimilated you can go on to the code word for 'maybe' which is a diagonal swing of the pendulum. It is also useful to have the code words 'good' and 'bad' (or 'positive' and 'negative') as a clockwise or counter-clockwise movement which can be used by your lunar self to let you know if a question was poorly phrased, or, for example, to detect spoiled food or what food/ vitamins, etc are needed by the physical body to maintain it.

There is another method for establishing pendulum responses which is far simpler than the first, although it deals purely with 'yes' and 'no' answers and can, therefore, be somewhat limiting. This method is less rigid and allows the lunar self to determine its own responses. To do this, hold a pendulum over any object, for instance an electric cable, and ask, 'Is this live?'. You can switch off the power supply, therefore discovering the 'no' response, then switch it on, to establish the 'yes' response. If you decide to use this method your questioning will have to be slightly adapted, as it will not be able to give a 'maybe', a 'positive' or a 'negative' answer.

Having established your means of communication, you can then go on to consult with your lunar self about a variety of things, learning about its beliefs and needs. Hoffman suggests that at first you should write down a series of questions and record the answers non-judgementally. These questions can be along the lines of:

Do you have guilt feelings about . . .?

Are you afraid of physical death?

Do you ever feel inadequate to a task?

Do you enjoy responsibility?

Do you believe you have ESP?

Does it hurt to be criticised?

Do you like . . .?

Do you believe it is wrong to have or want money?

Do you believe the saying, 'One pays for everything one gets'?

Do you believe you have to work hard to keep friends?

And so on. Make up your own questions along similar lines. Until you have done a fair amount of exploratory work in getting to know your lunar self, it is better not to overdo things. Assimilate the material your lunar self is providing and never force it into long sessions as it may bore quickly. It is also a good idea to begin any session with your lunar self with the query – 'are you willing to answer some questions?'

You can proceed from this basic pendulum work to test for various attitudes and beliefs held by the lunar self which can be at variance with what you consciously believe. For example, there can be in many women (despite strongly-held conscious feminist attitudes) a deeply-ingrained belief within their lunar selves that women are inferior. This can be due to early programming by one's environment or other factors. It is self-evident that such beliefs need to be addressed before a real sense of self-worth is experienced.

Make out lists of various belief statements and ask for a 'True or False' indication with the pendulum; whether your lunar self loves or hates certain things or considers others good or bad. These fixed attitudes held by your lunar self can be very revealing and get to the heart of many problems. What can be done when such beliefs or attitudes are found when one discovers a deep sense of inferiority or a belief that is negatively self-conditioning?

As your relationship develops with your lunar self and it realises that you are willing to listen to it you can utilise the fundamental technique of self-love and positive affirmation to change the experience your lunar self has of the world. It may seem a daunting task but there are many excellent books that can assist. Find new ways via the pendulum to know exactly what you can give to your body and lunar self to aid in its health and development. Make sure to write up this work in your diary.

BEAR THERAPY

This word is 'bear' as in the animal, not 'bare'. This exercise was passed on as an oral teaching during my training as a therapist as an excellent way to connect with our 'inner child' and as a gentle exercise to give our clients so that they may do the same. I found it easily adaptable for work with my lunar self and have inevitably passed it on when instructing others in the Huna system. The bear (or any other stuffed animal toy that appeals) is used as a symbolic representation of your lunar self. This can often be a valuable aid if someone is shy, unfamiliar or slightly uncomfortable with talking directly to themselves. Hold the toy lovingly and address it by the name of your lunar self, giving it love and assurance. In this exercise you will not be using the pendulum but nurturing your lunar self (rather than seeking answers to questions).

Many people will make this sort of link anyway with a beloved teddy or pet and this can often be a valuable source of comfort and health, for through both we make contact with our lunar selves. I have inevitably found that my own lunar self is extremely suspicious of people who are unkind or uncaring about animals. It usually bears out that they are also estranged from their lunar self. The same is true about children, and a rise in child cruelty and abuse in the West has been linked to the sense of alienation within our society from our 'inner child' and innate innocence.

THE GARDENS OF THE TEMPLE

We are about to embark on the next stage of our meditational journey within the Temple of Isis. Again I would suggest that you do this journey three or four times during a week and on other days you focus on exercises related to your lunar self, subpersonalities, or simple relaxation with meditation, perhaps on material already received. This work is quite intensive and while regular practice is very important for continuity, it is necessary properly to assimilate your experiences. If this vital process is not honoured, external pressures will intrude to make you take a break.

Certainly, while discipline and regular practice are important, other factors will sometimes demand your time. Never be embarrassed to take time off; it isn't 'backsliding'. The links you have made with the inner levels through your work will continue to operate.

Journey to the Island and the Temple of Isis and enter your room there. In this chapter's meditation a new area of the temple complex is to be explored. Your temple guide will lead you there from your room. Allow them to come to you and lead you forth. You will find yourself being escorted beyond the lotus pool to a large garden full of plants, shrubs, trees, rockeries and fountains. As you explore, try to bring in all your senses; smell the flowers, hear the songs of birds and the buzz of insects, reach out and touch the trees and feel the grass beneath your feet. Be aware that some areas of the garden are enclosed behind walls. Some of it is very formal, while other sections are more natural. Do explore it as thoroughly as you wish and write up your experiences.

You may well see others there – students or priests and priestesses of the Temple. If it is appropriate your guide will introduce you and this may lead to a dialogue. However, as the garden is a place where the initiates of the Temple come for rest and contemplation, privacy needs to be respected.

Also within the garden are to be found various small shrines containing figures of the Goddess honoured within the Temple complex. You will probably find over the course of your visits to the gardens that one of these shrines draws you more strongly and becomes special to you. Allow this process. Once you have identified such a shrine proceed as directed below.

A Personal Shine
Mention to your guide that you have found a special shrine. On your next visit within the meditation you are conducted

to this shrine and given both the materials and tools with which to create another small statue. It is possible to 'create' this statue merely through thought alone but it can also be helpful to imagine the process of creation.

This process of creation may take one session or more and the finished piece need not be an exact replica of the original statue, though it should convey the same energy to you. Once this is complete there will be a process of dedication on your next visit to the Temple.

In your next session visualise yourself bringing the completed sculpture to the original shrine within the garden. You will find there a priestess dedicated to the Goddess to whom you have been drawn. You will be introduced to her by your guide and the intention of dedicating this sculpture for a personal shrine will be stated.

Your sculpture is taken from you and washed carefully by your attendant guide in a basin of water. You are then asked to hold your sculpture, standing before the original shrine. The priestess carefully anoints your sculpture with sacred oil. Standing between you and the shrine, she reaches out and places her right hand upon the head (usually the third eye centre) of the original statue and enters into meditation.

Having achieved this, she reaches out and place her left hand upon the same spot on your statue, saying as she does 'between these two let there be resonance'. This is established as a vibratory wave that moves from the original statue to yours through the mediation of the priestess linking the two. Once this is completed, the circuit is broken. After giving thanks to the Goddess and her priestess, you are escorted back to your room with the newly consecrated statue. Place this in the recessed niche. You may from now on use this figure as a focus for meditation and place before it offerings of flowers, incense or candles.

You may of course also continue to meditate within the garden, at that place or elsewhere. However, the creation and dedication ceremony is done only once.

Return to your normal, waking consciousness as usual on completion of your meditation, close down completely and write up notes for your record.

An obvious off-shoot of this meditation is creating a sculpture for your own shrine. One thing to overcome is the sense that, if you have little skill in this artform, you should not attempt it. Given time and patience it is possible to create some form of figure. It is true that not many people have the facilities to fire clay though many schools and adult education facilities have pottery classes where kilns are available. It is also possible to obtain 'nu-clay' for children which does not need firing to create sculpture.

If this still feels beyond you, you can always obtain from a speciality shop or museum a reproduction of the Goddess you wish to have on your shrine. You can personalise it by painting it yourself. If you, in either way, obtain a physical statue to mirror your inner one, it is simple to likewise dedicate it in a ceremony combining visualisation, as given above. Cleanse and anoint the physical statue and physically hold it as you go through the meditation sequence. At the point the dedication is done by the priestess, make the mental link with the physical statue so that both the physical and visualised versions are likewise consecrated.

Chapter 8

Dreamwork and the Temple of Anubis

The focus of this chapter is upon working with dreams and using them to come into a better relationship with your lunar and stellar selves. I believe that our lunar selves are the major organising factors in our dream lives and can be considered the 'Dream Creator'. The improvement of our ability to communicate with our lunar selves improves not only dream recall, but also the clarity of the dream's symbolic content.

Dreams are a major link between our conscious and

unconscious minds. Jung considered dreams to be 'the royal road to the unconscious'. As stated in the last chapter, the lunar self is the channel through which we receive energy, guidance and information from our stellar selves and the inner realms. Learning to discriminate between which dreams are delivering such messages and which are part of the daily process of the unconscious is part of the process of 'dreamwork' which we shall be actively engaged in, in co-operation with our lunar selves.

Certainly some readers may have already worked with dreams or kept some form of record of them. Using dreams as an exploratory tool is crucial to the work of becoming self-aware. They also occasionally act as an interface with the collective unconscious in the form of a dream experience of a being or archetypal energy which imparts teaching and initiatory experiences. Later, I will touch on this sort of dream which can be a life-changing event.

However, let us start with the basics. The more common experience of dreaming and dreams is of fleeting and confusing images which are as often as not dispersed on waking, as everyday concerns take over. Some people feel they never dream, but this is not so. We all dream every night, but the ability to recall dreams on waking is where the problem comes in; the mind has simply not been trained to recall them!

It used to be thought that dreams were random, fleeting experiences brought on by some form of external or internal stimuli (a noise, full bladder, anxiety or eating certain foods before sleep). However, in 1953, at the University of Chicago, researchers carried out a series of experiments in which they monitored the electrical impulses of sleepers' brains with an EEG (electroencephalogram) machine. They noticed that brain wave activity changed throughout the night and that sleepers went through a regular cycle of stages of sleep, descending into deep sleep then ascending into a lighter sleep before descending once more. On the ascending arc, which would be produced about four or five times a night in a normal sleeping period of seven or eight hours, sleepers enter into a type of sleep typified by a number of physiological signals. The most significant of these was rapid movements of the eyeballs as though the dreamer was viewing something. It was found that when subjects are awakened during these periods of REM (rapid eye movement), about 80 percent reported vivid, detailed dreams. It was also found that closer to the end of a sleep period the relative time spent in REM sleep was considerable.

Researchers went further and also did experiments with dream deprivation: that is waking subjects up as they entered REM sleep, thereby depriving them of dream time. Although they had plenty of resting sleep, the subjects became very tense and anxious. When they were again allowed to sleep uninterrupted, they spent almost double their time in REM sleep as though they needed to catch up on their dreaming.

Thus research has rediscovered what the ancients were aware of. Dreams are necessary to both our emotional and mental health. They allow us to process experiences and order our realities. If you recall times when you have been under pressure to learn a new skill or in a new situation, you will often have found yourself dreaming about it. This is obviously part of the procedure for assimilating new material. It is also how we process, in a symbolic way, the daily stresses of our lives.

We all dream but the problem is that we don't all recall our dreams. Once they are recalled we are then faced with the daunting task of figuring out what they mean, or whether they are just the simple processing of daily experience.

The Dream Journal

Unless the dream is written down upon waking there is a tendency for the images and feelings to fade during the day and thus be lost to the dreamer. Therefore the first task is to improve recall of dreams. The simplest way is to keep a pad and pencil beside you as you are sleeping and to get into the habit of writing down dreams or dream fragments upon waking. Some people prefer to use tape recorders but they can be very awkward to start up in the middle of the night unless they are voice-activated. Whatever method is used it comes down to practice and discipline. Certainly it is usual to find, as you did with the lunar self previously, that once you start taking the trouble to pay attention to your dreams, they begin to become more accessible to you.

Keeping a special dream journal in the form of a book in which you transcribe your dreams and dream fragments on a daily basis is essential, though you may wish to combine it with your diary-record of meditation work. It is important to date your entries and to write down, briefly, any factors from the day before which may have contributed to the dream as these are likely to give valuable clues. Very often, a book, TV programme, video, conversation or encounter will provide images or themes for your dream. However, do not fall into the trap of letting these associations 'explain away' the dream. You may well consider why your lunar self chose these particular ones to act as trigger points.

For example, a day full of petty frustrations at home or work may trigger a dream in which that frustration is emphasised, or one in which you escape completely to a place where there are no such worries. Yet the dream remains a clear message that you were stressed out and that you need to find a way in which to cope with this in your waking life to avoid further problems.

Beginning Interpretation

In approaching themes and symbols, the main thing I would stress is that standard 'dream dictionaries' are next to useless and are best avoided. No one can really interpret a dream apart from yourself. You are your own best dream analyst. The best a dream dictionary can do is start the ball rolling on symbol association though, if used, you should be wary of accepting them as gospel. The same is true for another person's opinion, for while they may have interesting ideas about your dream, these will be, for the most part, based on the significance of certain symbols to themselves and not to you. Certainly it takes time and work to become confident in interpreting your own dream symbols and themes, but this is better than imposing an interpretation which may confuse the true message of the dream.

Different schools of psychoanalysis and psychotherapy will have their own dream languages. Freud, for example, thought that dreams were merely wish fulfilment and that most dream imagery was sexual in nature and referred to disguised genitalia and sexual acts which could not be expressed outside of fantasy because of repression. The Jungian approach, by contrast, looks at the broader, symbolic message of the dream, though there is still a tendency to consider dream themes as archetypal interplay when what may be happening is simply a passing on of information about daily life.

Dream dictionaries and 'classic' psychoanalytical literature does have the tendency to reduce dreams to the lower common denominator rather than taking into consideration the circumstances of the individual dreamer. Thus, for one person who loves cats, the appearance of one in a dream will have connotations of pleasure, comfort, adoration and all their association about cats; someone who abhors cats and considers them pests and nuisances will be receiving a very different message. Remember that, in essence, you are the producer and director of your dream (your lunar and stellar selves being parts of your totality) and probably the principal actor as well! Some aspect of you will have carefully chosen all the symbols you encounter.

The first thing to consider is whether there is a literal meaning to the dream before digging deeper. Dreams can be warnings about health. Dreams about one's car breaking down may be triggered by your lunar self having picked up on a subliminal signal the last time you were in your car. So before looking for subjective interpretations of such dreams it is advisable to look at the obvious. If work is getting you down or is especially demanding, you may find yourself dreaming of the work situation and this may have a simple message that your work place is a source of stress. Returning to an old place of employment may point to old issues being raised again in a current situation, and so on.

Certainly, there can be themes and symbols which tend to be practically universal. Houses in dreams are usually symbolic of the dreamer's or another's personality. It is 'where we live', as was the house you explored in earlier chapters. Likewise, vehicles can refer to one's own body or the journey through life, etc. Animals and children may refer to literal beings, or symbolise our lunar selves.

Ann Faraday, in her book *Dream Power*, gives three broad categories of dreams. The first of these 'three faces' of dreams concerns those which look outward. In this category she places reminder and warning dreams along with precognitive dreams and those in which we perceive in symbolic form people and situations in our daily lives.

The second category concerns what she calls the 'looking glass' dreams. She draws on the examples of the story of *Alice Through the Looking Glass* where things and people have an association with aspects of the dreamer's inner and outer life but they are, as it were, a created picture which may be a straight reflection or distorted completely. It is these pictures of houses, vehicles, people, creatures and objects that we must learn to read and relate. In this category we most often find fictional, historical and public figures featuring as well as people from our pasts.

The third category of dreams concerns those which look inward and give direct assistance with the process of coming to 'know thyself'. They can be considered to be ultimately coming from our stellar selves, assisting us with the process of coming to terms with ourselves in totality. They may be confronting, informative, healing, transformative; giving us insight into various aspects of our unconscious.

There is a further category of dream that relates to esoteric subjects, but I shall return to this later in the chapter. Right now let us look at some basic techniques of dream interpretation.

Obviously, the first step is to recall and record your dreams as previously suggested. Before sleep you may try simply suggesting to yourself that you will remember your dreams. Another technique is to have a glass of water beside your bed. Drink some of it before sleep, saying to yourself that when you drink the remainder on waking you will recall your dreams.

The exercises in Chapter 7 concerning communication with your lunar self may well have increased your dream recall already as you begin to allow your lunar self a voice.

You may only catch a fragment of a dream rather than a full dramatic piece but this too should be recorded and interpreted. You may find working on it brings back other memories linked to that dream or the symbols in it.

Let me include at this point a quotation from Dr Ann Faraday's second book on dreams, *The Dream Game*, which

I feel sums up, in a few clear and simple points, a set of basic rules/guidelines for successful dream interpretation:

The basic rules of the dream game at this point are:

1 The dream should always be considered literally in the first instance and examined for signs of objective truth, such as warnings or reminders, before moving on to metaphorical interpretation.

2 If the dream makes no sense when taken literally, then (and only then) should it be seen as a metaphorical statement of the dreamer's feelings at the time of the dream.

3 All dreams are triggered by something on our minds or in our hearts, so the primary objective must be to relate the dream theme to some event or preoccupation of the previous day or two.

4 The feeling tone of the dream usually gives a clue as to what this particular life situation is. For example, if the feeling tone of the dream is miserable, then the dream was sparked by some miserable situation in the dreamer's current life.

5 Common dream themes (such as falling, nudity, taking examinations, travelling, finding or losing valuables, sex, being pursued, meeting famous people, being lost) are likely to indicate common areas of human feeling and experience, but within these broad limits each theme can mean quite different things to different dreamers according to the individual's life circumstances at the time of the dream.

6 The same dream theme may recur from time to time in the dreams of the same dreamer and have a different specific meaning each time, according to the life circumstances at the time of each dream.

7 Dreams do not come to tell us what we know already (unless of course, it is something we know but have failed to act upon, in which case they will recur, often in the form of nightmares, until we do), so if a dream seems to be dealing with something you are quite aware of, look for some other meaning in it.

8 A dream is correctly interpreted when and only when it makes sense to the dreamer in terms of his present life situation and moves him to change his life constructively.

9 A dream is incorrectly interpreted if the interpretation leaves the dreamer unmoved and disappointed. Dreams come to expand, not diminish us.

In recommending books to students to complement the material given in the course I always suggest Faraday's books which contain many examples of dreams interpreted using her methods. Also the *Dreamwork Manual* of Strephon Kaplan-Williams (Aquarian) contains many techniques.

Identifying Dream Themes

Once you have collected a few dreams, the next stage is to identify their main themes. What is a 'theme' in this context? Well, it should be a brief sentence, which is a statement of that dream's content. This will often provide clues to the dream's meaning by suggesting further questions. For example, if in a series of dreams a person finds themselves set upon by lion, then perhaps what they need to ask themselves is 'what or whom do I feel attacked by in my life?' since the fear of an actual lion attack is unlikely to be the real meaning here.

The main point with identifying themes is to practise doing it. Some will be very obvious, others more obscure, but don't be afraid to try to chart the theme. Remember this dreamwork is something very private. It is not necessary to share it with anyone else unless you wish to. If you have a partner or friend who is also interested in dreamwork, sharing your dreams and interpretations can be a very fulfilling activity for both of you.

After writing up a dream you can begin to ask yourself questions about the main themes and symbols of the dream, finding these answers within yourself by association or in concert with your lunar self. For example, what are you doing in the dream? What are your feelings about this, both in the dream and now in considering it? What are the issues, conflicts or unresolved situations present? What are the main symbols within the dream and what is your relationship to them? Do the themes, places, people or symbols relate to other dreams you recall? To which of Faraday's categories do you feel it belongs? The answer to this last question may be multiple for dreams can easily have, like an onion, different layers of meaning.

Dream Symbols

Most dreams will contain certain symbols: people, places, objects, animals. Often these are familiar things. When they are, do keep in mind the first basic 'rule' – that the dream may have a literal interpretation! Even a stranger or famous person, for example, may, through their name, build, voice or personality, be actually pointing to a particular real person in your life and be attempting to express something quite literal about that relationship.

Another point to keep in mind when extracting symbols from a dream is that humour is often subtly present. Humour may seem an odd thing to look for in dreams, but our lunar/dreaming selves do have an often well-developed sense of humour, even a sense of the ridiculous. Ann Faraday makes quite an interesting case for how the unconscious will use puns, slang and colloquial metaphors, body language and literal pictorial metaphors in dreams.

Also, if the same or similar dream image or character appears frequently in your dreams, it is likely to have a similar meaning. For this reason it is helpful to compile a dream glossary of major symbols. This can be done in a loose leaf notebook (or on cards) indexed A–Z. This can be an immensely valuable exercise as you will be able to see when and if dream symbols do recur, as memory can often play tricks on you. This will also greatly assist your interpretation.

So how do you actually interpret a symbol? Here is the crux of the matter and the reason why people will often turn to dream dictionaries despite the fact that it may be a useless exercise. First of all, it is important to establish what you feel about any symbol. A snake as a symbol will be interpreted depending on how you feel about snakes. If, on the one hand, you hate them and consider them slimy, dangerous and loathsome, it will take on that symbolism in a dream. If, on the other hand, you like them and consider them a beneficent force or symbol of wisdom/healing, then that it is the meaning it will take on for you.

When writing up your dream you may also wish to jot down key words about a few of the symbols and also take a stab at interpreting the message of the dream. Do not worry about missing out on an opportunity to analyse a dream more deeply at this point. You will always be able to go back to dreams you have had previously and examine them in the light of newly acquired skills.

Symbol Dialogues

In order to dig deeper, especially with those symbols which recur or are illusive, there are two techniques which are very valuable. Each, in its own way, seeks to get the figure/symbol to answer the question using simple techniques of disassociation.

The first way is called 'inner dialogue'. In this you have an inner conversation with the people and symbols within your dream. First, formulate a few questions – such as 'what do you represent in this dream?' and write these down. Then call into your mind the dream figure and ask the question and write down, without evaluating it, the answer that comes into your mind.

Again, in your head, give feedback to that answer and, if appropriate, ask another question. At first this process will probably be awkward, but you will get used to doing it. Continue with the dialogue until it feels complete and/or you have enough material to work with. Read over the material and evaluate it in the light of your dream and other experiences.

The other way of interviewing figures is the 'Gestalt method' which acts out the process of questioning. Gestalt (meaning 'whole') therapy was founded by the late humanistic psychologist, Fritz Perls, and has as one of its basic premises the idea that all dream figures, things and situations represent aspects of the dreamer. That is, they are entirely subjective.

In Gestalt terms, if I dream about my best friend being married, I am actually dreaming about myself with no relation to her or her life situation. My friend is considered an aspect of my personality appearing in the dream. In order to decide whether to treat a dream as subjective or objective, a general rule of thumb would be to consider the dream to be subjective if the meaning of the dream is not easily apparent. Recalling our 'onion' analogy, a dream of this type could well be about an objective situation – my friend's longing for marriage – or represent part of my own unfolding process.

To work with a dream symbol within the Gestalt method decide, as before, on some basic questions and sit with an empty chair opposite you. Then imagine that the dream figure or symbol is sitting opposite you and ask it your question, such as 'what is your meaning in my dream?'. Do not answer in your head this time but get up and sit on the empty chair. Imagine that you are now that figure or symbol and allow an answer to come into your mind, then answer the question out loud. You then switch back chairs to write down the answer, give feedback and ask for clarification or another question. Continue the process until it feels complete.

This is a very powerful way of working and although it was actually meant to be used in either a group situation with a therapist, or one-to-one, it can still work when done by oneself. As a technique it can feel quite embarrassing even when you do it alone with no one within earshot. However, the process of stepping outside yourself in this way can produce quite incredible insights into the meaning of a symbol. Perhaps gently experiment with it when dealing with especially illusive symbols.

It can very often be a way in which to break into a particularly elusive dream image. An example from my own dream-life: since childhood I had suffered from the occasional vivid nightmare about sharks (particularly great white sharks). I would find myself floating in a pool or the sea and would realise that there was a shark in the water near me. I would wake up in terror although I lived many miles from anywhere I would be likely to encounter a real shark.

The dream resurfaced when I first began recording my dreams and it became a recurring nightmare for some time. I had attempted to interpret the dream using Faraday's guidelines but it was only using the Gestalt exercise that I discovered the great white shark represented my suppressed negative emotions. My big fear was that I would be 'eaten alive' by the shark. I learnt through this method that my shark was not just a monster but was seeking my recognition. A few days after I had used the Gestalt method, I had a dream wherein I became a member of an organisation to 'preserve the great white shark' from extinction.

This dream marked a transition point where I was coming to terms with the dream message. I also read some informative literature on sharks and began to appreciate their primitive beauty. The dreams did not cease on learning their meaning. Indeed I had to work for quite a long period of time at integrating those emotions. However, as I did, the symbol of the shark began to slowly change in my dreams from a figure of terror and nightmare to being an ally protecting me in certain situations.

These days I find that if I am avoiding powerful emotions, I will often have a dream that involves the sea or a swimming pool where I see from the sidelines the fin of a shark or I am told a shark has been spotted. On waking my response is to take conscious action immediately to examine what I am attempting to suppress. So the shark has changed from being an object of terror to a very clear 'early warning signal' that my conscious/solar self will sit up at, pay attention to and act on. It is this willingness to pay attention and, where appropriate, to act on dream messages which is a key way of letting your lunar/dreaming self know you are paying attention. The relationship between your waking and dreaming minds will then improve considerably.

Teaching and Lucid Dreams

It is likely that because you are regularly meditating and working with the mysteries some of your dreams will contain archetypal themes or symbols. These can be incredibly useful to chart your path of growth and can also be indicative of your attaining to certain states of consciousness. 'Magical' dreams containing goddesses and gods, mythological and legendary figures, fantastic animals or sacred places, journeys or encounters can be extremely transforming. You may find that you are, while in the dream state, being taught skills associated with the mysteries of the Goddess. There will be a very marked qualitative difference in these to ordinary dreams which will leave you in no doubt as to their special nature: deep emotions and a sense of spiritual connection are experienced. They may even manifest as out-of-body experiences or contain a sense of lucidity. However, the very fact of their infrequency does not mean we should despise or reject dreams that do not contain this quality but see that each has their place as a message.

Lucid dreaming is somewhat different, though may also contain powerful imagery. Basically, this is a dream wherein you become conscious and are aware that you are dreaming. This may be a fleeting experience or it may be sustained. There are various techniques to encourage lucid dreaming and to explore the boundary between this sort of dreaming and out-of-body experiences which are subjects for books in themselves. If you wish to explore either of these subjects, may I suggest the works of Patricia Garfield on lucid dreams and dream incubation (*Creative Dreaming* and *Pathway to Ecstasy – The Way of the Dream Mandala*) and for out-of-body experiences Robert Munroe's *Journeys Out of the Body* and J.H. Brennan's *The Astral Projection Workbook*.

We will return to the subject of dreams in Chapter 10. Meanwhile the meditations which conclude this chapter give two very powerful methods of working further with your dreams. These involve the use of the active imagination to illuminate the meaning.

Dreamwork Meditations

The two settings for the following main meditation work are the Inner Room, and the Temple of Anubis which is located in the complex of temples upon the inner island. In going within in this way you will be able to seek assistance for deeper dream analysis.

The Egyptian god Anubis is most usually depicted in the form of a jackal-headed man or as a black jackal. He was the son of Osiris and Nephthys, the sister of Isis. He was later adopted by Isis, becoming her guide and protector during her wanderings in the wilderness as she sought Osiris's body. His role within the Egyptian pantheon was as the guide for the newly deceased, and also as a god of magic and as a guide during visions and within the dream state. He is known as the Walker Between The Worlds and the Opener of the Way. He is a gentle and protective guide, who can be visualised accompanied by his mother, Nephthys. In the final meditation of this chapter you will be consulting the priests and priestesses of Anubis about the deeper meanings of your dreams.

However, this is not a journey that you will necessarily wish to make each and every day! Therefore, vary your routine. During the time you work on this chapter, you may wish on some days to remain within your Inner Room and on other days to journey onward to the Temple of Isis to consult those of the Temple of Anubis. While regular work is the key to self-development, sometimes it will feel more appropriate for you to do some simple relaxation and energising exercises, to meditate upon a dream image or key thought received in more formal meditations, or indeed to work on one of the other exercises.

Before working with any dreams within either the Inner Room or the Temple of Anubis, you should have done some form of preliminary work with the dream material as I have suggested. For this purpose you may use a current dream or an earlier one that has engaged your interest.

As to the place in which to meditate or ask for assistance with dream images, a general 'rule of thumb' is that those dreams which appear to deal with your everyday life and personal issues can be worked with in the Inner Room. Dreams containing archetypal images and symbols or those having a numinous quality can be brought to the Temple of Anubis to gain insight or for further exploration and teaching. Obviously what seems an 'ordinary' dream may sometimes contain symbols which actually reach much deeper. However, an indication will be given by your Guide in the Inner Room as to whether it is appropriate to take such a dream into the Temple of Anubis.

DREAMS IN THE INNER ROOM

After entering the wardrobe and descending the stairs, enter your Inner Room. Light the candle and be seated as normal. You notice on one wall there is a curtain covering something. Sitting there, call upon your Inner Guide and wait for them to come to you. You sit together and the curtain opens, revealing a monitor screen which you can watch together.

The dream you wish to work on now plays as though you were watching a film on video. Feel free to watch the action or freeze it, to rewind or fast forward it. (You may find you have either a remote control box for this or are able to do it with thought alone.)

The story or images may alter from what you recall of the dream. If this is so, the way in which they alter should provide you with insights as to their meaning. Feel free to ask your Guide for assistance, but try to find the answer that feels right for you through their guidance. It may be that you wish to dialogue with one of the dream characters or symbols. If you do, allow your guide to act as a mediator for the discussion. After you have finished, allow the screen images to fade, thank your guide and your lunar self (for providing the dream). The curtain should be closed. Now return as usual to normal waking consciousness and write up notes.

DREAMS IN THE TEMPLE OF ANUBIS

Journey as before to the Island and enter your special room. You find that dusk is falling and the air is full of rich scents. There is a clear sky and the moon is visible. The stars are beginning to show. Note the phase of the moon. Be aware, and open to the beauty of the night.

Your Temple Guide comes to escort you through the formal gardens, past the lotus pool, away from the main temple complex. There is a clear path leading into and through some trees. Still you are able to see quite easily – the path itself seems to shine with a pale light. You are led to a clearing with a pool of clear water in the centre, the moon and stars reflected in its surface. Beyond the pool is a temple whose entrance is guarded by two large statues in the form of recumbent jackals of ebony with golden eyes and ears. The temple is of onyx and marble. As you approach with your Guide you are met by either a man or woman dressed in indigo and black robes. This is the Priest or Priestess of Anubis who will be your escort. Your Temple Guide will wait for you outside the Temple and will lead you back to your room once you are finished.

You find that the temple is open to the night sky and is also lit by softly burning rush torches set into the wall. In the North is a large image of the enthroned Anubis, the Jackal-Headed Walker Between the Worlds who is both the Guide of the Dead and Guardian of the Mysteries. He also presides over the Dreamtime world. The walls of his temple are decorated with many scenes of him assisting travellers, and other scenes depicting his journeys as protector and guide of Isis.

Here, with the assistance of the attendant priestess or priest, you can meditate upon your dream and its symbols to seek its meaning in your life or, as in the Inner Room, you can see it played out. In the Temple itself there is another pool of clear water and, as you look into it, your dream images form in its depths. In this place it will be the Priest or Priestess of Anubis who functions as your facilitator should you should wish to talk with any of the characters or symbols. What happens on each visit here will be different according to your needs of the time. It may simply be that you just soak up the atmosphere, meditate before the image of Anubis or even see a new dream in Anubis's mirror/pool. You may even find that Anubis appears within the pool to speak with you.

Once you have completed your meditation, give thanks for what you have received in the Temple and leave, returning with your Temple Guide to your own room in the temple complex. Then return to the Inner Room and close down as usual. Write up notes on the experience.

Chapter 10 on the mysteries of the Moon Goddess will provide further information on dream symbolism and incubation. As always, the key to this work is the integration of these practices into your outer life. The practical applications of such realisations should always be a goal with this work – as within, so without!

Chapter 9

The Temple of Earth

In this and the next four chapters, the main meditation will concentrate on the construction of the Pillar of Isis. The Pillar is a conceptual model of the Universe which draws on the image of a tower-like structure with its foundation within the Earth, and culminating in the Stars.

The Tower as a traditional magical image was preceded by the World-Tree, whose roots were in the Underworld and whose topmost branches mingled with the stars. We have already seen in Chapter 3, that the Judaic mystical tradition utilises the image of the Tree of Life. It is a powerful symbol within Teutonic mythology as Yggdrasil, the Tree that links the nine worlds of that tradition. In shamanic traditions trees are considered to be the entrances to other realities and are climbed in visionary experiences.

When I first received the Pillar in meditation as a symbolic framework for the course I did envisage it as a tower. However, as my work with it developed, the name 'Pillar of Isis' seemed more appropriate for the Egyptian setting.

At each level of the Pillar is found a Temple to which are attributed certain symbols which you have already encountered in your work in Part 1. These include the elements, the Tattvas, the chakras and the Sephiroth of the Qabalistic Tree of Life. The Pillar is a very personal image, existing within your aura. As you build it, level by level, it shall become your gateway to the energies and worlds represented by its symbols. It may be helpful at each phase of its building to look back on the notes you have made of your earlier journeys and meditations linked to these associated symbols.

For each of the Temples we shall visit as we ascend the levels of the Pillar of Isis, we will look at some of the mysteries associated with Goddesses attributed to that Temple. Many Goddesses are capable, by the complexity of their natures, of being attributed to more than one Temple. Others are more obviously linked to a specific one, as Artemis is to the Moon. I do not expect that everyone will agree with my attributions and, certainly, I will be unable to cover all mythologies. Think of these ideas as starting points for your own researches. Like the Tree of Life or the Tarot, the Pillar is capable of being used as a mnemonic or esoteric filing system to assist you in your approach to these mysteries.

Let us examine some of the attributes and mysteries linked to the Goddesses of Earth. These mysteries tend to mark our own 'rites of passage' and cycles through life and death. As Janet and Stewart Farrar state in their book, *The Witches' Goddess* (Robert Hale 1987), 'The Earth Mother is the most vivid and immediate face which the Goddess presents to us. She is fertility itself, for mankind and for all creatures and plants.'

Certainly, the face of the Earth Mother is by no means

always benign as we have already seen in the myth of Ishtar/Inanna's descent into matter and her encounter with Ereshkigal. If we are to become conscious individuals it is necessary to come to terms with her Dark Face as well as her Bright One. For she is an initiator and an awakener.

The Goddess of Earth has many aspects. She is the Great Mother, the primordial Goddess of Life, Death and Rebirth, the faceless Goddess whose many images with ripe breasts and buttocks and pregnant belly have been discovered in Palaeolithic dwelling sites. She is the Goddess both of fertility and of the barren Earth. She is the Underworld Goddess of death and knowledge. She is the Grain Mother who teaches humankind the skills of agriculture. She is the Dark Devouring Mother who brings famine, earthquakes and pestilence as well the Bright Fertile Mother. Above all she is the Earth herself that contains all the life that exists upon this sphere in all its complexity and paradox.

We can encounter the Goddess in a very concrete way through our attunement to her aspect as the Goddess of Earth yet, as the Farrars also point out: 'as a planet she is a separate entity, existing and active on all the levels – one planetary entity among countless others, one 'organ' of the total cosmic organism, and we in turn are cells of that organ'.

The concept of the Earth Mother as the planet, although existing within many religions, has in recent years found a surprising ally in the Gaia hypothesis of Drs James Lovelock and Sidney Epton. The basic premise states that the conditions which enable life to exist upon the planet are so delicately balanced that the Earth and its biosphere 'seem to exhibit the behaviour of a single organism, even a living creature'. This idea that Earth could be considered a conscious living being and not just a random coming together of chemicals is another example of modern science rediscovering ancient concepts.

With the advent of the science of ecology, scientists are learning more and more about the delicate state of the Earth's ecosystem. We are also becoming aware of how that ecosystem is being disrupted by mankind's pollution and exploitation of the planet's resources.

Many people drawn to the mysteries of the Goddess are already aware at a deep level of the threat the planet is under, or quickly find themselves becoming more aware. Reconnecting the 'green movement' to its spiritual dimension has been greatly assisted by the work of scientists such as Lovelock and Epton as well as by countless others in both the scientific and esoteric camps. Many followers of the Goddess are seeking to bring about a union between a religion based on a love of the planet as our Mother and practical work on the local, economic and global levels to help restore the ecological balance.

The idea of rituals and meditations to direct healing to the Earth may seem like a daunting task in the face of the current ecological crisis. This Earth-healing work is seeking to restore the balance with Nature known to the ancients and to those indigenous peoples who still live in harmony with her. There is no doubt, though, that since this work began in earnest there has been a virtual explosion of Green issues coming to the forefront of popular consciousness. This is slowly beginning to have an effect even if the damage done is still vast and the fight for the planet's health far from over.

One very easy way in which to connect to the sphere of the Earth Goddess is to begin to take some form of active involvement in issues linked to ecology. Much can be done using active meditation and ritual but being conscious in your everyday life – using recycled paper products, recycling paper, cans, plastic and bottles, buying 'green', working on local conservation projects and getting involved in the bigger ecological issues through support and letter writing – will serve to make your own relationship with the planet more harmonious and will also 'earth' any meditation/ritual work you do. If these ideas seem threatening to you, you may be lacking a firm connection to the Earth level. It will probably be helpful to examine your resistances and attitude towards the Earth Goddess.

Lady of the Earth

The multi-faceted nature of the Earth Goddess is due to the richness of our experience of and within the Earth. Life and Death are the two great mysteries. All life begins in the mysterious depths whether within an egg, a womb or the Earth. It is back to the Earth that all life returns upon death;

the very stuff of life transmuted back into Earth matter. Thus the Goddess of the Earth is Lady of both the womb and tomb, she is Mistress of Life, Death and Rebirth.

She has many names throughout the world. For example, she is Rhea, the Mother of the Gods, Gaia the Great Goddess of the Earth, Demeter, Ceres, Cybele, Tellus Mater, Adamah of the Hebrews, Magna Terra, Astarte, Prithvi and Maya of India, Freya the Teutonic Fertility Goddess, Odudua of Nigeria and Brazil, Selkhet and Isis of Egypt, Ti-Mu of China, Papa of the Polynesians, Mama Alpa of the Incas, Inanna, Ceridwen, Rhiannon, and Dana the Mother Goddess.

She is Goddess of the caves, mountains, fields, plains, forests. She is the Goddess of physical matter – the city as much as the country, the cultivated land and the wilderness. There is a special link between the realm of Earth and that of the stars which may not be apparent until you reach out and meditate upon the Earth herself. The following exercise is best done lying upon the bare Earth but this is not always practical or possible so do feel free to adapt. The thing to remember is that wherever you stand upon this planet you are in intimate contact with the Earth Mother. Indeed your very body is part of her.

THE EARTH CURRENT

The Earth is full of energies, currents and tides that we can call gravity, magnetism or electricity. These energies and currents affect everyone and everything upon the planet. The mighty vibrations and rhythms are set up by the Earth's rotation about the Sun and on its own axis. The spin of the Earth sets up an intense pull to the North, for the North and South Poles are the poles of a huge magnet. Our everyday environment is affected by this North/South magnetic tension as well as by the pull of gravity. This exercise is intended to make you aware of these energies and to assist you in attuning to them.

Before doing this exercise it may be valuable to study diagrams of the Earth's inner structure to aid your visualisation. The exercise may be done lying upon the ground outdoors or, if that is unworkable, on the floor. Assume a comfortable lying position on a North-South axis. Allow your awareness to sink beneath you. If you need to, penetrate down through the foundations of the building you are in. Be aware of the Earth beneath you and the layers of rock beneath that. Extend your awareness deeper and deeper until you find yourself becoming aware of the fiery core of the Earth. Be aware of the energy and magnetism held within. Be aware of the Earth current. Feel it both as gravity and magnetism. As a tree draws upon the Earth's minerals and nutrients along with the more subtle energies of the Earth current, so does your body as you connect to it. Allow the Earth to nourish your energy body. Bring your consciousness back into your body and back to present time and space. Give thanks to our Mother, the Earth for the gift she has bestowed.

The Cosmic Earth

As you will have perceived in the above exercise, the fiery core of the Earth is of the same substance as the Sun, which itself is a star. Further than this the chemical elements which have been brought together upon the Earth as the simple and complex molecules that make up matter and life had their birth in the hearts of stars that exploded billions of years ago. This is not woolly esoteric thinking but physical fact. As Carl Sagan writes in *Cosmos*: 'All elements of the Earth except hydrogen and some helium have been cooked by a kind of stellar alchemy billions of years ago in stars, some of which are today inconspicuous white dwarfs on the other side of the Milky Way galaxy. The nitrogen in our DNA, the calcium in our teeth, the carbon in our apple pies were made in the interior of collapsing stars. We are made of starstuff.'

This is why so many of our ancestors related the Mother Goddesses to Goddess of the Sky and Stars as well as to the Earth. We will look into this further in Chapter 13. Certainly it is not uncommon for people to ache after the beauty of the sky and stars and abhor the density of flesh and Earth. This is, however, an error of perception as liberation from the physical plane does not come until the lessons of Earth are fully learnt and integrated. Even then, it is said that many Great Souls willingly and joyfully incarnate despite the apparent trials of earthly life. This is as much true of the story of a descent into the realm of matter such as Inanna's as it is of the story of Jesus Christ or Buddha.

During our time in incarnation it is to the Earth and the plane of matter that we owe our very being. The esoteric theory behind the reason for incarnation is that the very density of matter allows us to grow and learn within a concrete order and this is aided by the very solidity of this plane of existence.

The Goddess of the Elements

The Goddess of Earth is she who rules the Wheel of the Year as Goddess of fertility and the grain. The human race sustains itself upon the planet through agriculture and farming and in her role as patroness of agriculture we encounter her in many mythic tales. Before examining a few of these the following meditation will establish a direct connection with aspects of the Goddess as Mistress of the elements and seasons. It may also be used for problem-solving and advice.

FOUR GODDESSES MEDITATION

The initial setting for the meditation is a garden containing a richly carved seat. Taking your place upon this, close your inner eyes. There is a sense of rising in the air and you find yourself still seated but within a room.

At the centre of the room is a small round table divided into four quarters. Each section is coloured differently – the portion to the East is yellow, the South red, the West blue and the North brown. Also within each of these sections will be carved a symbol which each person doing the meditation will perceive differently.

There are four doors in the room, each one set in the centre of a wall. Each door will lead you to a short passage which will emerge into a landscape. The landscapes will be individual to each person taking the journey. For some the South may lead to a desert, for others a rain forest. However, each landscape will be consistent to your inner experience of that elemental quarter and season. As you travel within the landscapes you will encounter four aspects of the Goddess. As you visit them you will come to better understand your inner relationship with that aspect of the Goddess.

The four-fold Goddess to be encountered is as follows:

To the East. Quarter of Air and Spring. The Flower Maiden. She is clad in the colours of spring, her gown embroidered with buds, leaves and flowers. She wears a flower garland in her hair and bears a sword. She is attended by a stag.

To the South. Quarter of Fire and Summer. The Warrior Maid. Sits before a cauldron emblazoned with the figure of a dragon and in which burns the flame of wisdom. She is clad in red with a white mantle and she wears upon her head a golden helmet. She holds a spear and is attended by an owl.

To the West. Quarter of Water and Autumn. The Queen and Guardian of the Grail Castle and the Treasures of the Land. She is clad in white, blue and silver and her head is crowned with a diadem of silver and stars. She bears the Grail of Love and is attended by a white mare.

To the North. Quarter of Earth and Winter. The Crone. She is clad in simple black robes and wears a black veil. Upon her brow is a circlet in the form of a serpent and she holds a stone or shield. She is attended by a bear.

The attributes and magical weapons of the Goddesses are based on Celtic symbolism. These are suggestions only, as the visualisation is adaptable to personal taste. For example, you might utilise the four Egyptian goddesses from the first ritual in Chapter 4: Hathor (East), Bast or Sekhmet (South), Isis (West), Nephthys (North). A Greek version could be Artemis (East), Athena (South), Aphrodite (West), Hecate, Demeter or Persephone (North).

You may wish to do this journey on four separate occasions or combine them in two segments. To do it all in one session can be a bit of a marathon! After your exploration return via the passageway and door to the central room. Sit once more in the chair. You are aware of a shift and find yourself back in the garden. Return to your normal consciousness. Close down as usual and write up the meditation in order to ground it.

In order to use the meditation for problem solving, write

out clearly the issue on which you seek advice. When in the central room visualise yourself placing a note with the question in the middle of the table. Then become aware of the presence of your Inner Guide with you. Allow your Guide to lead you to one of the four doorways – be it East, South, West or North. Then explore the environment you find. You may receive the advice you seek from the Goddess of that direction. Even if you receive no definite answer, when you return to the central room, retrieve your paper from the table and come back to ordinary consciousness. You will either have some sense of an answer then or it will come later in a flash of inspiration or within a dream.

The Mother of the Grain

Although Isis is one of the most complex of Goddesses, often known as She of Ten Thousand Names, her primary role in Egypt was with her husband Osiris as the great teachers of farming and agriculture to humankind. Together they instructed humans on the planting of wheat, barley and flax. Isis and Osiris were honoured as the Lady and Lord of bread, beer and green fields. Isis was especially venerated as the Goddess who embodied the yearly inundation (flooding) of the Nile which brought fertility to those lands by the Nile and allowed Egypt to prosper despite being surrounded by desert.

As with other Grain Mothers such as Ceres and Demeter, Isis has a close relationship with the Underworld. Her mythology links to the death and rebirth cycle of her brother-husband Osiris. The myth tells of how Osiris and Isis ruled Egypt wisely. However, Osiris was murdered by his jealous brother Set. His body was placed within a coffin and thrown into the Nile. Isis, after much wandering, retrieved the coffin and his body. However, Set found it again, tore Osiris's body into many parts and scattered them throughout the realm. Eventually Isis retrieved the scattered pieces and was able to magically reconstitute it except for the phallus which was eaten by a fish. She managed to fashion another and through magical means conceived a son, Horus, who grew to avenge his father's murder.

Isis's magic had made Osiris immortal. From that time he ruled as King of Amenti, the Egyptian realm of the dead. When Egyptians died and went through the funeral rites of the Book of the Dead, once judged and found pure, they were believed to become immortal within Amenti. In wall paintings and papyri, Isis is shown attending Osiris in Amenti though she also exists in the Middle World of Earth and the Upper Realm of the Gods as well. Osiris was venerated as a god of vegetation, the Green Man, who died to be reborn continually. Similarly the myths of Persephone, which we will examine next, had her function as the Queen of Hades, the Greek Underworld, as well as being the embodiment of the Spring.

The Goddess and the Rites of Eleusis

The Eleusinian Mysteries are probably the most famous of all the classic initiation rites. They were observed at Eleusis, some twenty kilometres from the city state of Athens. They celebrated the mysteries of the Grain Mother Demeter and her daughter, Persephone, the Kore or Maiden.

Briefly the myth is as follows: Persephone was dancing with her companions in the meadows of Nysa, when her attention was attracted to a narcissus flower. As she gazed at it the Earth opened and she was carried off by Hades, God of the Underworld. Her mother, the Goddess Demeter, heard her cries but could not find her though she searched and searched. Finally with the help of Hecate and Helios, she discovered Persephone's fate and that Zeus had allowed this abduction. In anger and grief Demeter left the realm of the gods and wandered the Earth in mourning.

She stopped at Eleusis where she was welcomed though not recognised. When she was eventually revealed as the Goddess, and spoke of her loss, she instructed the King and Queen to build at Eleusis a temple to her honour. She then would instruct the Queen in the sacred rites. For a year Demeter remained at Eleusis and during that time withdrew all her energy from the Earth, and famine came upon the land. The Gods and Goddesses pleaded with her but she was unmoved until finally Zeus negotiated with Hades for Persephone's return. However, as Persephone had eaten a seed of the pomegranate while in Hades' realm she was bound by the laws of that place to remain there for part of the year. This Demeter reluctantly accepted and allowed her energies to flow back into the world.

The myth is a complex one and has many levels and interpretations. Persephone is an extremely passive Goddess in her early myth both in relation to her mother and to her abductor/husband. However, there is development in her mythic cycle when later she is encountered by various heroes and heroines who descend to the Underworld realm. She is there to receive them as its Queen and to act as their guide. As Jean Bolen remarks in her chapter on Persephone in *Goddesses in Everywomen*, 'none found her absent. There was never a sign on the door saying "Gone Home to Mother"'. In my experience Persephone functions very much in the role of a walker-between-the-worlds and in walking with her, we are able to gain a sense of the eternal cycle of return of our own souls.

At the heart of the Eleusinian mysteries are the familiar themes of life, death and rebirth, bound up in the cycle of the seasons and vegetation. Although these rituals involved rites of passage and the coming to terms with mortality, there was also the conferring of certainty, not faith, upon the initiate that in their participation in these rites they too would conquer death as had Persephone.

The Eleusinian mysteries are one of the enigmas of the ancient worlds for nobody initiated into them ever violated the oaths they took and therefore there are no written records of the heart of these mysteries. However, the clues which have been left and the knowledge of how mythic drama was, and is, used as a source of initiation allows us to delve quite deeply into the Eleusinian mythic cycle.

The use of mystical drama to initiate has been touched upon in Chapter 4 where we utilised the myth of Ishtar's descent into the Underworld to enact a rite of self-initiation. At Eleusis there were at certain times of the year mass initiations into the Lesser and Greater Mysteries. Following pilgrimage, fasting and rites of purification coupled with meditation, the candidates empathised with the characters enacting the parts of their gods in the sacred drama.

Those taking these parts were themselves priestesses and priests who were trained to be channels for the gods, rather than merely to 'act out' the parts. Through years of intense training and ritual preparation, they became for a time the gods themselves. This is a form of divine possession wherein the priestess or priest allows themselves to be as 'a garment' for the Deities. This process is known as mediation or the 'assumption of godforms'. This can manifest as a gentle symbiotic relationship or be a more intense trance, where for a time the consciousness of the priestess or priest is eclipsed by that of the Deity.

Demeter was the Grain Mother who, like Isis, gave instruction to her peoples and spread the knowledge of agriculture. Demeter, as with other agricultural goddesses, was also associated with domesticated animals and was at times represented as a Grain Mare with a horse's head and mane, and sometimes as a cow. The harvest cow was annually sacrificed with a sickle at the sanctuary of Demeter at Hermione. The pig also plays an important role in Demeter's mysteries and sows and piglets were sacrificed to Demeter and Persephone and thrown into chasms in the Earth. Later their remains were collected and mixed with seeds to be spread upon the newly planted fields to bring fertility.

It has been seen time and again that the early animalistic forms of the gods and goddesses became the animal most often sacrificed to that specific deity to gain their favour. Of course this form of gift is considered unnecessary and inappropriate in our Western culture, although there is no doubt that within certain cultures there is still the practice of animal sacrifice. In our own culture, however, as with the later Greeks, the gift has become the transformed grain and fruit in the form of bread and wine. This is the love feast shared in communion with the gods. This is as true for the Christian communion ceremony as it is within a pagan celebration.

Lady of the Trees

My incense is of resinous woods and gums; . . . because of my hair the trees of eternity.
(The Goddess Nuit, The Book of the Law, 1904)

The Goddess of Earth, as Goddess of vegetation, has under

her protection trees and woodlands. I have already commented on how the tree is utilised in various traditions as a symbol of the Cosmos and there is no doubt of its importance for all of life upon Earth. Trees function as lungs for the planet.

The veneration of trees is worldwide both as deities in themselves or as the dwelling place of gods. Celtic Druids were sometimes referred to as the 'knowers of trees' as they spoke to trees and worshipped amongst them; and shamans of all cultures have recognised trees as having a special relationship to humanity. Tree lore throughout the world is vast and is a study within itself. However, the best way to connect with trees is to experience them directly.

Learn to identify various trees in your locality. You might like to experience the aura of a friendly tree. Sit under it with your back to its trunk. Just relax and become aware of its physical presence and aura. As you become aware of the comfortable, warm sensation of its energy merging with your own, you might like to reach out in your thoughts to the spirit of the tree. Be receptive to its voice as it may speak to you in the language of the trees of its history and the magic of the tree people. Trees can be great energisers. Also, if you are feeling a little ungrounded, sitting for a time against a tree's trunk or embracing it in a hug can serve to assist you in connecting back to the earth and everyday reality.

The English writer, J.R.R. Tolkien, who created *The Hobbit* and *Lord of the Rings*, conveyed in his writing an enduring love and respect of trees. Although a modern creation, the roots of Tolkien's mythologies lie in his Anglo-Saxon scholarship and in his inspired dreams. As a mythological system, I consider it as valid as any.

In *The Silmarillion,* the source book for the mythology of Middle Earth, he writes of the Valar, who functioned as the gods and goddess of Arda, the Kingdom of Earth. Of these Yavanna Kementari is the Queen of the Earth. She is the Giver of Fruits and loves all things that grow in the earth. 'All their countless forms she holds in her mind, from the trees like towers in the forests long ago to the moss upon stones or the small and secret things in the mould.' When Yavanna takes the form of a woman, she is robed in greens and gold. However, she is often seen in a form 'like a tree under heaven, crowned with the Sun; and from all its branches there spilled a golden dew upon the barren earth, and it grew green with corn'.

For those wishing more in-depth material on tree lore and magic in the European tradition I would recommend, for example, *The White Goddess* by Robert Graves. There are many other works mentioned in the Bibliography.

Our Bodies and the Earth

Working with this chapter, it is appropriate that we should look once more to the body and our experience of it both outwardly and inwardly. Our body is the source of both our greatest pleasure and our greatest pain. The exuberance of life and movement that typifies childhood; the vitality of youth; the passion and release of sexual pleasure; the maturity of the body which is inevitably accompanied by increasing aches and pains as we move towards old age; and, the culmination of our life's journey in the death of the physical body.

Of course, pain is not confined to old age. Illness can strike at any age. In our Western society we have divorced ourselves from death. It is a virtually taboo subject in our society and due to this we do not see it very often. When it does occur, even with old age, it is considered as something unnatural. There is little sense of preparation. Indeed, in a culture where youth and beauty are considered the paramount virtues, the very processes of aging are considered abhorrent. In mistrusting and fearing the inevitable way in which we, like all living creatures, mature and age, we have again disconnected from the Earth Mother. The most unacceptable aspect of the Goddess for the majority of people is the Crone, the Cailleach because she is rightly attributed to Death. Yet she is also the Gateway to new life just as the fallow period of winter is part of the natural cycle of growth.

THE GROUND BENEATH OUR FEET

I have mentioned grounding more than once in the course of this book. To ground something, whether it be a meditation, dream or idea, is to anchor it in the realm of the Earth. Our feet are our point of contact with the Earth and are a symbol of grounding and incarnation.

Have some plain paper and coloured pencils or crayons at hand. In this exercise simply stand, barefoot if possible, and allow yourself to become aware of the Earth energy and its pull and exchange. Be aware of what this feels like and be receptive to images and thoughts. Then sit and allow a picture to come to you and draw it. Consider the picture as illustrative of your relationship with the Earth and write of any feelings you have about this image.

When I first did this exercise my experience contained Celtic images including a scene from Macbeth, dolmens, a well within a wood, the sun shining on standing stones making a connection between the Earth and sky. I noted that I 'felt my ancestral roots in the Celtic tradition'. The picture I drew was of two standing stones and on analysing the drawing I noted that 'the left stone is much stronger in contrast to the weaker right. Lack of confidence to assert myself in the world? My right leg affected by severe riding accident with a tendency to 'draw up and away' from contact with ground. But accident also catalyst for my entry into mysteries and development of right-brain (left-side) faculties.'

In the West, and increasingly in areas of the world where Western scientific materialism is gaining ascendancy, there is considered to be a split between the mind and body. This attitude is not new but has been about since the time of Descartes who proposed that the body was a machine which like any other machine could be 'mended' when something went wrong. The idea that an illness could be related to emotional and mental factors does not fit this paradigm. While the work of those practising psychology since the late 19th century has done much to reverse this idea, there is no doubt that it continues to dominate Western thought and especially the practice of medicine.

The roots of medicine in Greece and Egypt were extremely 'holistic' in that techniques such as purification, ritual and dream incubation were utilised to gain insight into which remedies would effectively treat certain conditions. Over long periods of time these became standard allopathic cures, though much of this knowledge was lost during the time of the Dark Ages.

There is no doubt that the modern medical attitude which often treats the body as purely mechanical can be very effective on a physical level. However, it can often violate the soul of the patient leaving them feeling a sense of dis-ease and alienation. A doctor who has a good 'bedside manner' may do much to reverse this effect. Also, recent innovations in nursing practices are looking at the whole person, taking into account the stress-related aspects of illness. Unfortunately, these doctors and hospitals are relatively rare compared to the number of doctors who prescribe pills for anything and everything.

Alternative forms of medicine such as homeopathy, aromatherapy, herbalism, acupuncture and the like seek to approach the patient as a whole and treat the body, mind and soul. On a deep intuitive level these treatments appeal to people because of this recognition of connectiveness. In the language we have been building one might say it is their Lunar Self which is then sought to be engaged upon the treatment of the illness.

The exercises you have been doing in Parts 1 and 2 will have been strengthening your subtle body and are likely to be having a positive effect on your physical body as well. Again, to define this subtle energy body as separate from the physical, as some writers do, sets up a false sense of division and disassociation from the physical body rather than seeing these as a whole. One might say that our bodies are like potential temples, unaware of their sacredness.

It is to be hoped that your work with the exercises and especially the Pillar of Isis meditations will serve to bring about an awareness of that sacredness and of the Goddess you are carrying within your body.

Movement with the Earth

An effective way in which to connect gently with both our physical and subtle bodies is through meditative movement. While meditative states are usually considered to be something that occurs when sitting quietly with one's eyes closed, this is not the entire case and movement, especially dance, can be highly effective in bringing about altered states of consciousness.

One very accessible example of this is hatha yoga; the type of yoga which is usually offered when 'Yoga' is advertised. These are slow and precise movements and postures which are linked to breathing. Advanced practice combines the movements with visualisations upon the chakras which are being stimulated.

However, many people who jog, walk, or do aerobics will, at times, find themselves entering an altered state of consciousness through the regularised movement. This can be part of the 'high' that comes from exertion which is a traditional way shamans and others have used to induce altered states.

MOVEMENT

You had the opportunity to explore movement in ritual at the end of Chapter 4, in the circling of the central altar. Dance is a very effective way in which to move in a meditative way. Choose some music that you feel at ease with. It may be song or instrumental; classical, New Age, pop or rock. Wear comfortable clothing which allows for free movement, be barefoot or in light slippers which allow contact with the ground. Make sure you have privacy for this, as with every exercise, for this is your dance and not a display of skill. There is no judge of technique, only your own enjoyment of movement. It is not necessary to be trained in any form of dance to do this type of movement.

First relax and centre yourself and then begin to play the music. Without consciously trying to move your body (unless you feel instantly moved to do so) allow the music to flow through you and to move your body. Be especially aware of the connection between your feet and the floor, the subtle pull of gravity. Move with the rhythm and beat. Continue this for as long as feels appropriate. After this type of movement session you are likely to feel relaxed and energised and receptive for more formal meditation and to receive inspiration.

The Goddess and Crystals

Crystals are very special children of the Earth Goddess; they are, as are stones, formed from the body of the Earth Mother. As humans have rediscovered their relationship to the Goddess of the Earth and honour her once more, she is restoring to them the ancient knowing linked to working with crystals, which embody her spirit in the form of frozen light. This knowledge includes the utilisation of crystals for healing, artistic inspiration, energising of the physical and subtle bodies, the enhancing of psychic abilities, as gateways to other worlds and as connectors to our lunar and stellar selves.

Crystals are minerals in which the molecules have been 'frozen' into a three-dimensional lattice formation, taking many forms and colours. They are probably the most visible sign of the growing popularity of New Age thinking. Whereas a few years ago wearing a quartz crystal pendant openly would have provoked comment, now as with alternative medicine, meditation, and 'New Age' music, they have become an accepted part of popular culture. There are many books on crystals which explore their properties and uses. These range from the inspiring and useful to the wacky and repetitive.

Such books can be of assistance, though the best way to learn about crystals is by forming a relationship with one and listening to its unique voice. To choose a crystal which will be right for you to work with, let your lunar self do the choosing. By this I mean pick the crystal which you are instinctively drawn to.

Once obtained, cleanse it in cold running water, which is a natural way of removing any unwanted energies from it, and place it upon your shrine to the Goddess for a few days to dedicate it. If it is a crystal that you will wear daily or for meditation or ritual, this is an ideal place for it to remain when not with you.

As stated earlier, the concluding chapters of this book centre around the work of building the Pillar of Isis within your aura. Each temple room or antechamber built up along the way links to one of the seven sacred chakra centres as well as to a station of the Qabalistic Tree of Life. Insights and experiences gained during your work in Part 1 can be referred to here, both to identify any imbalances in the form of over- and underactive centres and to chart the changes experienced as you continue to work with and refine these energies.

The Pillar, although generally outlined here, will be personal to you alone. As with the Inner Room in Chapter 5 these meditations, along with the supplementary exercises, are assisting you in undertaking the alchemical process of transformation and service in the mysteries of the Goddess. Again, how you approach these exercises is left to your own ingenuity. I would suggest that you undertake the journey that concludes this chapter two or three times a week and on the other days work on dreams in the way outlined in Chapter 7, meditate in your room at the Isis Temple or concentrate on one of the supplementary self-awareness exercises.

THE TEMPLE OF EARTH

In the following meditation you will be focusing on forming the Temple of Earth, the first level of the Pillar of Isis. This Temple forms the base of the Pillar, that which connects to, and is of, the Earth. This is the place we will both enter and exit in all subsequent journeys. In doing this we acknowledge our connection to the Earth plane.

Within the system of the Qabalah, the Temple of Earth is attributed to Malkuth, the Kingdom; the final manifestation of the creative impulse which created all the worlds. This Temple is also attributed to the element of Earth, the Tattva Prithvi and the muladhara/base chakra.

In the company of your Temple Guide walk within the far groves of the Gardens of Isis. You go further than before into the depths of the Island and come to the shores of a lake surrounded by many trees. There is a mist lying upon the lake which slightly obscures your vision, yet you can make out the image of a small island in the middle of the lake. Upon this island stands a column of white stone. It is a tower-like structure whose top is shrouded in the mist. There seems to be no door or entrance, though high up are some windows that must look out upon the Great River and the desert beyond. Your Guide does not say much but you may wish to ask the significance of this place.

Then you return to your room. Build up this initial journey over a week or so. Journey to the lake and return. You will come to realise that this is a place you will enter shortly and will indeed take this pattern and make it part of your own psychic structure.

The day comes when you begin to return and your guide hands you a dark-coloured cloak and leads you not back to your room but to an earth mound by the path on which you have come. You have not noticed this mound before. There is a low door set within a recess here and before it sits an elderly woman dressed in black and veiled. She appears ancient yet her eyes are bright and lively. Your Guide introduces you – take a few moments to acknowledge this guardian figure.

You feel her glance penetrate your heart and you know that you are being tested. If it is not the right time then depart with your Guide to meditate upon the experience. However, if you feel that there is an acceptance then she hands to your guide a key in the shape of an ankh which will unlock the door. She then stands aside and lets you enter. On each journey you make to this place she will be present both to allow you to pass deeper into the experience and to hold the door open for your return.

There is a stale and musty smell as the door swings open. You see in the dim light that there is a flight of carved steps leading down and westward in the direction of the lake. You receive a lamp from the Guardian which will light your way. Your Guide will accompany you on the first journey though on subsequent journeys you may choose to have them await you at the entrance.

You travel down the steps into a long passageway that you realise passes under the lake bed. It is dark and your lamp gives little illumination. At times you may feel a little panicky; if you do you may either turn back or take the hand of your Guide. Always remember you are perfectly safe. All that is about you is the stuff of matter, earth and rock. There is a sudden change of temperature and your light blows out. Suddenly you are in the deepest blackness of night yet within a few moments this passes as you become aware of a soft glow ahead. This is the shining light of phosphorescent rock, which could not be seen in the light of fire, the earth light of crystal and gem.

Notice the colours all around you. Walk in this gentle light, looking at the structures of rock and the elegant carvings. The passage opens up into an underground cavern, its floor scattered with crystals and semi-precious stones. The walls of natural rock have in some instances been carved into figures, fantastic animals, lions, dragons and birds of flame. You realise that not all of these have been carved, some are the natural shape of the crystalline rocks.

There is also a spring feeding into a small stream that is carried away into the western recesses of the cavern. You are aware of a gigantic figure in the North of this natural temple formed by the cavern. A statue of a woman carved of black basalt seated upon a simple throne. There is a stark and primitive beauty in her face and form as though you look upon the essence of the Earth. Her spine forms a gigantic column and her head touches the ceiling forming a foundation for the structure above. She is the virtual base of the Pillar of Isis upon the lake. You are present beneath its waters within the Earth.

Before the figure is a slab of rock forming an altar and carved upon its surface is the equal-armed cross of the elements surmounted by a circle, a symbol of the Earth. Upon the altar are a number of natural objects which have been placed there as gifts to the Earth Mother. These include stones, minerals, seeds, flowers, leaves and little wooden carvings. Be aware of these. Your attention is drawn to one specific object among them. Your Guide informs you that this is for you to take as a token from the Earth Goddess of your physical body.

They hand you a soft pouch which is carried upon a green cord to wear about your waist. Take the object, examine it and finally place it within the pouch (as this is inner reality whatever its size it will fit without difficulty). On your return, you may meditate upon the symbol and find out what it tells you about your relationship to your physical body. On subsequent journeys you will keep this object with you.

Also feel free to explore the cavern. You are aware that it stretches for some distance into the recesses and there are vast cave systems leading from this place. When your exploration is complete, return to the statue of the Earth Mother and in your own way salute her and give thanks.

Your Guide gives you the lighted lamp once more and its steady glow lights your way as you both return the way you have come, handing back the key and lamp to the Guardian, who then locks the door.

You may find on some journeys the Guardian may journey with you, leaving your Temple Guide to ward the entrance. She also functions as the Priestess of the Earth Mother. Hers is the Voice of the Goddess and she will both answer your questions in the form of oracular utterances and impart teachings to you about the nature of the Earth Goddesses and their mysteries. She can also assist you in integrating the earth energies into your consciousness or may lead you upon a symbolic journey wherein you meet the Earth Goddess as a living presence.

Come back to full waking consciousness and ground yourself fully. Heed any experiences you have and write them up. You may also wish to write down your feelings about the Earth, about Gaia, but however you approach it for this period, remain focused on the Goddess at the level of the Earth. Do not attempt to transcend this level of the Temple until you have gained a solid experience of it. All levels are equally holy in the eyes of the Goddess, she is present in all things, and you should experience her at all levels to be fully initiated into her mysteries.

With respect to the token you received, in due course you will receive such a token at other levels of the Pillar of Isis. It would be worthwhile for you to find a way of expressing this symbol upon your own shrine. You may be able to sketch it or find a comparable token to represent it. The symbol may appear within your dreams in the future and is also likely to change over a period of time; a reflection of inner transformations at that level of consciousness. In the present instance a change in the symbol represents a change in your relationship to the Earth and your physical body.

On subsequent journeys here you will not need to take another token from the altar but you may wish to bring with you some fruit or grain offerings. Or perhaps take some of the crystals strewn about, cleaning them of sediment in the spring, and place them before the statue. Although this is only an image, allow yourself to commune with her and see what comes into your mind. Here you may meditate upon the mysteries of the Earth, of matter and the physical plane and seek to integrate the energies of these throughout your consciousness through the experience of the Earth Mother Goddess. Feel free to speak with her and be open to her inner voice speaking with you in return.

Chapter 10

The Temple of the Moon

She is the ruler of the tides of flux and reflux. The waters of the Great Sea answer unto her, likewise the tides of all earthly seas, and she ruleth the nature of woman.

Dion Fortune

Having considered and explored the mysteries of the Earth Mother we move our attention to the Moon and the mysteries of the Goddess of the Moon.

The Moon is the familiar cosmic image of the Divine

Feminine. With her phases she is ever-changing yet remains constant above us. She is the three-in-one, the Triple Goddess. Throughout world mythology the Triple Goddess is found and honoured in her aspects as Maid, Mother and Crone. While the depiction of the Moon is not universally attributed to the Goddess, there is no doubt that in classical Western mythology and popular thought, the Moon is experienced as the embodiment of the Goddess.

It is important to make the distinction, as we did with the Earth, that the Moon is a symbolic representation of the Goddess and not the Goddess herself. The Moon is in actuality a small satellite of the Earth which is devoid of an atmosphere and of life. But its physical influence is very important to marine life, growing cycles and the weather. Its gravitational pull affects the tides of the Earth's waters and all living things in ways that are not yet fully understood. To the heart and imagination, however, the Moon is much more.

The Full Moon rising, the sliver of the New Moon's crescent, the waxing and waning moon have the power to inspire and move us. In Victorian times there was a distinction made between people diagnosed as insane and people suffering from 'lunacy'. Greater leniency was shown in the courts toward the latter. It is acknowledged that during the time of the Full Moon there is a rise in crime rates. There is more blood lost in operations performed around the time of the Full Moon. There is also the legend of the werewolf, a human transformed during the time of the Full Moon into a wolf which may be a memory of the lunar powers of the shape-shifters and shamans.

Cycles of the Moon and Women

The Moon is closely linked to the female of the human species as its cycle of 28 days corresponds to the roughly 28-day cycle of the menses. The four phases of the Moon are associated with the four phases of this cycle: the pre-ovulatory phase corresponds to the New/Waxing Moon; ovulation to the Full Moon; the pre-menstrual phase to the Waning Moon and menstruation itself to the Dark of the Moon. The word menstrual is derived from the Latin word *mensis* for 'month', which itself means 'moon'. The measuring of time by the Moon's phases was the basis for the first calendars. Although the conventional calendar has been changed to a solar one, even the Judaic-Christian-Islamic religions calculate the dates for their festivals from the lunar calendar.

Before the advent of the patriarchal societies, the onset of menstruation was celebrated as the mark of womanhood, the blessing of the Goddess. With patriarchal values came the association of menstrual blood with contamination and taboo. In some cultures women are still segregated at the time of their menstruation. Though no longer overtly practised in western society, the shadow of these taboos remains with us in the embarrassment, shame and social perception of women as unreliable due to their menstrual cycle.

The Wise Wound by Penelope Shuttle and Peter Redgrove was a ground-breaking study of the historical and cultural legacy of menstruation combined with the authors' own creative interpretations of menstruation as the true evolutionary force. Their essential message was, and is, 'the idea of the menstruation and its "wise blood" as a precious and powerful thing' and that the menstruation phase of the cycle is the time when women are able to make a deep connection to imaginative and creative energies and to function as initiators to the hidden realms of being.

In 1983, Barbara Walker's *The Woman's Encyclopedia of Myths and Secrets* appeared, containing a treasure house of information and lore associated with menstrual mysteries. The Women's Movement and Women's Spirituality Movement have done much to bring back to women a sense of the sacredness of their bodies and to reconnect us to the ancient heritage of honouring the menstrual cycle. Rituals that mark the menstrual rites of passage are being widely circulated and enacted.

How do we make contact with the Moon and the Moon Goddess? The easiest and most effective way for either sex is to look to the sky and begin to notice the phases of the Moon. These can be used in conjunction with meditation or simple rituals to attune yourself to the Moon, her phases and the aspects of the Moon Goddess.

Certainly for a woman a key way to be sensitive to the

lunar cycle is through her menstrual cycle. A woman's menstrual cycle may not be a perfect 28 days or link to the phases of the Moon, in ovulating at the Full and bleeding at the New Moon. There is some evidence that this used to be the order of things but that the amount of artificial light in our environment combined with the conditioned disconnection from our bodies has changed this.

A woman can observe her menstrual pattern, not only the physical manifestations of her cycle, but also the patterns of her dreaming, moods, energy and creativity, as well as waking events. This information can be transferred onto a menstrual mandala. The circle commences with 'Day One', the date of the onset of bleeding and continues with each sub-section marked with the day of the cycle, the date, as well as transferring any significant observations as above. The Moon phases can be drawn in on the appropriate days. Over a period of months this mandala will enable a woman to be more conscious of her relationship to her own body and to the Moon's energies.

However, what if a woman is menopausal, post-menopausal, or has had a hysterectomy? This is no barrier for she is free from her biology and able to attune herself to the Moon and to the vibrations of the Moon's phases as they actually take place in the sky at night. Thus she can move freely through the tides of the Moon's changing.

Men and the Moon Mysteries

How may a man attune to the Moon? Men, like women, are affected by the Moon on a biological level, but it is more subtle and a highly controversial subject for which extensive research has yielded no firm answer. In their Afterword to the revised edition of *The Wise Wound*, Shuttle and Redgrove write of this controversy and the inconclusive results: 'The reason for this seems to be that the man's own inherent rhythms, if they exist, are often overlaid by the menstrual rhythm he picks up by reflection from his female partner (and it would appear, in childhood from his mother)'. They go on to say that 'the mechanism may be pheromonal, as with menstrual synchrony between women . . . but the fact remains that if you look for a menstrual rhythm in a man who lives with a woman, you will find it.' They go on to explore ways in which a conscious couple can work with the menstrual rhythms and this book may be considered a primary source of inspiration for a Tantra for the West.

Therefore, if a man is in a relationship he may become sensitive to the cycles of the woman he is closest to and this can be a shared experience. However, if he is not in a relationship where this is possible or appropriate, he is then free to attune himself to the phases of the moon.

Another way in which the sensitive male can link to the moon is through relationship to his Muse. The Muses were nine sister-goddesses of ancient Greece, each of whom was regarded as the protectress of a different art or science. When we speak of the relationship of a poet or other artist with his 'Muse' it harks back to this source of inspiration from the Goddess. Nine is the number of the Moon in Qabalah tradition as Yesod, the Ninth Sphere on the Tree of Life. Nine is the triplicity of the Goddess tripled.

Moon Magic in the Novels of Dion Fortune

Two major works within esoteric literature on the mysteries of the Moon are *The Sea Priestess* and *Moon Magic* by the occultist and writer, Dion Fortune. These were written in the late 1930s and have been widely reprinted in recent years to become classics of occult literature. Alan Richardson, Dion Fortune's biographer, writes in *Priestess: the Life and Magic of Dion Fortune* that within the pages of the first of these novels, *The Sea Priestess*, 'nothing very much happens . . . It is no more than a tale about how a rather dreary and asthmatic estate agent, Wilfred Maxwell, falls for an older woman yet ends up marrying his secretary . . . Nothing much happens and yet it is a masterpiece'.

In the opening pages of the novel, Wilfred is drugged and semi-delirious following a severe bout of asthma. The curtains of his room are left open and he lies there 'watching the full moon sliding across the night sky . . . and wondering what the dark side of the moon was like, that no man has ever seen, or ever will see'. On subsequent nights he allows his mind to wander and begins to commune with the Moon.

> . . . now I cannot tell what I said to the Moon, or what the Moon said to me, but all the same I got to know her very well. And this is the impression I got of her – that she ruled over a kingdom that was neither material nor spiritual, but a strange moon-kingdom of her own. In it moved tides – ebbing, flowing, slack water, high water, never ceasing, always on the move, up and down, backwards and forwards, rising and receding; coming past on the flood, flowing back on the ebb; and these tides affected our lives. They affected birth and death and all the processes of the body. They affected the matings of animals, and the growth of vegetation, and the insidious workings of disease. They also affected the reactions of drugs, and there was a lore of herbs belonging to them. All these things I got by communing with the Moon, and I felt certain that if I could only learn the rhythm and periodicy of her tides I should know a very great deal . . . I found that the more I dwelt with her, the more I became conscious of her tides, and my life began to move with them.

A little later in the text he comes into relationship with the mysterious Vivien Le Fay Morgan, who is the Sea Priestess of the title. Together as priestess and priest they investigate the mysteries of the Moon and Sea.

Towards the end of the novel, with the departure of Miss Le Fay Morgan, Wilfred eventually undertakes with his new wife the type of dynamic relationship suggested by Shuttle and Redgrove, and together they explore the Moon mysteries. When written it was unacceptable for the menstrual rhythms to be mentioned in print, though a modern-day reader can 'read between the lines'.

The second book, *Moon Magic*, continues Vivien Lilith Le Fay Morgan's story, and within its pages are detailed the mysteries of Great Isis, as Goddess of the Moon, as well as much practical lore gleaned from years of work undertaken by Dion Fortune and her circle of initiates. As she writes:

> I place my trust in Nature and regard it as holy, and I represent it to myself under the glyph of Great Isis whose

symbol is the moon. The cult of Great Isis I believe I have served down through the ages . . . we who would return to Great Nature, the All Mother, are driven down into the catacombs for our worship.

It is the map of the labyrinthine path from those catacombs which is the legacy of such women as Dion Fortune to her magical daughters who are re-establishing the Mysteries of her beloved Goddess in the light of the Moon and Sun.

Moon Goddesses and their Mysteries

Throughout the world, many Goddesses are attributed to the Moon, either directly or through being depicted as triple in nature, reflecting the changing phases of the Moon. Some pantheons and traditions attribute gods to the Moon, though an exploration of this is outside the brief of this particular work. Whenever this does occur it is often, though not always, in a polarity with a feminine Sun Goddess. It is also common to find that many mortal or semi-divine heroes are considered to be the Son/Consort of the Virgin Moon Goddess.

The mysteries of the Moon Goddess are, like the Moon, very varied. A number of books have been devoted entirely to this subject. In this work, I am striving to give you a thumbnail sketch and hopefully the guidelines to continue with more in-depth research if desired, using the Bibliography which contains relevant source material.

We have already touched upon the primal lunar mysteries at the beginning of this chapter. As with the mysteries of the Earth Goddess, the Moon Goddess's mysteries also link to fertility upon the physical level. They also relate to health and fertility upon the etheric level of energies which are very influential upon the physical. One might say that the etheric forms the matrix upon which the physical level of existence is based.

The Moon Goddess rules the patterns into which plant, animal and human grow. She also rules the magical moment of conception and planting. In the latter instance this links to the knowledge of the right time to both plant seeds and reap the harvest so that the seeds are imbued with the right potentialities with which to bring forth the next crop. Although modern farming methods may have dismissed the lunar almanac as superstition, there are still many farmers who trust the old ways and will still turn soil and plant their crops on a particular phase of the Moon. Being aware of the Moon's phase when planting and gathering is still very relevant to herbalism.

As the Moon Goddess rules the element of water, it is fitting that she rules our emotional lives, their tides and phases. Whether or not we have access to these, our emotions change constantly. They are fluid and seemingly change without warning or reason, sometimes from moment to moment.

Certainly in the West women are given greater permission to be in touch with their emotions and this strengthens this Moon-woman symbolic linking. However, men are just as much ruled by the Moon but they are often unable to express this consciously. They may project their emotions outwards onto a particular woman or upon women in general. Although I am vastly simplifying this process of projection, for many men and those women who are unable to cope with strong, fluctuating emotions, it is common to find that they will have a partner, parent or close friend who will take on this role for them.

As with the Earth Goddess, the Goddess of the Moon has many names both familiar and strange. In some cultures, such as the Hindu and classical Greek, each aspect of the Moon's phases is acknowledged as a separate goddess. In other cultures the Moon in totality is honoured as the Goddess who changes with the phases, sometimes fruitful, other times sterile.

Within the Egyptian pantheon Isis was also identified as Goddess of the Moon and Sea. She is often shown wearing a crown depicting the Full Moon, held within the crescents of the Waxing and Waning Moons.

Because of their nocturnal nature and the 'waxing and waning' of the pupils of their eyes, cats have long been associated with the Moon Goddess as a form which she takes or as her sacred animal. The daughter of Isis, Bast, depicted as a cat or as a cat-headed woman, was considered the personification of the Moon. Her lunar mysteries were associated with fertility, healing and midwifery. The Moon was one of her eyes, the other was the Sun, for she was also venerated as a Solar Goddess. This will be explored in the next chapter.

The Goddess of the Moon is closely linked to the tidal waters of the Earth and so is also often honoured as the Goddess of the Sea or depicted in the form of a mermaid as is, for example, Yemanja of Nigeria and Brazil. Yemanja is also portrayed walking upon the waves of the ocean and adorned with the crescent Moon.

The primary surviving mystery of the Triple Moon Goddess in the West has been witchcraft/wicca, the Craft of the Wise. Wicca has become the primary way in which pagan religion is celebrated in this culture. The Women's Spirituality Movement has focused on Wicca for the expression of women's mysteries. The magical rituals, meditations and spells of the Craft are done in harmony with the Moon's phases. In their worship they honour the Lady of the Moon in her aspects of Maid, Mother, and Crone.

The Triple Moon Goddess of Greece

The Greek pantheon contains perhaps the best known of the Triple Moon Goddesses with Artemis (Virgin of the New Moon), Selene (Mother of the Full Moon), and Hecate (Crone of the Waning and Dark Moon). Connecting to these goddesses allows for a further experience of the Moon mysteries. It may be thought that in this material I have neglected my male readers. However, the Moon Goddess, because she is the most visible aspect of the Goddess, offers men the opportunity for close relationship with the Lady of the Moon as her son and lover, consort and pupil as well as priest when he achieves her initiation. In coming to know her he comes to know his soul.

Let us begin with the Maid – Artemis. She is ever-virgin (meaning one-in-herself, belonging to no man). In Artemis's realm wild animals roam free. The virgin forest is a fruitful place which has multiplied without the hand of man. Contrast this abundant wildness to the orderly rows of trees imposed by any country's Forestry Commission!

Artemis was the protectress of the young and especially

of young women. In ancient Greece, girl-children of 9 to 12 years of age who were called to the cult of the Goddess Artemis were known as the 'arktoi', the bear cubs of Artemis. This period apart from the world allowed them a time and place of protection under the mantle of the goddess where they were able to learn skills such as hunting and to fend for themselves. Deep within the woods they danced the dance of emerging animal life as do hares when they dance in the moonlight.

The phase of the Full Moon is attributed to Selene. The Full Moon is the Mother and Queen of the Night shining with beauty and light. She nurtures the soul and gives healing and comfort. She is fertility itself and is both passionate and transformative in her love-making.

The final phase of the Waning and Dark Moon belongs to Hecate who is so often misunderstood and misrepresented. She is the Wise One, the Elder, the Guide and Teacher of whatever age who teaches from experience. Her name means the 'distant or remote one' and in our consideration of the dark face of the Moon, which is never seen from Earth, it is indeed remote.

Hecate is the protectress of wild and remote places as well as being the guardian of the crossroads. She is a triple goddess within herself and is often depicted with three faces or in tri-form bearing her sacred symbols – three torches to illuminate the path, a Key (to the Underworld as its guardian and guide), the Scourge and the Dagger, as symbol of ritual power. The latter two symbols have found their place within Wicca as Scourge and Athame.

In this triple aspect she is described as a goddess of the Moon and as such had dominion over the sky. But she also walked the Earth as a mistress of magic and resided in the Underworld wherefrom she bestowed wealth and the blessings of everyday life. She oversaw the mysteries of human life – birth, life and death. The Guardian whom we encountered at the entrance to the Temple of the Earth was fulfilling this role of Priestess of Hecate. Her key opened the door and her torch accompanied us in the form of the lamp. In this case her scourge was her gaze and her questioning of our intention.

Hecate is often depicted with three animal heads of a horse, dog and boar and these animal forms are probably totems; a subject we will consider next. These animals also have connections with the Great Goddesses within the Celtic tradition – Rhiannon, Epona and Ceridwen. The owl was Hecate's messenger and the yew tree and willow her trees.

Dream Animals and the Moon

Our work with dreams is going to be taken one step further in this chapter through working in the dream state with totems and dream incubation.

Firstly, what is a totem? A totem is a Native American word meaning an object or animal which has personal symbolic meaning to either an individual or to their family, tribe or clan. In recent years within parts of American society there has been a strong movement among whites to connect to the mysteries of the land in which they live through connecting to the teachings of the Native Americans.

However, it is important not to see this as merely a fashion. I believe it denotes a deeper movement within the collective consciousness of North America to make reparation for the attitudes of their forebears whose greed for land and sense of superiority practically destroyed these indigenous peoples and their ancient cultures. Some Native Americans have welcomed this interest and others resented it. It is a complex issue though the impulse feels essentially a healthy one. It may be the spirits of the land itself which are calling to the inhabitants of the Americas to become in tune once more with them, just as the spirits of rock and tree and the ancient heroes of the British Isles sing their own special songs which have called for a revival of their mysteries.

We are to focus here upon the totem as a special animal which functions in your inner life either consciously or unconsciously. Even the Bible speaks of God relating to Job 'through the medium of all creatures, real or imaginary . . .'.

The moon speaks of our emotional relationship to the world and animals appeal to our emotions. We may be attracted or repelled, or we may love or fear various animals.

So how to find your totem (or, rather, totems as it is likely that you will have more than one)? It is quite easy to identify them – just ask yourself what animals you like. What wild or domestic mammals, reptiles, fish or birds have some special meaning or significance for you? Also what imaginary creatures appeal to you? Do you have special little knickknacks or pictures of any particular animal or recall any from childhood which you were drawn to.

Fabulous animals such as winged horses, dragons, griffins, chimeras, sphinxes and unicorns populate myths and fairy tales and can feature in our sleeping and waking dreams as well.

Within many pantheons and mythic cycles various gods and goddesses have the power of transmutation and, as shape-changers, of taking the form of animals. In the story of the birth of the Welsh poet Taliesin, he is granted this power by accidentally partaking of the three drops of wisdom broth brewed by the Goddess Ceridwen. She is furious with him and pursues him as he takes many shapes and likewise changes her shape. The ability to shape-shift in this way is a primary magical power granted by the moon-wisdom. It is a skill which illustrates how people are intimately related to the animal kingdom. Even in the recent film *Highlander*, the protagonist, Conner McCloud, is introduced by his mentor to the ability of becoming one in spirit with a stag while in human form.

Perhaps part of the almost universal appeal of the Egyptian pantheon is that many of their gods and goddesses were depicted as animal-headed and often were represented in the form of animals. Therefore, goddesses such as Bast and Sekhmet were cat or lioness-headed or took the form of a cat or lioness. Ra and Horus were hawk-headed but also depicted as hawks. The mother Goddess Mut is depicted as a vulture-headed goddess or a vulture; Anubis is a jackal or jackal-headed. This speaks of a deep bonding and recognition of a union at an inner level.

If you find that no totem animal springs to mind or if you allow yourself to be inspired in this choice, then follow the meditation given below. In it you will meet with the Guardian of the Totems who will grant you a special totem animal to assist you in this work.

TOTEM MEDITATION

Relax and prepare yourself for journeying as usual. Imagine there is a door before you and see it opening upon a woodland scene. Walk through the door and find yourself walking along a clearly marked path within the forest. Be aware of the air upon your face, the ground beneath your feet as well as the scent of the forest and the movements of animals within the undergrowth and trees. You come to a clearing within which stands a mighty and ancient oak tree. As you stand there you are aware of two figures, a male and a female, emerging from the depths of the forest. They are the spirits of the forest, the Lord and Lady of the Woods, and they speak to you of the responsibility involved with having such a bonding as you seek with a beast, fish or fowl. As they speak with you, feel free to answer and ask questions of them. You become aware that a variety of animals and birds have come out of the woods to be close to the Guardians. If the time is right for you to work with a totem, then one animal, bird, reptile or other creature will come to where you are standing. One of the Guardians will guide you to make the connection with that creature. If it is a creature of the water that is to be your totem, you will be led by a Guardian to a place where this contact can be made.

Take time to strengthen this contact. Then allow your totem animal to go back to its place in the wild and give thanks to the guardians. You will now be able to call this animal to yourself when you wish.

Working with Totems

Once you have identified your totem (or totems) utilise the natural history section of your library to find out more about this animal. The section on folklore can give you some ideas of the way in which it has operated on a mythic level. Find some way to have this represented on your shrine in the form of a picture or statue. You may wish to obtain a piece of jewellry that you can wear depicting your totem which will strengthen the bond between you.

Art is a positive way of 'capturing' the spirit of an animal, and if you have any artistic skill you may wish to draw or sculpt it. As you gain a sense of other totems you may create a 'coat-of-arms' for yourself. You may find that your family name already has some associations with fabulous or mundane creatures through an actual 'coat of arms'. These can be traced within books on the subject by yourself or by a genealogical society for a fee. Discover the oral history of your own family and any special animals associated with it.

Feel free to have more than one totem. Enjoy the process of working with them. You need not be interested in the shamanic tradition to do this or to work with 'power animals'. Put together a scrapbook of images of your totem(s) and other information about them. If you have the skill draw a picture of yourself and the totem standing together. Make a collage.

Consider the thought that mankind was appointed as stewards to the natural world and its inhabitants. How do we fulfil this in our daily lives? Where do we betray this trust? It is an excellent idea to find a way in which to give support to that animal, if it exists in the real world. You can join an organisation dedicated to its protection whether it is some broad-based group such as the World Wide Fund for Nature or a protection league for that animal or bird. There are many simple and effective ways of honouring your totem. As with a special name it is best not to speak too openly of the nature of your totem except to those people you trust.

While it is not possible to support all causes, there is an important talismanic function in choosing one or two charities. You can balance the animal charity with one concerned with humanity's problems of poverty or health. If you are not in a financial position to make a donation or pay a yearly subscription you may be able to offer your time as a volunteer which can be extremely rewarding.

As someone who has had the fortune of being able to make my living working for a charity for some years, I realise how important it is to have volunteers willing to give a few hours of their time on a regular basis or to lend a hand for a flag day or special fund-raising events. Whether with money or time, it is a sharing of energy on the level of the lunar self. It allows for a sharing of the energy on one level or another.

TOTEMS OF THE FOUR
DIRECTIONS/CHAKRAS

Meditate upon the qualities of the four directions and their elements in turn. Allow some form of animal or bird to come into your mind. You will have four totems, each associated with the elemental quarters. Work them into a simple ritual of protection where you visualise them as guardians of your home.

You can also do a similar exercise with your chakras. Do the relaxation and energising exercises. Allow your mind to focus on each chakra in turn, allowing an image of an animal or bird to come for each of your seven chakras. In this way you can connect to your own totem pole. When you are feeling as though certain chakras are under- or overactive you can communicate through meditation or movement with the totem associated with this centre to assist you in balancing your energies.

Totems within Dreams

When the totems you have chosen or discovered in meditation appear in your dreams, they are likely to be conveying special messages. You can dialogue with them as you would any symbol. Likewise be receptive to the animals which spontaneously appear in your dream life for these may be indicative of animal energies that are coming into your life.

On retiring I often do a small guided meditation for myself as I fall asleep, in which my totemic animal and I begin to explore a landscape. Once you are used to having your dream totem with you in this way, you will be able to call upon your totem as a helper or guide if you find yourself in a difficult dream situation.

Dream Incubation

The process of dream incubation can be as simple or as elaborate as you wish to make it. In simple forms, you can, through words and writing (placing the request under your pillow), ask your lunar self to provide you with a dream linked to a certain issue you would like clarification on.

Write down any dream or fragment on waking the next day. If you do not recall a dream that night, continue the practice for three days. Once you have captured a fragment or the dream, you can use dream work exercises to interpret it or take it to the Temple of Anubis for clarification.

You can elaborate this process by combining it with meditation. If you have the facilities you might arrange to have a 'temple sleep'. In order to do this I would suggest you do not sleep in your usual bed but make up a spare bed or cushions in a separate room. Have your shrine there also. Cleanse and purify the room and do some form of ritual to create sacred space. Take a ritual bath perhaps with essential oils such as lavender or camomile to promote relaxation. Before sleep meditate upon your request. You may like to combine this incubation with a visualised journey to the Temple of the Moon within the Pillar of Isis.

Again on waking write down any dreams or fragments. Work on these. If no dreams are received, repeat the process for a further two nights. If there are still no results you may wish to wait until the Moon's phase changes before attempting again.

THE TEMPLE OF THE MOON

Here you are to ascend to the next level of the Pillar of Isis. The Temple of the Moon corresponds to Yesod on the Tree of Life and the svadisthana chakra which is located in the area of the lower abdomen. The elemental association is with Water and the tattvic symbol of the Silver Crescent. It will repay you to refresh your memory by looking back through your notes of the inner journeys you took associated with this element and the chakra work.

As you move from the Temple of the Earth to the Temple of the Moon you will do so through a spiral stairwell decorated with scenes depicting the Eleusinian mysteries. In these Persephone, Demeter and Hecate represent the Triple Goddess of the Moon as Maid, Mother and Crone. We have already encountered this myth in the previous chapter but here it is used to illustrate a way of moving between two states of consciousness, from the realm of the Earth to the Moon. The mysteries acknowledging the relationship between the fertile earth and the underworld realms also form the road which brings us to the sphere of the Moon.

Repeat the journey to the Temple of Earth. However, now as you stand in the Temple of the Earth Mother you become aware that behind the statue of Gaia is a small alcove. As you move around and behind to examine this you are aware of a silvery light streaming down and illuminating it. You find that within the recess is a narrow winding stair which spirals upwards to the right. There is a rail set into the wall to assist you in climbing.

Upon the walls of the stairwell are a number of carved images which depict the myth of Persephone and Demeter as a universal theme of the seasons' renewal. You may see these very vividly or only partially. Ascend the stairwell which is still bathed in the soft silver glow from above. You emerge into a circular chamber, into the walls of which are set emblems in silver, moonstone, jet and obsidian of the Moon in her four phases. The East shows the crescent of the New Moon; the South the dual symbols of Waxing and Waning Moon; in the West the Full Moon and in the North a black mirror.

Before each symbol are shrine tables of silver, ebony and moonstone upon which lie treasures from the sea and representations of the Moon Goddesses and Gods throughout the world. The room is lit with nine silver lamps and in the centre is a deep circular pool of crystalline pure water. Its depths plunge into the heart of the earth beneath as it is fed by the springs of the Earth Temple.

As you gaze into the pool you see that in the soft light it shimmers and you become aware of a figure reflected within the pool, a woman robed in white and silver. Her dark hair is bound in a filigree of silver and she wears a silver crown emblematic of the Moon. Note the details of this crown and other symbols she may wear.

You look up and see that indeed a Priestess of the Moon stands before you. Behind her you are aware of the symbol of the Moon glowing as if charged from within. Be aware of which phase of the Moon this is. This may change on subsequent visits. She greets you and speaks with you.

On your first visit she will lead you to one of the moon shrines and give you from it some object which is your token for this level. This will remain with you and be either carried in your pouch or worn in some way every time you make this journey. This token is symbolic of your emotions and astral body. As with your other token it is worthwhile to meditate on it and to find a way of physically representing it. If you have questions about its meaning do ask the priestess.

She is your teacher and guide to the Moon Level. Each time you enter the Moon Temple she will be present. Listen carefully as she tells you of the mysteries of the Moon and of its magic. Feel free to ask questions and to seek her advice. Each visit to this place will be different. She may lead you to gaze within the magical mirrors of the moon – the silver mirror of the Full Moon or the obsidian black mirror of the Dark Moon. In these mirrors you may see pictures and scenes – dream images, heroic quests or images like films. Some may have relevance to past-life experiences; while it is not advisable to pass within the mirror it is likely that you will learn much from observation.

At other times you may be aware that you are being shown things in the mirror where healing or other help is required. Upon these levels much help can be given and you should let your own training and instinct guide you as to whether this be in the form of prayer or in sending positive energy and help. Find ways of bringing this into your daily life – sending thoughts of comfort, prayer or lighting candles as a symbolic act.

Within the Temple of the Moon lie many experiences and the Priestess is your guide to these. Also, as this place is linked to the Sphere of the Moon, it is important that you are aware of the actual physical Moon throughout the period of your meditations.

After you are complete, return through the stairwell and Temple of Earth as before. Come out of the meditation and close down fully and write up your notes.

Chapter 11

The Temple of the Sun

Hail to thee, Sekhmet-Bast-Ra, We invoke Thee Lady, Great of
  Magic
Thou who art the Mighty One, who utters the Words of
  Power
In the Boat of Millions of Years!
Oh, exalted Sekhmet, Thou art the Great Cat,
The Avenger of the Gods, the Judge of Words
The Queen of the Sovereign Powers, and Guardian of this
  Temple.

Save us from terror, save us from the burning heat of the
  desert sun!
Save us from the darkness of our own fears.
Save us from the danger of being devoured by our own
  unconscious.
Light in us the spark of your healing Flame!
That we may not perish in your fire, but be transformed.
Praise and Homage to Thee, O Sekhmet.

To the Lady of the Sun, from Her devotee, Sunflower

As we prepare to enter the Temple of the Sun, it is
important to make a connection with our own inner sun:
the solar self. As through the solar plexus and heart
chakras, we make contact with the element of Fire as well
as the radiant presence of the Sun through our solar self.

There is a common misconception that the Goddess and
the feminine principle are inextricably linked to the Moon
and Earth and that deities associated with the Sun and Sky
are always masculine. This is blatantly not true. Goddesses
of the Sun appear worldwide in mythology. Janet
McCrickard in her work *Eclipse of the Sun* strikes out
forcefully against the 'underlying orthodoxy' concerning
the Sun and the Moon inherent in feminine spirituality,
Wicca and Theosophy that underlies the philosophy of the
New Age Movement.

Likewise the elements and Quarters of Water/West and
Earth/North are considered 'feminine' and 'receptive'
whereas the Air/East and Fire/South are considered
'masculine' and 'active'. When you actually work with these
energies you discover that they transcend the qualities of
gender and instead rely upon an internally cohesive
polarity. Therefore it is entirely possible in practice for a
man to resonate more easily with the Moon/West/Water
and Earth/North and a woman to Sun/East/Air and
Sky/South/Fire.

The fact that polarity is a movable phenomenon and not
fixed by gender runs contrary to the orthodoxy that
McCrickland strikes out against. It has been found that a
woman who functions as Priestess of the Sun will be able
successfully to work magically with another priestess who
attunes naturally to the Moon as well as she could work
with a Moon priest. There is a heterosexual bias and great

fear of homosexuality underlying much of the Wiccan and the more conservative Western Mystery philosophies and attendant practices. There is much wariness of workings wherein polarities are expressed through participants of a single sex, even though it is not expected that physical sexual relations are a part of such working relationships. Certainly, there is an exchange of energy upon many levels between the participants in any ritual work that is 'on line' and it is important to approach such exchanges from a place of inner centredness and maturity.

The actual experience of single-sex workings can be extremely rich and fertile. Women are often perceived as priestesses of the Moon alone which is a very limited magical role. A woman may naturally resonate to earthy, lunar, solar or stellar energies. The natural polarity between these energies may thus be expressed through, for example, a solar priestess working in ritual opposite an earth priestess, etc. The magical interchange between two women is therefore potentially extremely rich and valid. My own magical workings where my natural tendency to mediate solar energies has been balanced by another woman with lunar contacts have resulted in a subtle and powerful interchange of these energies – no less than working with a man.

Needless to say this is also true for men as they too can polarise with one another and break out of the mould of only mediating as energies of a solar nature. Certainly, on the leading edge of the contemporary magical community in Great Britain much practical work and exploration of potentialities which transcend physical gender are being explored by men and women in both single-sexed and mixed groups.

Ultimately the aim of the sort of training one receives under the aegis of the College of Isis (and indeed in other such mystery schools) is to give the aspirant the opportunity to work actively with all aspects of polarity rather than fixating on one alone. For polarity needs to be integrated in the individual, so that they are whole-in-themselves, rather than sought outside as compensation for a lack within. Thus, as we are moving through the Levels of the Pillar of Isis, you will be experiencing these various energies singularly and in polarity to one another.

The aim is to come into a balanced relationship with them within and to express these in your life in all its aspects. These phases of development are usually traced through years rather than months.

Mysteries of the Sun Goddesses

In exploring the mysteries of the Sun Goddess we will concentrate mainly on the Egyptian and Celtic/Northern traditions. For a further exploration of the subject and a compendium of Sun Goddesses worldwide, the reader is referred to *Eclipse of the Sun*.

As we are working within the Temple of Isis, let us first examine the Goddesses of Ancient Egypt. Firstly there is Bast, a goddess who makes a natural link between the levels of the Moon and the Sun. Bast mediated both energies as the Right (Solar) and Left (Lunar) Eyes of Ra. Her lunar mysteries have been commented on within the chapter on the Moon Temple. In her solar aspect she is the kindly goddess who represents the beneficent powers of the Sun. The worship of Bast was celebrated through dance, music and joyous worship. Her priesthood would participate in light-hearted barge processions and orgiastic ceremonies. Bast was a goddess of healing but very specifically emotional and psychological healing. Some of this was linked to the practice of healing through the use of sexual rites and some priestesses of Bast were sacred prostitutes.

Bast is commonly depicted in the form of a cat or as a cat-headed woman clothed in red and carrying a sistrum, a sacred rattle. She carries a basket containing kittens or, alternatively, kittens will be found clustered at her feet. She was the protectress of children and of women during childbirth. Her other concern, especially as her worship is expressed in the 20th century, is as protectress of animals. Much healing work for animals is done in the name of Bast.

The other prime solar goddess of the Egyptian pantheon is the lioness-headed Sekhmet who was known as the 'Lady of Flame'. Sekhmet is depicted as a woman with the head of a lioness and wearing the solar disk with the serpent crown of Egypt. She carries the ankh, symbol of eternal life and often bears a lotus wand.

She was the Protectress of the Divine Order. It is said she represents the destructive power of the sun. In her main legend Sekhmet is sent by the Creator/Sun god Ra to seek retribution upon humankind for their misdeeds. However, she becomes maddened with blood lust and is on the verge of wiping out mankind, when Ra has to resort to trickery to stop her. He does this by spreading the earth with a mixture of red ochre and beer. Sekhmet gorges herself on this thinking it is the blood of her victims and become too intoxicated to continue her rampage.

This is not the only aspect of Sekhmet. Her priesthood, as that of Bast's, was concerned with healing. They were physicians possessing a detailed knowledge of the workings of the heart and were actually surgeons. Surgery is a form of medicine that seems bloody and destructive but its end is healing.

These two goddesses are often combined in the form of Sekhmet-Bast-Ra. One hallmark of women and men who resonate to Bast and Sekhmet's energies is their relationship to the animal kingdom and especially to cats which has echoes of the relationship of the priesthood to the sacred temple cats of Egypt.

Here is an example of how the Sun Goddess can manifest in the life of an aspirant. In 1975 I underwent a period of devotion in order to ready myself to become a priestess. I chose to work with the Goddess Bast because I had always been drawn to cats of all kinds. I found myself during this period having powerful dreams of my following cats wearing golden collars. On one occasion I vividly experienced giving birth to a kitten which I interpreted as my birth as priestess of Bast.

I also dreamt of being in a temple wherein I found graceful gardens and a sacred lotus pool around which lay recumbent lionesses. I incorporated this dream image into a visualisation sequence. In using this in meditation I made an inner contact with a High Priestess of Bast who was accompanied by a lioness. (Bast in her solar aspect was sometimes depicted with the head of a lioness.) This relationship has continued to this day, as the priestess stimulated my own far memories of my time as priestess in Egypt and introduced me to the inner Temple of Isis. My prayers/invocations to Bast celebrated the Goddess in her many aspects: Lady of the East, Flaming Eye of the Sun, Daughter of Isis, Soul of Isis. In the following section of a ritual to Bast, I wrote of her as Mother, which reflected my experience of being nurtured and sustained by her solar energies:

> I adore Thee, Mother
> For Thou art called a Mighty and Terrible Goddess
> Yet Thy kitten is held within Thy
> Mouth of Velvet.
>
> During the hours of the night
> I am laid to rest beside
> Thy soft belly.
> The sound of Thy Heart
> The music of my dreams.
>
> I am suckled with sweet milk
> From Thy Breast.
> Tender Mother
> I call unto Thee
> That Thy child may know Thee.
>
> She brings me unto Life
> And unto Death
> She brings me into the presence
> of the Gods
> Blessed is She.

In the years that have followed this period of devotion, I expressed my service to Bast by training as a psychotherapist and combining the insights gained with my work with others in the mysteries.

Another example of the way in which meditative contact with an inner temple can be utilised to receive teachings in devotional practice is expressed in the experiences of another priestess with the cat/lioness Goddess of Egypt. In her 'Path of the Solar Priestess' (from *Voices of the Goddess*), Sunflower writes of her visualised journeyings:

> . . . towards the middle of the second month, I became aware of a large inner courtyard beyond the pleasant

gardens . . . the room was dark and sombre in atmosphere . . . I could smell the pungent odour of animals, accompanied by the smell of blood. As my eyes grew accustomed to the light, I could make out a hall lined with pillars and shapes of several large beasts lying just ahead of me – they were lionesses . . . Behind the pillars of the hall were more rooms . . . These were the rooms of the three lioness priestesses. Sometimes I would catch sight of them, walking across the room, the animals following them with a lazy, self-assured stride . . .

In the last month of her devotion Sunflower entered the inner sanctum of the Goddess wherein she found herself 'at the edge of a large fire-pit, fed from an unknown source below'. In time she came to visualise herself daily standing

> . . . in the fires of Sekhmet. Each time I stood in the blinding light, heat and noise of the fires, it was like being in the alembic of the alchemist, the repetition building on itself, calcining and purifying. The alembic of the fiery temple was both my womb and heart.

In the final week of her devotion she crossed over the pit and entered the doorway of the building she had seen beyond the smoke.

> At last I was in the awesome presence of my Goddess. She sat enthroned some distance from me, much larger than I expected. A mighty black lioness, a fire-spitting cobra raised to strike upon Her brow.

Following this climax of her devotions Sunflower asked Sekhmet's permission to become her priestess and she received the reply that 'although I had gained much inner knowledge of Her, I now had to serve Her in the outer world as a healer'. Then in the months and years that followed she found that 'opportunities did come my way in the next year to do healing both for individuals and groups. I mediated healing solar energies.'

The teachings experienced in such inner contacts as these, and indeed in the work that you are undertaking here, is lifelong. It extends and deepens beyond the initial experiences.

Sekhmet's energies are very powerful and resonate to the solar plexus chakra.

The final aspect of the Sun Goddess within the Egyptian pantheon is Hathor. Hathor is depicted as a beautiful woman, a cow-headed woman or as a cow. Hathor is also a Goddess of Love and awakens the heart to both physical and spiritual love.

She also has a strong connection with Sekhmet, as it is said in some versions of the legend already mentioned that it was Hathor whom Ra sent to punish humankind and she then took on the form of Sekhmet. Among Hathor's titles is 'Mistress of the Mansion of Sekhmet' and, like Bast, her worship was associated with music, dancing and joyous revelry. As Bast makes a link between the energies of the Moon and Sun, so Hathor makes the link between the energies of the Solar and Stellar Temples. For she is also a Goddess of the Stars and in this form can be visualised as a cow whose body is made of stars and who wears the solar disc between her cow horns. From her body she gives birth daily to the Sun. Lest we forget, the Sun is also a Star! Hathor brings great joy and comfort to her celebrants and is the source of much creativity.

Each of these Goddesses has relevance to the material contained later in this chapter on the dynamic polarity of Love and Will and when we come to work with this later on it would be a good idea to access into your experience of the Sun as Goddess to understand your relationship to Love and Will.

I should now like to consider the Goddess of the Sun as found within the various Celtic/Roman-British/Northern Traditions. Within the Northern tradition the Sun is the Goddess Sol and is envisioned 'Like a young queen in flower'. It is from Sol that we get the name 'Sun' and 'Sunday'. In Celtic mythology the Sun is Sul or Sunna. Likewise in Irish-Celtic tradition the Sun is depicted as Grainne. Each of these goddesses can be visualised as a beautiful woman with long, streaming golden hair, robed in red and gold and bearing a burning sun-wheel before her breast or standing within the Sun itself.

As has already been mentioned there is an obvious connection between the Sun and the element of Fire. Goddesses who are associated with the Sacred Flame can also be approached as ways to access Fire/Sun energies, for example, Sulis-Minerva and Brigit. Sulis (Sul), the British Sun goddess, was honoured by Bladud by his building a shrine to her at the hot springs of Aquae Sulis, the modern-day city of Bath. Here was found a perpetual fire that was burned in her honour. The invading Romans combined the qualities of the British Sulis with Minerva, their martial and wisdom goddess. Sulis-Minerva is a complex goddess as she also has aspects of an Underworld and Stellar Goddess. The reader is referred to the works of Bob Stewart listed in the bibliography for a deeper exploration of this Goddess.

Brigit (Fiery Arrow/Power) has a complex history and a wealth of symbolism associated with her that can only be touched upon here. She is a Celtic Goddess of fire, fertility, healing and poetic inspiration who was identified as St Brigit (Bridget) by the Christian Church. She was said to have been midwife to the Virgin Mary and had a role of protectress to both Virgin and Child. At the Abbey of St Brigit in Kildare, Ireland, a perpetual flame was tended by nine maidens. Brigit is an aspect of the Divine Feminine which, when worked with, easily links the Pagan and Christian mysteries and can generate much understanding of the compatibility of these mysteries on the higher levels.

Brigit was also identified with the Northern British Goddess Brigantia, a warrior-goddess, and again, as with the Egyptian Hathor-Sekhmet relationship and with Sulis-Minerva, we have the combination of the solar qualities of inspiration and wisdom with those of a martial nature.

Brigit is known also as Bride and her main festival is Imbolic/Candlemas where, as the Virgin Bride, she can be viewed as a manifestation of Sol, the Solar Goddess. As we have seen in the Egyptian pantheon, some goddesses act as natural bridges between the levels and Brigit, through her manifestation as the Virgin Bride, connects to Solar and Stellar aspects of the Goddess.

GROVE OF THE LADY OF FIRE

These Fire Goddesses can be approached by visualising yourself standing within a sacred woodland grove. Before you is a large dish/cauldron from which burns a perpetual flame. Before the flame, clothed in bright red robes, is seated the Goddess and she is the guardian of the Flame of Wisdom and Inspiration.

As the flames rise higher they emit a dazzling white light which reaches out to you. This is the ever-burning flame of the Goddess. The light encompasses you first as white light and then it changes through the colours of the spectrum and your body is bathed in these colours which invigorate each of your chakras in turn. First from white to red . . . then orange . . . to yellow . . . to green . . . to blue . . . to indigo . . . and finally to violet. Accept these healing and vitalising energies. Bathe in them as you breathe deeply. When you feel you have had enough, visualise the flames leaving your body. Give thanks to the Goddess for her gift.

The Sun and the Sense of Self

As our progressive journey through the Pillar of Isis continues so does the building-up of self-awareness/knowledge. In order to do this we now move to seek an awareness of the waking consciousness which observes and stands – the ego or personal self which I have earlier termed the solar self. Connecting with our solar self we connect to our inner sun.

Look again at the 'egg' diagram in Chapter 6 and how it depicts the transpersonal self projecting down into the field of consciousness, a reflection of itself which is called the ego or 'I'. This depiction is in line with esoteric theory, which states that the self has an existence in non-physical reality and that it chooses to incarnate in order to learn certain lessons, to fulfil part of the Divine Plan which is unfolding in the world.

However, the natural density of the physical plane means that the self is limited by the process of incarnation. In order to operate effectively one must surrender to the experience of physical form which is vibrating at a much lower frequency. It is the natural denseness of matter which brings about a distortion of both the self (ego) and those transpersonal qualities of the 'super-consciousness' we touched upon in Chapter 6.

SELF-IDENTIFICATION

The following classic exercise from psychosynthesis was developed to encourage the process of dis-identification with the contents of our consciousness and to gradually re-align the self to the transpersonal self through self-identification.

1 Become aware of your body as you did in the exercise in Chapter 5. Do not judge or seek to change what you feel -- just observe and quietly say to yourself: 'I have a body but I am not my body'.

2 Move on to your emotions. Again just observe without judgment the various feelings that have occurred throughout the day or that you feel often. Consider both the positive and negative feelings. As you reach the end of this process say to yourself: 'I have feelings but I am not my feelings'.

3 Move your attention to your desires which may be very mundane, such as a desire for a chocolate biscuit, or more abstract. Observe how much your daily life revolves around such desires (or not) and finish by repeating: 'I have desires but I am not my desires'.

4 Move your attention to your mind and its thoughts. Observe the strings of thoughts that you have – the stream of conscious thoughts that emerge one after another. Again as you get a sense of this say to yourself: 'I have a mind (thoughts), but I am not my mind (thoughts)'.

5 Review your various subpersonalities and as you do so affirm: 'I have subpersonalities but I am not my subpersonalities'.

6 Finally, consider who it is that is observing all these aspects of body, feelings, desires, mind and subpersonalities. It is your self and once you get a sense of this repeat to yourself 'I am the self – a centre of pure consciousness'.

I suggest that you do this exercise daily for a month and observe the results. After this either use the exercise on occasions as a prelude to your main meditation work or when you feel the need to centre yourself in this way.

ANTECHAMBER OF THE SUN

With respect to the Qabalah, the Antechamber of the Sun is attributed to the Sephiroth of Hod and Netzach, which on the Tree of Life are linked to the planets Mercury and Venus. The chakra associated with the Antechamber is the manipura located in the region of the solar plexus.

You will now go a stage further in building the Pillar of Isis. Make your way to the chamber of the Moon by your usual route. The Priestess of the Moon greets you and moves to indicate a door which had been concealed by one of the hangings. The door is made from a silver-grey metal and upon it is carved a symbol. The symbol will be unique and will assist you in making the journey on subsequent occasions, so be aware of it – you may wish to draw a picture of it later. The door opens and you see that beyond it there is a spiral stairwell leading upward. The priestess indicates that you may proceed onwards. You ascend slowly.

After a few moments, you emerge into a small room. All about the walls are murals depicting the Sorrows of Isis which comprise the story of Osiris's murder by his brother Set and Isis's task of re-assembling the parts of his body which were scattered. At first these images may seem remote but, as you continue to visit the antechamber, you begin to see the colours more clearly. There is a seat in the centre of the room from which you can observe the paintings.

You may wish to refer back to the material in Chapter 9 on the myth of Isis and Osiris or read it within a book on mythology. This will assist you in this process of bringing the antechamber to life.

The story of Isis and Osiris is linked to the seasons and the circular nature of crop development which is associated with the sun's passage through the circle of the year.

You should build up these pictures daily so that you gain a sense of their reality. You may even find that it is possible to see the story of Isis and Osiris like a moving picture. Remain as the observer – do not seek to identify with the characters. Seek to understand what message you gain through observation of this mystery tale.

At the far side of the room is a golden doorway emblazoned with the symbol of the Sun. Flanking the doorway are two statues: on the right is Isis in her aspect of Queen and Nature Goddess and on the left is the Ibis-Headed God of Learning, Thoth. There is no handle or key hole on the door and you become aware that in order to enter the next chamber you must purify yourself.

In order to do this, it is necessary to remain at this level for a time and to meditate and contemplate your path so far. You may wish to combine this waiting time with the exercise given above or with one that follows. When the time is right you will have a strong sense of being called to the door leading to the Temple of the Sun.

Return to normal waking consciousness as usual.

True Will and the Solar Self

The fiery solar goddesses we have explored in the first section of this chapter could easily be described as 'Goddesses of Will'.

If you refer to the earlier material in Chapter 7 on Huna, you will see that 'will' is attributed to the solar self. What is meant by will or 'the will' in this context? My dictionary defines will, when used as a noun, as being the 'conscious adoption of a line of action' and 'the power of making a reasoned choice or decision or of controlling one's actions'. The definitions make clear that the will comes from the conscious mind. Will Parfitt, in his chapter on 'Purpose and the Creative Will' in *The Elements of Psychosynthesis*, writes: 'Our will power is the dynamic energy that brings us into the world and if we consciously connect with this energy it gives us the ability to be and do and become whatever we wish'. We shall look at ways of further connecting to this faculty.

Beyond the will of the solar self is the will which emanates from the stellar self. This is termed 'true will' or spiritual purpose, and is the agenda with which we have incarnated. It may manifest as a specific task or series of tasks which are necessary for our personal evolution or for the transpersonal good of the Earth, human or animal kind.

There are many people who connect to their true will as a matter of course and may not be aware that they are doing any such thing. They just get on with it. However, for most of us 'will', whether it be aligning to the true will of our stellar self or the personal day-to-day will of our solar self, is hard to sustain.

I list here some of Piero Ferrucci's suggestions from *What We May Be* for reviewing and strengthening the will:

> Look at your own will. Are you frequently: pushed around by the will of other people, is it subjugated by your feelings, such as depression, anger or fear; paralysed by inertia or lulled to sleep by habit, corroded by doubts? Are you able to do what you wish, from the depths of your being because you have willed it, or does some other factor prevail.

Certainly the common human experience is to feel as if we have no 'will'; to feel a victim of circumstances and of others, as well as to our own desires and urges. Moving from this to having control and choice in our lives is an extremely rewarding experience. As you gain this sense of your will with respect to your solar self, it will be easier to connect to your true will and find a way in which to manifest it in your daily life. The exercise on 'Self-Identification' is also likely to have brought with it a stronger sense of your true will.

The best way of building a stronger sense of will or of gaining access to your latent will, is to treat it like a muscle and use any number of small, mainly insignificant gestures which will slowly strengthen it. It is also an idea to make this fairly light and playful and not to be too attached to the outcome. In meditating regularly you have asserted your strength of resolve and one of its side benefits will have been to strengthen your willpower. You can also devise any number of small 'will-building' exercises such as doing something extremely slowly, dropping a certain word or phrase from your conversation for a few hours or breaking a habit. Exercises which include positive affirmations can be very helpful here.

The Place of the Heart: the Dynamics of Love and Will

The Polarity of Love and Will is a complex subject and a full discussion of these is beyond the scope of this present work. The English magician, Aleister Crowley, in his numerous magical writings, makes much of the theme of Love and Will. The prime axiom of Crowley's magical philosophy is encoded in the phrases: 'Do what thou wilt shall be the whole of the Law' and 'Love is the Law, Love under Will'. Though it has been open to misinterpretation, the will Crowley is referring to is the true will of the stellar self. As to the second part of this axiom, I am grateful to Steve Wilson, Priest of Nuit, for pointing out that 'Love under Will' need not mean that love is dominated by the will but that love is the foundation upon which the true will rests. When we encounter the transpersonal (true) will it is experienced at its highest resonance as 'Love in Action'.

Will Parfitt writes again in *The Elements of Psychosynthesis*:

> One result of moving towards our centre and making our acts of will more conscious and purposeful is that we find there is another aspect of the will, sometimes called the 'good will'. Acts of will that are made from the heart, that are filled with sympathy, love, understanding and warmth, are all manifestations of the good will. Psychosynthesis sees the good will as a synthesis of the archetypes or energies of love and will.

Love, of course, is intimately connected to the heart and it is within the heart centre that we experience the communion of unconditional love. Allow yourself to reflect upon love in its many aspects. Contemplate the idea of love as the keystone of the Universe. You can hold this as a seed-thought within your mind or combine it with a visualisation of a red rose which is first seen as a bud and then slowly opens under the golden rays of the sun to its full glory. Open your heart to Golden Aphrodite or to Hathor, the Egyptian Goddess of Love and Beauty, and allow these goddesses to inspire you. You may wish to select some appropriate music to accompany your meditation.

As the meeting place of the synthesis of love and will is the heart centre and this in symbolic terms is the place of the Sun. When we function from a place of connection to the good will we cannot help but add to the healing energies between people, nations and levels of being. From this centre of unity between love and will comes unconditional love which is a dynamic acceptance of others' inherent self.

Within the Western Mystery Tradition a key symbol of love is the Holy Grail, the cup which was said to be used at the Last Supper and to have contained the blood of Christ. However, as writers such as Marian Zimmer Bradley and John and Caitlín Matthews have expounded, the Grail was and is a powerful symbol of the Goddess. It is a further example of a way in which the Goddess's mysteries have survived, encoded within the Grail and Arthurian texts.

We balance this image of the Grail of Love with the Sword of Power and the Will, Excalibur. This sword was given to King Arthur by the Lady of the Lake, the otherworld representative of the Goddess. For theoretical and practical exploration of the Arthurian and Grail mysteries, the reader is referred to the works of John and Caitlín Matthews.

THE GRAIL AND SWORD

In order to experience your own relationship to love and will you may like to undertake a visualised journey up a mountain upon which you will find the Grail of Love and Sword of Power. Rather than using a constructed guided meditation, it is more appropriate in this case to allow for a spontaneous journey in which you seek these hallowed objects.

For best results this should be done with a partner who can make notes from your spoken words as you report what you encounter on the journey. The nature of your journey and the finding (or not) of the Grail and Sword, as well as the form in which these objects manifest to you, should give you much information as to how you relate inwardly to these two principles. You may like to take the journey in the company of your Inner Guide or when you have found them to seek your Guide's assistance in exploring their properties and significance to your own process of self-development in this area.

SALUTATIONS TO THE SUN

Here it is suggested that you begin to salute the sun each day. This does not have to be anything dramatic but a small acknowledgement of the four stations of the sun's day; that is: sunrise or upon rising, noon, sunset and midnight or before retiring for the night. This can be a simple hand gesture of holding your right palm up as is shown in Egyptian paintings. You may elaborate the salutation by writing your own short acknowledgment prayer which you can quietly say aloud or to yourself. You can also extend this practice by visualising images of various goddesses within the orb of the Sun and incorporating invocations to them in your salutations. You can focus on the Sun Goddess in one aspect, say Grainne or Sul, or attribute each station of the sun's passage to a separate goddess. For example: Bast, as Lady of the East for sunrise; Sekhmet for the noonday sun; Isis, as Lady of the West, for sunset; and Hathor, as Stellar Cow, representing the midnight sun.

THE TEMPLE OF THE SUN

With respect to the Qabalah the Temple of the Sun is attributed to Tiphareth, the central sphere of the Tree of Life. Also, the polarity of the Qabalistic spheres of Chesed, representing Love, and Geburah, representing Will, may also be expressed within this Temple. The chakra associated with this level is the anahata or heart centre. The tattvic symbol is Tejas, the red triangle and the element is Fire.

Make your way to the Antechamber of the Sun by the usual route. Your attention is drawn to the golden doorway with the symbol of the Sun and the statues of Isis and Thoth. Now is the time for you to request entrance to the Sun Temple. You knock on the door and it opens inward to reveal a short flight of steps leading upwards. On subsequent visits you will find this door opens to your touch.

The way is lit by torches. On the walls are painted murals which recount the tale of Isis and Ra, the Sun and Creator

God. They tell of how she tricked Ra into giving her his secret name which she then passed to her son Horus.

This myth holds deep significance. Ra is described as very old and decrepit. Isis deliberately places a scorpion in his path. As with most gods associated with the sun and seasons Ra is seen to grow and diminish through the course of the day and seasons of the year. In symbolic terms the scorpion is the sign of the month when winter begins. Ra is poisoned and seeks healing from Isis who has the antidote. She gives him this only when he passes to her his true name. Thus with rather blatant trickery, Isis won from Ra his magical secrets and the right to wear the solar disc as well as the horns of the moon. She also gave birth to a daughter named Bast (whose name means 'daughter of Isis') who is, as we have seen, goddess of both sun and moon. Isis then passes the name again through a mind-to-mind link to her son Horus.

The importance of this myth can be considered in light of the fact that in ancient Egypt the pharaoh was considered to be the earthly avatar of Horus, son of the Goddess Isis. In this tale lies the practice of passing on, through mind-to-mind contact, the secrets of the sacred kingship and a direct initiation into that office by Isis. This is similar to the Celtic tradition of the Goddess as Lady of Sovereignty initiating, through her priestess, the King in a sacred marriage with the land.

As you reach the end of the steps you see another doorway before you which is flanked by two statues of the lioness-headed Goddess Sekhmet carved from black basalt and gilded in gold. You pass between them and enter the Temple of the Sun. The Temple has four archways opening to the outside, one to each quarter. These allow you to look out beyond the Pillar and to view the sun's progress in the sky throughout the day. In this temple is found a red sandstone statue of Bast and beside her stands a priestess, robed in red and gold and bearing a golden sistrum.

Open yourself to the Priestess of the Sun as she instructs you in the mysteries of the Sun Goddesses. These will include attunement with the Sun, mediation of healing energies and how your salutations to the sun will energise you and align you to this healing power. All of this will not come immediately for, as with the other Temples, your relationship to the Sun Temple will deepen over a period of time. Either on your first or next visit, the priestess will give you two personal tokens which you place in your pouch. The first relates to your creativity and will and the second to your experience of love. Again it will be valuable to meditate on the significance of these symbols and to mark how they change as your own transformation continues.

Cross to the windows and be aware of the desert lands which surround the great river and how the Sun can be experienced both as beneficent to life or inimical and a destroyer of life. Its fire needs to be tempered with the elements of Water and Air in order that the Earth be fertile and not barren like the desert.

Gaze upon the Sun and within its radiance become aware of the presence of the Goddess of the Sun in whatever form she appears to you. A path of sunlight extends to you and enters your heart centre. Allow the rays of the Sun to infuse your body bringing with them a sense of healing, energy and joy. You may feel as though you could travel in your spirit body into the heart of the Sun. If it feels appropriate, do so, though you must remember to return to the Temple of the Sun before concluding your meditation.

Rather than having to trek back and retrace your steps entirely to your room within the Temple, you can now link from the Sun Temple back to your statue of the Goddess and return from there directly to normal waking consciousness.

Before you complete your meditation, take a minute or two to send forth the healing rays of the Sun Goddess and to share them with other beings or levels of existences as feels appropriate. Close in the usual manner and write up your meditation notes.

Chapter 12

The Antechamber of the Stars

In your meditational journey through the Pillar of Isis you are about to enter a mysterious place, the Antechamber of the Stars. If you refer back to the material in Chapter 3 this equates with Daath, the mysterious eleventh sphere of the Qabalistic Tree of Life, and to the throat chakra. To it are also attributed the element of Air and the tattvic symbol of Vayu, the blue circle.

We also call this place the Gateway to the Stars. Gateways are places which are imbued with power and mystery for what lies beyond. You have already passed through several gateways in your meditations. A gateway can be a physical place or part of a state of mind, a crossing over place. It is symbolic of the frontier – a place of mystery and possibility. In science fiction and fantasy literature gateways are used as a device for characters to travel between worlds of possibility. The spectacular Star-Gate which the astronaut passes through in *2001: A Space Odyssey* and the magical wardrobe which serves as a gateway to the world of Narnia in C.S. Lewis's *The Lion, the Witch and the Wardrobe* are popular examples.

The overall emerging face of the Goddess which we have encountered in each of the Temples has been one which is ever changing, She of Ten Thousand Names and Titles yet who is One in Herself. The Lady, the Goddess, Mistress of the Mysteries of Life and Death and Rebirth – whether that involves the processes upon the physical plane or the more subtle death and rebirth of initiation. The realm of the Gateway Goddesses is linked to Air and the attainment of knowledge. Her changing is not based upon the cycle of the Earth's year of fertility and barrenness, nor the phases of the Moon, nor the increase and decrease of the Sun's power, although she may also partake of these energies. Her changing comes from her power to do so as she wills.

The Goddesses associated with the Gateway are teachers and way-showers or are in some form of exile from their own realms of the Otherworld. Often they are associated with the functions of Time and the weaving of the threads of life and death. They stand in the in-between places, straddle the abyss which we have to cross in order to gain the goal of self-knowledge and therefore they will act as our guides and initiators upon this quest. They walk with humankind as companions or may be mortal women who, through their individual quests, gain immortality.

She guards magical places and has under her protection fabulous creatures. Sometimes she is perceived as evil, the one who imprisons innocence in a sheer-faced tower, or who seeks the death of the protagonist. She may be an ambivalent figure appearing within a story or our dreams of whom we are unsure; the serpent and the dove.

Overall the Goddess of the Gateway is a tester and she may well manifest in any mythic cycle as quester, helper and adversary. In this final aspect she often appears as an enchantress, the mistress of a castle or magical island where a great physical or metaphysical treasure lies. In the Greek myth of Perseus, she is the Gorgon Medusa and also Athena, his half-sister, who gives him the magical weapons and formula to defeat the Gorgon.

She also is Ariadne, princess and priestess of Crete, whose magical distaff and thread assist Theseus in his quest to find the Minotaur in the labyrinth, thus ending the time when the maidens and youths of Athens were its sacrificial victims. She manifests as the champion against any injustice.

In European myth she finds many expressions, often in the guise of the one with the ability to move between the worlds or as the tester/initiator. As the Lady of the Lake, she gives and receives the sword Excalibur and is guardian of that magical realm of Avalon. Also she is Morgan Le Fey, half-sister and adversary of King Arthur and yet at the end of his life the healer and comforter who carries his body to its rest in Avalon.

She is Arianrhod who dwells in the Castle of the Silver Wheel upon an island whose ambivalent relationship with her magician brother, Gwydion and their son, Lugh, is central to the Fourth Branch of the Welsh epic the *Mabinogion*. She is a Goddess of reincarnation for her castle within the upper realms, Caer Arianrhod, is the place where souls dwell between incarnations. The stars representing her realm, the Corona Borealis, are associated also with Ariadne in the Greek interpretation of the constellations.

The Goddess of the Gateway also is represented by the Welsh Goddess Rhiannon, who is associated with the great horse Goddess, Epona. As well as originally being an Otherworld Goddess she became the Great Queen amongst the Celts and her complex story makes up the First and Third Branches of the *Mabinogion*. Along with Rhiannon, the Gateway may be associated with the Queens of Faerie, whose relations with those who encounter her and her retinue can, again, be quite ambivalent.

She manifests in Teutonic myth as the Goddess Frigga who has the power of magical transmutation using a cloak of feathers and has the ability to travel between the nine worlds of the Teutonic cosmology. She was a Goddess of prophecy and her priestesses, known as 'volvas', had many of the abilities we associate with shamanism. She also manifests as the Norns who govern the fate of all that lives. They are sister weaver Goddesses: Urd, the ancient one who governs the past; Verandi, depicted as a mature woman who sees only the present; and the youngest, Skuldi, who looks far ahead to the future and who is depicted as veiled to indicate the uncertainness of what lies ahead. As with many of the Gateway Goddesses who are depicted with wings or take on the shape of birds, the Norns sometimes visit the world in the shape of swans.

There is a link here with the Fates of Greek legend, again taking the form of a Triple Goddess consisting of a young, mature and ancient woman. The Fates are Clotho, whose distaff spins the thread of life, Lachesis who measures the thread and Atropos who cuts the thread.

Indeed throughout the world she takes many forms. In Egypt she manifests once more as Isis in her aspect as Lady of Magic. Also as Nephthys, who like her child, the jackal-headed Anubis, guides dreamers and travellers upon the inner quest and is the guardian of things hidden.

Throughout the world, those Goddesses who somehow descend to or otherwise enter the Earth realm to teach, guide or comfort, also correspond to the place of the Gateway. Into this aspect we place Aradia, daughter of Diana and Goddess of the Witches, who descended to Earth to teach the Lunar Magic to the witches, and Tara of the Buddhist tradition who is known as the Saviouress.

Storytelling and the Eternal Quest

The theme of the quest is very central to the mysteries of the Gateway. Stories of quests have always enthralled us. Ancient sagas and modern interpretations still have the power to stir at deep levels. The quest may take many forms. It may be for love, for knowledge, for wisdom or for treasure. We must not forget this latter more materialistic type of quest for it, too, has its place and has been the theme of many tales and legends.

The role of story and story-telling is not to be underrated

for it is the gateway to the imagination. If we think back to our childhood, such stories usually feature as strong memories which inspired our imaginations. Whilst 'realistic' fiction is thought to be the proper diet of adults, there is no doubt of the popularity of genre fiction. These allow for our imaginations to be fed by the fantastic; to travel to alternative worlds in space or to the past of this world, and to realms where magic is acknowledged and fabulous beings walk the earth. The number of sword and sorcery, fantasy and science fiction books published, and the enduring quality of books, television and film where fantasy is allowed its day, speaks of our need for the art of storytelling and myth. In these, archetypal themes are played out again and again. Although some might call it escapism we learn through identification with these characters of the eternal quest for enlightenment and wisdom.

We identify with people within stories, whether hero or heroine. Whilst we are reading and identifying with the characters, this becomes our story. This also is true within films. Thus we are free to cross gender, race, creed, country and even species to identify with an enfolding story. What we gain from this may be a momentary respite from our ordinary lives or something more precious.

For children, the playing of games utilising the imagination is part of the wonder of the formative years. Stories, especially imaginative ones, can form the basis of infinite worlds wherein children learn various skills of cooperation as well as having terrific fun. This play can be very serious, with scenarios being carried on for days and weeks among a group of friends. An extension of this imaginative play which has come from the upsurge in imaginative literature is role-playing games.

Role-playing first gained popularity within the United States in the mid-1970s as a direct result of the success of *Lord of the Rings* by J.R.R. Tolkien, and of its descendants. Role-playing games are not usually played on a board but in the imagination of the players, directed by the 'Dungeon Master' who plans the campaign and is, in a sense, the 'god' (or 'goddess') of their world. No one's fate is determined by this person for each character is free to respond independently to the unfolding game. Also, much is determined by luck in the form of dice rolls. It is a game wherein people can develop their visualisation skills and exercise their creativity. Each game is an on-going quest. It is possible for one's character to be killed in combat or die in some other fashion. However, when this happens the player is in the position to 'generate' another player character which may be very different than their last one. As with reincarnation one is expected to learn by one's mistakes and successes, carrying these forward into their new 'lives'.

Although these games have their detractors and may seem trivial compared to real life, or the more sombre nature of true quest, they can be preparatory for the road to the mysteries by offering an experience of group cooperation and a chance for people to extend their awareness into other worlds. Marion Zimmer Bradley, the writer well known for her books of imaginative fiction, has written of this in her book *The House Between the Worlds*. In this the game of 'Dungeons and Dragons' serves both as a training devise for those who would walk between the worlds and as a monitor for the alternative worlds that this Worldhouse served as Gateway to.

Role-playing games are still approached mainly for entertainment, although something of the same idea can be utilised for more serious work in the mysteries. One exercise, which can be done individually or by a group of like-minded friends, is to work through a book with an archetypal theme. I, amongst countless others, did this instinctively with books such as *The Lord of the Rings*. When I had a ritual to produce in 1986 for a ceremonial magical group, I based it on a quest theme utilising Tolkien's mythology. The result entitled 'The Voyage West' was kindly incorporated by Gareth Knight in *The Magical World of the Inklings*, his study of the mythopoeic worlds of Tolkien, C.S. Lewis and others.

I am grateful to Lauren Bleach of Norwich, England, who introduced me to further applications for using imaginative fiction. When I first met her, Lauren and her group were working through Jules Verne's *Journey to the Centre of the Earth*. Each member of the group consciously identified with a member of the party engaged on the journey. They would take a chapter and work through it together utilising reading, meditation and spontaneous ritual. They also linked this to the work they were doing in relation to cleansing and healing sacred sites and the energy centres of their locality. To do this they visited local sites that they had psychically identified as being connected to the inner landscape of the book and used the storyline as part of their healing work.

Lauren also inspired those close to her to seek their own stories and books using synchronicity and contemplation. That is, a story reflecting the archetypal processes we are each unconsciously or semi-consciously living out in our lives.

If you wish to do a similar process to 'discover' your own story, allow yourself to choose a book with a positive archetypal theme. Something about the story will draw you, whether it be an appealing dust-jacket, a favourite author or the rediscovering of a story from childhood. Allow your lunar self to guide you. For women looking for stories with women as the protagonist, very few classical stories have survived with heroine figures, though work is being done by women to reclaim these fragments to redress the balance. Certainly contemporary imaginative literature abounds with quests undertaken by women as well as men. Writers such as Marion Zimmer Bradley, Julian May, Ursula Le Guin, Diana Paxton, Louise Cooper and many more have written novels with strong female leads. A book in an imaginative setting with some form of journey or quest as its theme is probably the most ideal for this purpose. When you are scanning the library or bookstore shelves keep in mind that children's literature and plays are an excellent source of such material. Horror stories are not suitable for this process as they are deliberately written to disturb the imagination and are unlikely to have a positive transformative theme.

Read the story with consciousness, allowing yourself to become identified with the heroine or hero or one of their companions. It is quite an easy process as it is something you do naturally when you become enthralled in any film, play or book. Writers and film-makers count on this identification and it is this which allows us to empathise with the characters. We get personally involved with these characters but rarely stop and examine why. The exercise that follows allows you to connect with your own internal library where a special book can be identified.

THE PLACE OF STORY

Recall the house you have previously visited in your imagination in Chapter 5. After relaxation and centring, travel there in the company of your Inner Guide.

As you enter this familiar building, your attention is drawn to a stairway that leads to the upper level of the house. There is a sense of light and beauty as you climb higher. Do feel free to explore this upper level of the house of your personality, noting the various rooms and how they are furnished.

Somewhere in the upper level of the house you will find a library. It may be large, taking up an entire room, or merely a bookcase. When you enter this room, your attention is drawn to a specific book upon a shelf. What draws you may be the colour or design of its cover or you may recognise the title or author. It may be a story that you already have known in your life or one which you will know. It may even be a story that is not yet written and you will be the one to give it physical expression. Open it and begin to get a sense of its theme and characters. Speak with your Inner Guide about this story and its significance to your path in the mysteries so that together you can understand how to work with it.

One woman who was working with this exercise discovered in her library a book with a cover depicting a unicorn which had for many years been a special symbol in dreams and her imaginative life. In working with the story she found within its pages that the unicorn became her companion on inner journeys which she has woven into magical stories for her children. She is an excellent illustrator and may one day seek to have these stories published for others to enjoy. The imagination is an important creative tool and to translate your experience into a story, whether long or short, a poem or a picture, can be an extremely rewarding exercise.

When working with a story and, as suggested above, reading through it visualising yourself as a character, you can approach it in an informal way or construct for yourself, or with a group, a series of meditations and inner journeys around the book. This can be a pleasurable and exciting experience and can be approached in the spirit of play, although this is not to trivialise the experience. You may also find that symbols that occur to assist the protagonist on the quest will also occur in life. Indeed, you may find that reality begins outwardly to reflect some of the experiences you are going through within the book in symbolic terms. We all have battles to fight figuratively, puzzles to master, adversaries to overcome, as well as a need for the joy which is a reward of a quest fulfilled.

Your imagination and ability to focus on possibilities can also be utilised to enrich your personality in a more direct way as is outlined in the following exercise.

THE IDEAL MODEL

What do I mean by an ideal model? It is the achievement of your deepest yearnings and goals, the process of unfoldment towards your own purpose and destiny. Consider your life as a piece of art, as your personal masterpiece. When we utilise the Ideal Model exercise, we are allowing for positive change to be effected in our life.

This sort of creative visualisation can be utilised when you want, for example, to change your body image. It is quite common these days to assist in a programme of exercise by backing up physical work-outs of whatever nature with visualising yourself as healthier, trimmer, etc. Likewise with sports or dance. However the technique of the 'ideal model' focuses not on some physical attribute or change but an inner one. Basically, you choose a quality you would like to be enhanced in your life – say joy, strength, courage, love, wisdom, etc and follow these steps.

1 Choose the quality which you feel would help you in your emerging life purpose.

2 Imagine yourself imbued with this quality in its highest degree of purity and intensity.

3 Imagine yourself walking into this image and becoming one with it. Experience how this feels.

4 Finally imagine how you will in real life situations express this quality. Again bring as much sensation and awareness to this visualisation.

The idea behind the ideal model is that you have free will and are free to choose the manner in which to express yourself and fulfil your destiny.

We may also choose ideal models from people we know and are associated with or those from history or current affairs, writers, film and music personalities. These are people who actualise qualities that we desire or wish we could bring into our lives more fully. Sometimes they will turn up in our dreams in some fashion and in our dream diaries it is important to note them. If they are people in the public eye and not personally known to us, they will be symbolic of that quality or characteristic we associate them with.

Psyche's Quest

In the main meditation for this chapter, as you climb to the Antechamber of the Stars, the murals found on the stairwell walls depict the myth of Psyche and Eros. This mystery drama has the theme of a search for what is lost, in this case the beloved of the soul, Eros, the son of Aphrodite, Goddess of Love. The fullest version of the myth comes down to us contained within the *Golden Ass* by Apuleius.

The placing of this mystery at this Level indicates that we stand on the threshold of a new experience and we find that it is love which draws us to the higher levels. It may be the yearning for divine union, for the sacred marriage with a soul-partner or the search for one's life purpose which initiates this search as much as any sense of loss. As I retell this myth, allow your mind to imagine pictures which you can use to 'paint' the murals. You may also like to read C.S. Lewis's *Till We Have Faces* which is an eloquent and insightful re-telling of the myth from the unusual perspective of one of Psyche's sisters and has much to say on the nature of love and its quest.

The name Psyche means 'soul' in Greek and thus refers, in its essence, to both sexes. The myth tells how Psyche's mother offended the Goddess Aphrodite by claiming her daughter's beauty surpassed that of the Goddess. Aphrodite was angered by this and ordered her son, Eros, to punish Psyche. Shortly afterwards an oracle of Apollo conveys to Psyche's father that, under threat of terrible calamities, she is to be taken to the summit of a mountain where she will be the prey of a monster. As Psyche awaits the fulfilment of the oracle, she is gently lifted in the arms of the winds and carried to a magnificent palace. In the darkness she is joined by a mysterious being, who explains that he was the husband for whom she was destined. He disappears before dawn and extracts a promise that she will never attempt to see his face.

She is happy for a time, but when she visits her home and tells of the palace and her husband, her sisters sow the seeds of suspicion in her heart that he is actually a monster. Therefore one night, in spite of her promise, she lights a lamp as he sleeps and looks upon his face. Thus she discovers that he is Eros, the God of Love. A drop of wax from the lamp burns his shoulder. He wakens and flies away. The taboo being broken, he cannot remain with her. The palace vanishes and Psyche, knowing herself totally alone, despairs. She entreats the gods for aid. Aphrodite unwillingly sets Psyche tasks that she might win Eros back. Each of these are seemingly impossible but she completes them with mysterious assistance.

Through the working out of these, Psyche gains the deepening and maturation of her soul. Her first task is to sort a huge pile of seeds before nightfall and this she accomplishes with the help of ants. Psyche's second task is to obtain some fleece of the fierce Golden Rams of the Sun. This time she is assisted by a reed growing by a river's edge. It whispers to her that she should not confront the sheep but gather the wool that has stuck to the briars where they have grazed while they sleep in the afternoon sun. By this subtler route, Psyche gains the element of the masculine energies she needs, symbolised by the Rams of the Sun, to make herself whole.

The third task set by Aphrodite is to fill a crystal goblet with the Waters of Life found on a mountain top guarded by dragons. Once more she is aided in the fulfilment of this by a totem helper, an eagle, who flies past the guardians and obtains the sacred water.

The final and most difficult task given to Psyche is to journey to the Underworld. There she is to ask the Queen of Hades, Persephone, to place within a casket some of her beauty which is to be conveyed back to Aphrodite. Psyche believes that Aphrodite has triumphed, for the only way she can reach Hades is by dying. She climbs a tower in order to throw herself off. The tower speaks to her and tells her of a secret way to Hades which involves very precise and complex instructions to be followed both going and returning. These include the injunction that, once obtained, she must not, under any circumstances, look within the casket. She completes the task successfully, but cannot resist looking within the casket just as she is leaving the realm of the dead, with the result that she falls into a death-like sleep. However, Eros intervenes at this point, awakens her and, after petitioning Zeus, flies her to Olympus where Zeus confers immortality upon her and they are then wed.

This is one of the most enduring and powerful myths of initiation for a woman. It has been explored psychologically and mythically in many texts, including Erich Neumann's *Amor and Psyche*, Jean Houston's *The Search for the Beloved* and Robert Johnson's *She: Understanding Feminine Psychology*.

I am grateful to Brian Burgess for his attribution of Psyche's tasks to the four levels of the Pillar so far covered. The seeds, often distributed by the winds, to Air; the Rams of the Sun to Fire; the goblet of spring water to Water; and the descent into Hades to Earth. We can thus consider Psyche's journey in terms of a series of elemental initiations which culminate in her spiritual rebirth.

The Antechamber of the Stars

Begin your journey as usual. However, this time when you find yourself in the Temple of the Sun, you notice a stairwell and spiral stairway leading further up the Pillar. Follow this and you see upon the walls as you ascend murals depicting the story of Psyche and Eros. Look at these pictures which seem to be almost alive, as you pass them. Think again about the meaning of this myth and its relevance to your own search.

You emerge into another room where there are no windows. It is quite dark, being lit by a single blue coloured lamp set in the centre of the ceiling. You are aware of a small altar set upon one of the walls, upon which is marked the form of a spiral. In its centre lies the distaff representing the Goddess who spins and weaves the patterns of your life.

Above the altar is a dark mirror which glows slightly from the light of the lamp. There is a door in the far wall made of black obsidian and above the door is a carving depicting Isis with her winged arms outstretched as if in greeting.

However, it is not yet time to travel through this door to the Star Temple.

You see in the centre of the room a long, low couch upon which you may lie. This is very comfortable and as you lie there, reflect on why you have made this journey. Be aware of the cycle of your own life and the way that has been shown to you in order that you should be here at this time. The simplicity and relative emptiness of this place allows for your consciousness to range wide and yet also to find an inner stillness and peace. This is a time to seek purification and a sense of making a vigil before moving on to the Stellar Level of the Pillar.

On this first or a later occasion you are joined by the Priestess of the Antechamber, robed in grey with a pale veil covering her head. She may guide you to the mirror and within its depths you see flashes of another time, another place, other lives. You may find yourself just observing or being drawn deeper into the life shown therein. Whatever happens at this time the priestess will remain with you and will assist you in gaining a sense of perspective on what is shown, as well as its meaning in the overall unfolding purpose of your destiny. In the Mirror of Time you may also see scenes from your life, recent and memories of long ago. Again, the priestess will help you to understand the larger story and to see the threads of connection spinning out to your here and now. You may even get a glimpse of the future: this life, or others, and will always gain from this. Be open to the experience, and let the priestess who has mastery of this Mirror of Time guide you in the journeying.

You may find that once you come out of the meditation

and write it up that other insights come to you. You should include these in your diary as well. You may find the themes of scenes viewed returning in your dreams and they should be considered as further dreams to aid you in your quest for self-awareness. Not all that you see will be pleasant, indeed it might be distressing, but try to keep a perspective of this place between the worlds. The Priestess is there for you and you can always call on your Inner Guide for positive inspiration and comfort.

Return to your body by either returning down the Pillar or via the 'short-cut' explained in the last chapter. Remember that you need not do the entire journey every day but can visit the Temple of Anubis or relax in the Temple Gardens or do some of the other exercises.

At this Level I have not mentioned your symbolic gift. This will come to you after you have integrated the experience of the Antechamber. You may not know when you are ready but the Priestess will. At that point she will direct you to the altar. On it will be an object to place in the pouch you carry. Look at it closely for it is symbolic of your relationship with the element of Air and your mental processes. This is also the signal that on your next session you will be entering the Temple of the Stars.

Chapter 13

The Temple of the Stars

In coming to consider the Star Goddesses we leave behind what is known and enter the sphere of the cosmos in our search to comprehend the mysteries of time and space. Thus to this Level are attributed the Stellar Goddess from whose bodies, it is said, was born the whole of creation. Here is found the Egyptian Goddess Neith, who was not born but from whose body the gods and all creation came; Spider Woman of the Native American tradition who weaves the stars and the spaces between them; Tiamat of

Babylon who brought forth the heavens and the earth from her body.

Nuit, the Mother of Isis, whose starry body is depicted as arched above the Earth, gives birth daily to the Sun. With the words she speaks in the received Book of Nuit (*The Book of the Law,* 1904) she describes herself: 'I am Infinite Space, and the Infinite Stars thereof' and counsels those who would worship her to 'Come forth, o children, under the stars, and take your fill of Love'.

This is markedly similar to the Charge of the Goddess used in Wiccan rituals, where the Goddess through the mediation of the Priestess speaks to those gathered in worship. 'Hear the words of the Star Goddess, the dust of whose feet are the hosts of heaven, and whose body encircles the universe: For I am the soul of Nature, who gives life to the Universe. From me all things proceed, and unto me all things must return; and before my face . . . let thine innermost self be enfolded in the rapture of the infinite. Let my worship be within the heart that rejoiceth; for behold, all acts of love and pleasure are my rituals.'

The Star Goddess is the Known and the great Unknown. She is veiled and yet naked in her brilliance as we gaze upon the splendour of the night sky. Her body is often depicted as the starry heavens, the milk of her breasts the Milky Way. She inspires us to truth, wisdom, altruism and transpersonal love.

In some traditions Star Goddesses include those linked to specific stars and constellations such as Bahu, the Hindu Goddess associated with the constellation of Leo; Astraea, the Greek Goddess of Justice who abandoned the Earth to become the constellation Virgo; the seven sister goddesses of the Pleiades; Isis, in her winged aspect, associated with Sirius.

To the Star Temple I have also placed Goddesses of Wisdom and Truth including the Shekinah, the feminine aspect of the Hebrew God still honoured in their Sabat rituals; Athena, Wisdom Goddess of Greece; the Gnostic Sophia, spirit of Divine Wisdom who takes on the form of a white dove; Maat, the Egyptian Goddess of Truth.

Many Goddesses who are stellar in nature are given the title, Lady or Queen of Heaven and are depicted crowned with stars or clothed in starry raiments. Those familiar with the Christian tradition will recognise that the Blessed Virgin Mary is honoured here. There is often a close connection between Star Goddesses and the sphere of the Moon, although not all Moon Goddesses are Star Goddesses and vice versa. Many of the Great Goddesses, those whose attributes span the spheres of creation and can be considered Goddesses of the Underworld, Earth, Moon, Sun and Stars are also placed here.

Both the stars and the moon have a relationship with the sea, for the 'sea of space' is likened to the seas of our planet and images such as stellar craft associated with sea-going vessels continue to inspire our imaginations. The voyages of ancient travellers such as Odysseus, Jason and the Argonauts and others are mapped out in the constellations.

The Stellar Age

Awareness of the stars comes into three areas of study: astronomy, astrology and cosmology. World cosmologies tell of how the world and often the universe were created. As modern science discovers more about the universe, it seems these poetic analogies may be closer to the truth than was first realised.

Every indigenous culture and the classic pantheons spin stories about the constellations. Sometimes these relate to creation myths or the abode of the gods. Also they tell of how certain people and animals were placed amongst the stars so they would endure forever in the heavens.

The most familiar star lore is related to the art and science of astrology. To the level of the stars we attribute all forms of prophesy, divination and the foreseeing of events linked to individuals, nations, the planet and cosmos. Myth-makers and magicians turn to star lore for their inspiration for ritual which will allow us to journey beyond the Earth. We range out on the wings of our imagination into the star fields and learn of our destiny as it has been played out within this life and others in the past and to come.

Connecting to the stars we touch a sense of the eternal. Although we know that the universe exists in finite time, the time spans involved are so vast that to our human consciousness they are meaningless in real terms. We speak of hundreds of millions of years contrasted to our lifespan of under a hundred. Yet there is part of ourselves which does resonate to millions of years and that is our divine spark within: what I have called the stellar self; that which has its true existence upon the non-physical planes of existence and projects a portion of itself into each incarnation we have upon the physical plane.

We look to the stars with a deep intuitive longing both to reach out to touch them in some form, and for oneself to be touched by them. Recent films and novels have played out this theme of contact with star people. There is also an entire fringe culture concentrating on communication with extra-terrestrials. There also seems to be a deep ancestral memory of contact with other species either physically or on other, subtler planes of communication.

One esoteric idea which has begun to make itself heard in recent years is the idea that not all souls which are incarnate upon the earth have their origins upon this planet. These 'star-born' or star people have, it seems, incarnated upon this planet in order to assist in the environmental and social crises this planet faces as the birth pangs of the New Aeon or New Age are felt. What is this New Age? It is called by some the Age of Aquarius; by others, the Aeon of Horus, the Child of Isis and Osiris, and reconciler between the Goddess and God. It is the time of an emerging global consciousness during which human-kind begins to recognise its place in the Cosmic Order and, it is believed, we will find that we are not unique within the universe and will begin to function within a greater community of the galaxy.

Again this theme has been explored in genre literature and film and also has a life amongst the New Age and magical communities. Many people who are not part of these sub-cultures have seen strange lights in the sky, had some form of 'close encounter' or numinous dream in which they encountered creatures not of this earth yet possessing a wisdom and detachment of the stars.

Some have suggested that these creatures have always been with us in the form of the little people or fairy folk and these are merely 20th-century encounters with the Otherworld. This may be true on one level and it poses another question: what and where exactly is the

Otherworld? Is it above us or within? Is it the place between the worlds or is it an other world. It may appear as all of these – and none.

Many people who have encountered astral projection and near-death experiences find themselves leaving the planet Earth behind and entering a place which matches their view of heaven. A place where Beings of Light act as mediators and guides, giving them both love and an understanding of why they are incarnate upon the physical plane. Sometimes these people encounter trials which test their courage and determination. Yet always there is a sense of love, not a mushy love but the often hard cosmic love which has in perspective the eternity of the Spirit and not the relatively short life of the body. It is this perspective of the eternal which is the consciousness of the stellar self; for the stellar self is well aware of the trials of pain and loss we face while incarnate upon the physical.

From the stellar self comes a sense of perspective and a stepping outside of our physical limitations to consider the whole. It cuts across the animal instincts of survival. The following exercise is to open up a direct connection with the stellar self.

CONVERSATION WITH THE STELLAR SELF

Our movement to the Stellar Temple of the Pillar brings us within the realm of the stellar self. This part of one's self is known by various names depending upon which esoteric tradition you are encountering. It may be called the self or higher self, the Buddha Nature, Oversoul, Holy Guardian Angel or the God or Goddess Within. Here, for reasons I have explained in Chapter 7, I use the term star or stellar self. During the course of working with your dreams and various exercises, you may have already had some experience of your star self. The following exercise encourages this connection through an inner dialogue.

Get comfortable, close your eyes, relax and centre yourself as usual. Do some brief energising exercises and after this, focus your attention on your crown chakra. Be aware of this as your link to the transpersonal level of your star self and be aware of the formation of an image therein. You may see a symbol of some kind such as a star or a sun image; or a being such as an angel, Goddess figure, Wise Old Man or Woman or a Being of Light. Be aware of the great love which radiates from this image of your star self. Although the messages they relate to you may be quite serious they will never be authoritarian or judgemental.

Once you have a sense of their presence engage them in conversation and be open to the guidance they give you related to the life situations you find yourself in. You may find this comes verbally or in the form of symbolic images. Spend as much time as you need with your star self and gain whatever clarification you need. It is likely you will get a sense of an 'otherness' about your star self because of an awareness that their consciousness is so much more than yours. It is important to keep in mind that they communicate from the viewpoint of eternity.

When you are ready to disengage, give thanks to your stellar self for having come to you, allow yourself to return to normal waking consciousness and write up the experience. When you have gained some experience of this connection you will probably find that it is not necessary to do an elaborate meditation to make this connection but just to 'open up' on a special frequency. It is possible that during the dialogue your star self will give you their Name. This Name must always remain a secret and never be shared with anyone. It is a word which will summon your stellar self at will and thus has great power. Finally to further earth the experience do write it up for your record.

Stellar Magic

It has been said that 'the stars are silent' and the power to be silent and to keep secret certain aspects of the work is vital. No matter what is written and revealed in print, the true secret of the mysteries are experiential and cannot be revealed. This is especially so of the stellar mysteries for the vast physical distances of both time and space that separate us from their light bars us from true experience. The ability to travel upon the Inner Realms is granted not through skill but through purity of spirit and the inner integrity of the individual.

The best way to connect to the stars is to go outside on

a clear night, away if possible from an area that is lit by artificial means because of light pollution and to look upwards. The night sky is ablaze with light. Some constellations may be known to you, others unknown. It is important to be aware of what you are looking at in order to attune yourself with the vibrations of that particular star system. Some star systems such as Sirius, Ursa Major, the Pleiades, have strong mythological and inner connections with the Earth. It is said that beings from these planets came to earth to instruct us, and they may also have been our forebears.

The Cherokee of North America and the Maya before them believe that the stars of the Seven Sisters (Pleiades) were their ancestors. In many mythologies there are legends of people coming from the stars and mating with indigenous earth beings. These sources include the Bible where the myths are related to angelic hosts. Theosophical thought talks of 'swarms' of divine sparks coming to this earth from the depths of stellar space and entering into incarnation here. The writer Doris Lessing, in her celebrated *Canopus in Argos* series, paints a picture which is quite detached and at times coldly expedient in its depiction of the process of the star-seeding of the planet Earth.

It seems that we have lost much in the awareness of star lore which is being rediscovered at this time. The ancients had many more deities who were stellar in nature and later, as the world-view shrunk, this changed in favour of gods and goddesses linked only to this star system. It is believed, within some sections of the esoteric community, that this star wisdom was lost at the time of Atlantis's demise when humankind, through the misuse of magical power, lost its connection to the stars. The remnants of this stellar tradition were scattered to the 'Four Winds' and can be found in Egyptian, Hyperborean, Mayan, and other traditions.

In recent years there has been in this country, and no doubt in others, a movement within the magical field towards a preoccupation with 'star magic'. This includes seeking communication with the stars and the star 'Speakers and Watchers' in order to find answers to the planetary predicament we find ourselves in. For this the aforesaid fragments of the lost stellar tradition are being brought together for ritual exploration. Into this magic is woven material linked to the discoveries of astronomy and astrophysics.

This work involves not only 'spacing-out' from the Earth level but also seeking to connect the stars with the Earth. This is approached in various waves. Much of the experimental work I have been engaged upon, with others, is linked to this aspect of the mysteries. This also involves an establishment of the stars upon the Earth; that is, a linking of cosmic patterns with those existing on the Earth. These patterns are often expressed through the existing grids of Earth-energy manifesting as sacred sites, ley lines and sacred geometry.

As this material and work is highly experimental, much is unlikely to be openly expressed in print for some time, if ever. Because of the nature of star magic, and the fact that it is not tried and tested territory, it is not recommended for beginners. With the material contained in these pages, if you have been assimilating and integrating the previous exercises of the Pillar slowly, you will be able to approach the gentle Goddess-inspired exercises of this last chapter with no difficulty. As always, I want to stress the proper earthing of the energies. Some people may be over-sensitive and I feel it best to caution all my readers for those few who might have difficulty. Therefore, if you find that you are experiencing mood changes, any sense of disconnection from daily life, or disturbance of your sleeping, eating or menstrual cycles, cease meditating for a few weeks. Or concentrate upon working with the Earth and Sun Temples until you stabilise.

However, for those wishing to explore this material and the Stellar/Earth link further, some books and groups working with these ideas include: *Surfers of the Zuvuya: Tales of Interdimensional Travel* by José Argüelles; the World Ascension Network, coordinated by Juliette Sweet under the imprint Goddess Press (369 Montezuma Suite, 221 Sante Fe, New Mexico, 87501, USA), *The Star-Borne: A Remembrance of the Awakened Ones* by Solara (Route 7, Box 191B, Charlottesville, Virginia 22901, USA) and *Ancient Egypt: The Sirius Connection* (Element) and *Practical Atlantean Magic* (Aquarian) by Murry Hope. The first three consider developments emerging from the 1987 Harmonic Convergence. The first book by Hope examines both the historical links between Egypt and the star system of Sirius and techniques of Sirian Magic, while the second is a study of the science, mysticism and theurgy of ancient Atlantis, which sheds further light on the Sirian connection. It is likely that Argüelles and Hope will be eventually publishing further on this subject.

The Muses

As we approach the Temple of the Stars from the Antechamber, we encounter murals which depict the Nine Muses of Greek mythology, the daughters of Mnemosyne (Memory) and Zeus. Each Muse is depicted dancing with a sphere of energy linked to the planet she is attributed to. The symbolism of a nine-fold sisterhood appears again and again within the Goddess's mysteries: the nine maidens of the Cauldron/Grail; the nine priestesses tending the perpetual flame of Bridget in Kildare, Ireland; the nine sisters of the Isle of Avalon, the nine daughters of Oya, the African River Goddess; the nine daughters of each of the Greek Creation Goddesses, Nyx, Tethys and Gaia.

The Muses were, and indeed are, goddesses linked to the patronage of the classic arts and sciences; to connect to one's Muse is to make a creative link with a deep inner source of creativity. The attribution of the Muses to the 'sacred' planets derives from Renaissance magical and astrological texts. I shall, later in this chapter, give brief descriptions of these planets though you may wish to enhance these with your own reading.

The Muses are classically depicted as young women dressed in long, flowing robes who gather together in special sanctuaries to dance. One such place was Mount Helicon, where there were two magical springs which, when drunk from, conferred artistic inspiration. Likewise, as you connect to the Muses, they will inspire within you the blessed waters of inspiration and creativity. How you express this will be an intensely personal experience. Indeed, your relationship with the Muses is likely to have been stimulated already by your work with this book.

The first is Urania, the Muse of Astronomy and Astrology. She can be visualised in white holding a celestial globe and compass. It would also be appropriate to attribute the science of physics to her and she is assigned to the planetary sphere of the Fixed Stars (the Zodiac).

The second sister, attributed to Saturn, is Polyhymia, the Muse of Sacred Hymns and Storytelling. She is clad in black and crimson and is veiled.

The third sister, garbed in blue, is Euterpe, the Muse of Lyric Poetry and she is attributed to the sphere of Jupiter. She bears a flute.

The fourth is Erato, the Muse of Erotic and Love Poetry; she is clad in red and carries a small drum. She is attributed to Mars.

The fifth sister is Melpomene, the Muse of Tragedy, attributed to the Sun and clad in golden robes and a tragic mask.

Terpsichore, the Muse of Dance and Song is attributed to Venus. She is clad in green and golden robes and carries a lyre.

Calliope, the Muse of Epic Poetry, attributed to Mercury, is clad in robes of orange and bears a tablet and stylus.

The Muse of History, Clio, is attributed to the Moon. She is dressed in robes of violet and silver and bears a water-clock.

Finally to the sphere of the Earth is attributed Thalia, the Muse of Comedy. She is robed in the colours of Earth; russets, browns and greens, and wears the mask of comedy and wreaths of ivy.

The Planets and the Goddess

Within the actual Temple of the Stars we will not only encounter the Fixed Stars and Constellations and those Goddesses associated with these, but also Goddesses connected to the planets of our solar system. You will be able to use these planetary symbols as gateways to connect with the Goddesses attributed to the planets and, if you so choose, to explore your natal horoscope.

We begin with Mercury, the planet that links to mental processes and all forms of communication and travel. It symbolises the ability to express oneself, to be mentally agile and knowledgeable. Mercury is the psychopompos, guide to the traveller and the dead into the Otherworld. It is also the messenger of the Gods and the ruling planet of medicine. Traditionally, gods such as Mercury, Hermes and Thoth are attributed here. With respect to Goddesses we will attribute Sophia, the Gnostic Trinuine Goddess of knowledge and wisdom who was and is the patroness of the hermetic arts. Also Iris, the Greek Goddess of the Dawn, who heralds the approach of the sun and guides the dead to Hades. We will also attribute Ariadne, whose golden thread guided Theseus within the Moon Labyrinth of Crete, and Hygeia, Grecian Goddess of healing.

Venus is the planet of love and relationships and also rules art and beauty. Here, of course, we attribute the Goddesses Venus and Aphrodite, Lakshmi of India, Erzulie of Haiti, Ishtar of Babylon, Hathor, the Norse Freya and all Love Goddesses of the World.

Mars is a planet of action which when frustrated can become aggressive. Traditionally it rules war. In its positive aspect, it is a planet of assertiveness and sexual energy. Also attributed to this planet are justice and sports as well as surgical medicine. Attributed to Mars are Goddesses such as Sekhmet of Egypt, Pallas Athene, the Morrigans and Macha of Ireland, Durga and Kali of India, Pele, the Volcano Goddess of Hawaii, Brigit of the Celts and the Valkyries of Teutonic myth.

Jupiter is the planet of expansion and beneficent energies and rules civilisation. To it are attributed the Great Queens such as Hera and Juno; Vesta, guardian goddess of the hearth fire; Hathor, as the Great Cow of Heaven; the Goddesses of Sovereignty, the Virgin Mary as Queen of Heaven; Inanna of Summa; Ayida Wedo, Rainbow Goddess of the Afro-Caribbean tradition; Sarasvati of India and Kwan Yin of China.

To Saturn are attributed the Goddesses who limit and contain Time. Here we find Kali, the Hindu Goddess of Time and Death; Maat, the Egyptian Goddess of Truth in whose hall the dead are judged by having their hearts weighted against her feather of truth; the Norns – the Teutonic Goddesses of time and fate, and the Fates of Greece – Clotho, Lachesis, and Atropos.

To Uranus, the planet of magic and the occult arts, we attribute Isis, the Great Enchantress; Arianrhod of the Silver Wheel; Frigga who transforms herself into animals; the Queens of Faerie; the Enchantress Morgan of Avalon; the Tibetan Dakinis; Hecate and Aradia, Goddess of the witches.

To Neptune, the planet of dreams and mystical revelation, we attribute the Virgin Mary; Cleito, the Nymph who is said to have been a goddesses of lost Atlantis and Goddesses of the Sea including Yemanja of Africa and Brazil, T'ien Hou of China, and Tiamat of Babylon.

The Seven Ways to the Goddess

The seven planets encountered above can give us a further map to contemplate our relationship to the Goddess. For this we return once more to psychosynthesis theory which in its 'typology' provides maps of the ways in which we seek transpersonal and spiritual realisations. To each of these 'ways' I have made a planetary correspondence. Understanding this, for most, will mean using a combination of two or three ways of approach in our quest for the Goddess. Through better knowledge of the 'ways', we can also appreciate the paths that others follow which are different than our own.

The first is the way of Will, also called the Heroic way. This is attributed to the planet Mars. Many myths and stories use this way as an inspiration. It involves dedication to a cause outside of oneself, or may involve some form of quest, physical or spiritual. Much of the work done by the Women's Movement could be attributed here as an expression of the Amazon spirit. It is a very clear and direct way.

The second is the way of Love and inner illumination and is attributed to Venus. This sense of the Love and Light of the Goddess is gained through meditation and an increasing sense of enlightenment. The love one experiences allows for a greater love for all beings and creation.

The third is the way of Action. This entails the consecration of all activity in the world to the Goddess and an experience of the sacredness of all life and action. It also involves renunciation of the fruits of one's labours and an overall dedication of one's life to the spiritual quest. This way is attributed to the planet Saturn.

The fourth way is the Aesthetic Way and is the realisation of the Goddess as immanent through beauty both in nature, living creatures and art. This way can be expressed through the creation of images which embody the sense of beauty and the Goddess, or in some way telling her story through writing, acting, dance, etc. It is the way of the creative artist and the way of one who gains a sense of the Goddess through their experience of art. It also links to a transcendent experience of the Goddess through an appreciation of Nature. This is attributed to Jupiter.

The fifth is the way of science and is attributed to Mercury. Here the Goddess is approached through the intellect. That the intellect and the scientific method can lead to an experience of the Goddess may seem a contradiction in terms to those of a more devotional bent. However, I have known many who have experienced her within a contemplation of mathematics or of the abstract formulas of quantum physics. It is a way of discovery which honours the Goddess in creation, and does not attempt to explain her away.

The sixth is the way of Devotion and is attributed to Neptune. This is probably the best-known route to the Goddess and involves mystical experience through worship and devotion. While similar to the Way of Love, this is more passive attunement where the Goddess is not sought but awaited.

The seventh is the way of Ritual and Ceremony and is attributed to Uranus. It involves the use of colour, sound, symbolic action, invocation and rituals of initiation and sacred drama where an experience of the Goddess is sought. This is the way of magic and ritual.

One might consider that the way of the priestess and priest ultimately seeks to synthesise all these ways. In this way one's whole life becomes a quest for the Goddess, an active seeking, a passive waiting, a dedication of one's life to the unfolding of the Goddess's plan. Indeed the rainbow path of her mysteries.

TEMPLE OF THE STARS

This Temple of the Pillar is attributed to the brow chakra, the Third Eye, and to the Qabalistic sephiroth of Binah and Chokmah on the Tree of Life. It is also linked to the fifth element of Spirit, represented by the tattvic symbol of Akasa, the indigo or black oval. The crown chakra and the Sephira Kether are attributed to the space above the Star Temple's dome.

Continue the meditation sequence. Journey to the Antechamber of the Stars. You will have received your gift there and can thus travel onward. Night has come to this inner land. Upon the shrine of the Goddess of the Gateway you find a key which will allow you to open the obsidian door. Once this is open you are able to pass through to find another spiral stairway leading upward. In the stairwell is painted a mural depicting the Nine Muses as detailed earlier in the chapter.

At the head of the stairway is another doorway, studded with precious gems in the shape of the constellation of the Great Bear, sometimes called the Plough or Big Dipper. Use your key again and this door will open. Before you is a large circular room. As you are about to step forward, you have the impression that you are stepping out into a star field for it seems that the floor is not solid but made of space and stars. However, you do step forward and find that the floor is made from a luminous black substance, like obsidian. As you look up you see that the ceiling is a pure, transparent crystal dome which allows for the night stars to be reflected upon the floor giving the illusion that you are walking in the far-flung star fields. About the walls you see set out the astrological symbols of the planets Mercury ☿, Venus ♀, Mars ♂, Jupiter ♃, Saturn ♄, Uranus ♅ and Neptune ♆. These correspond to the seven sacred planets mentioned previously in the text.

As you come to the centre of the room, the figure of a white-robed, veiled priestess steps out from the walls and greets you in the name of the Goddess of the Stars. She wears upon her brow a circlet of silver, with a translucent crystal at its centre. As in your previous encounters allow the Priestess of the Stars to introduce you to the mystery of the Temple of the Stars and, indeed, to the mysteries of the stars themselves. Open yourself to her teachings and ask whatever questions come to you, including how you can work with the symbols around you. In due course the priestess will give you a symbol which you can place in your pouch. This is symbolic of your star self and spiritual path.

She encourages you to approach the symbols upon the walls and you see that before each is a small shrine dedicated to the Goddess as she relates to that planet. There is also at the opposite side of the Temple an altar cut from pure crystal upon which is a representation of the Star Goddess.

On any occasion, you may request the priestess to light the candles upon the planetary shrine you wish to work with. You may then find yourself becoming aware of the symbol softly glowing. The candles grow until they become two pillars. The planetary symbol becomes a doorway through which you may pass with the priestess to experience the inner world of that planet and the associated Goddess(es).

You may also wish to connect directly to the Star Goddess. To do this you approach the main altar and in your own words address the Goddess. A pure white radiant light pierces the dome of the temple and a beam of starlight illuminates the altar. You find yourself drawn up in your spirit body. Up the beam of light, through the top of the dome and out into the night sky. Faster than light you travel up into the night sky. Below you is the Earth, the Moon and the planets. In the distance is the Sun yet you are drawn even higher and find yourself within the galactic star fields. You may be drawn to visit another star system or the Palace of the Star Goddess which made of pure crystalline light. Here you may meet with the Lady of the Stars and speak of many things.

When it is time for you to return to the Temple you do so in a magnificent ship made from a glistening white wood and in the shape of a swan. This is the ship of the Star Goddess. It brings you swiftly back to the Pillar of Isis where you alight and drift down to find yourself once more within the Temple of the Stars.

Give thanks for your experience and return to your body as usual. Close down and ground yourself. Write up your notes of the experience.

Chapter 14

Symbols Within the Pillar

The material of the next two chapters focuses on further uses of the Pillar of Isis. This chapter discusses in detail the accompanying diagram, on which have been placed correspondences within the outline of the Pillar and its various temples. This is to supply you with the means, if you so wish, of extending your work within the Pillar by using it as a base from which to explore the mysteries of the Goddess as they apply to astrological, planetary and Tarot attributions.

In my suggestions of Deities associated with the Pillar I have also included some Gods. Some of my readers may feel uncomfortable with bringing aspects of the God into this place and wish to keep the Pillar as an expression of the Goddess only. I leave this as a matter of personal choice.

Also, the 33 rituals of the fellowship of Isis's Liturgy (see Bibliography) may be placed within the Pillar of Isis. However, these have not been detailed here. Readers wishing details of these correspondences may write to the Lyceum of Isis-Sophia directly (see page 306).

The Pillar and the Tarot

With respect to the Tarot Trumps, I will mention each Trump and the Suits of the Lesser Arcana cards as they are attributed to each Temple. There is such a wealth of books on the subject, as well as Tarot packs, each one with its own particular interpretation of the symbolism, that I could not truly do the subject justice in the space I have remaining. However, I will include a key-word or phrase associated with each Trump.

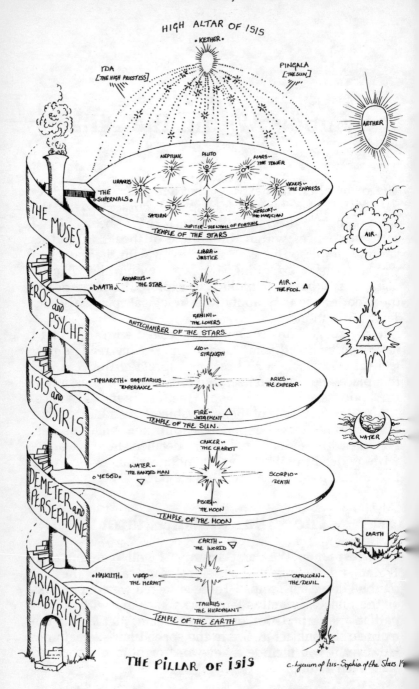

HIGH ALTAR OF ISIS
• KETHER •

IDA [THE HIGH PRIESTESS]   PINGALA [THE SUN]

AETHER

NEPTUNE   PLUTO   MARS — THE TOWER
URANUS   VENUS — THE EMPRESS
THE SUPERNALS
SATURN   MERCURY — THE MAGICIAN
JUPITER — THE WHEEL OF FORTUNE
TEMPLE OF THE STARS

AIR •

THE MUSES

LIBRA — JUSTICE
AQUARIUS — THE STAR
• DAATH •   AIR — THE FOOL △
GEMINI — THE LOVERS
ANTECHAMBER OF THE STARS.

FIRE

EROS and PSYCHE

LEO — STRENGTH
• TIPHARETH • SAGITTARIUS — TEMPERANCE   ARIES — THE EMPEROR.
FIRE — JUDGEMENT △
TEMPLE OF THE SUN.

WATER

ISIS and OSIRIS

CANCER — THE CHARIOT
WATER — THE HANGED MAN ▽
• YESOD •   SCORPIO — DEATH
PISCES — THE MOON
TEMPLE OF THE MOON

EARTH

DEMETER and PERSEPHONE

EARTH — THE WORLD ▽
MALKUTH • VIRGO — THE HERMIT   CAPRICORN — THE DEVIL
TAURUS — THE HIEROPHANT
TEMPLE OF THE EARTH

ARIADNES LABYRINTH

THE PILLAR OF ISIS

c. Lyceum of Isis - Sophia of the Stars 1...

SUMMARY CHART

Temple	Symbolic Shrine	Tarot Trump	Tarot (Other)	Some Suggested Goddesses/Gods
Earth	Earth	XXI World/Universe	Pentacles/Discs	Gaia/Demeter/Persephone
	Taurus	V The Hierophant		Skadi/Tauropolus (Crete)
	Virgo	IX The Hermit	Princesses (Pages)	Dana/Vesta/Ceres
	Capricorn	XV The Devil		Oshun/Inanna/Herne/Pan
Moon	Water	XII Hanged Man	Cups	Arianrhod/Mannanan/Tiamat
	Cancer	VII The Chariot	Queens	Virgin Mary/Mother Goddess
	Scorpio	XIII Death		Cerridwen/Cailleach/Melusine
	Pisces	XVIII The Moon		Triple Goddesses/Tanith
Sun	Fire	XX Last Judgement	Wands	Brighid/Paravati/Horus
	Aries	IV The Emperor	Kings	Durga/Amon-Ra/Athena
	Leo	VIII Strength		Sekhmet/Bast/Freya
	Sagittarius	XIV Temperance		Epona/Rhiannon/Brynhild Artemis
Ante-chamber of Stars	Air	0 The Fool	Swords	Mut/Neith/The Shekinah
	Gemini	VI The Lovers	Knights	Tefnut/Eve/Lillith/Psyche
	Libra	XI Justice		Muses/Astraea/Maat/Kwan Yin
	Squarius	XVII The Star		Aradia/Tara/Sophia
Stars	Spirit/Pluto	—	—	Peresphone/Devi/Nuit
	Mars	XVI The Tower		The Morrigan/Athena/Kali
	Venus	III The Empress		Aphrodite/Freya/Erzulie
	Mercury	I The Magician		Sophia/Hermes/Minerva
	Jupiter	X Wheel of Fortune		Hathor/Hera/Zeus/Odin
	Saturn	—		Nephtys/Norns/Fates
	Uranus	—		Morgan/Isis-Urania/Themis
	Neptune	—		Yemaja/Nimue/Sea God/desses
Beyond Pillar	Moon energy	II High Priestess		Isis/Inanna/Diana (Aradia)
	Sun energy	XIX The Sun		Grainne/Isis/Ra/Apollo

See Chapters on Temples for other associated Goddesses.

Although I personally favour classic Tarot images, there are a number of Tarot decks which have been produced with a strong feminine theme to compensate for the perceived patriarchal bias of the usual decks. These include *The Book of Aradia, Daughters of the Moon Tarot,* and *The Motherpeace Tarot.* As these utilise 22 Trumps they can be used in place of the ones I have mentioned.

With respect to the images of the Tarot, these, while popularly considered a system of divination, are used extensively within the Western Mystery Tradition as keys to gain experience of the Inner Planes. The 22 Trumps of the

Major Arcana are attributed in esoteric lore to the 22 letters of the Hebrew alphabet and to the 22 paths of the Qabalistic Tree of Life that were mentioned in Chapter 3.

Working actively with the images of the Tarot, themselves based on archetypal energies, can lead the traveller to an experience of the inner reality behind those energies and touch on other realms of existence. This type of inner journey is usually called 'pathworking' as the way chosen is one of the symbolic paths of the Tree of Life which connect the various Sephiroth. Referring back the Tree of Life in Chapter 3 delineates these pathways and the Tarot Trump commonly attributed to them.

The usual format of a pathworking is that the card chosen will form a doorway through which the inner traveller passes. At a certain point in their journey they will see the astrological, elemental or planetary symbol associated with the Trump and the associated Hebrew letter as well as approaching the Temple of the Sephiroth which lies at the end of their journeying.

For example, the first Qabalistic path encountered as one journeys is the 32nd which begins at Malkuth, the sphere of the Earth, and terminates at Yesod, the sphere of the Moon. Within the mind's eye will be visualised the Temple of Malkuth with appropriate symbols and in the East will be placed a doorway upon which is visualised the image of the Tarot Trump the World. For those not familiar with this image it is usually that of a Goddess or hermaphroditic figure dancing within a wreath of stars attended by the Four Holy Living Creatures, which represent the fixed astrological signs; the Bull (for Taurus), the Lion (for Leo), the Eagle (for Scorpio) and Man (for Aquarius).

Whilst the pathway may vary in imagery, due to the various teachings of the group writing it or the imagination of the traveller, certain themes will prevail. As the path from Malkuth is the Gate of Life and Death there will be some form of symbolic passage from this world to the next. This may be crossing over a river or descending into a cave. There may be some form of symbolic encounter with the Goddess of Death in some form where there is a realisation of the continuity of consciousness. At some point the planet Saturn will be seen in actuality or its sigil along with the Hebrew letter attributed to the path. This will indicate that the path is being followed correctly and the traveller is not just wandering. The pathway will be complete with an experience of the Moon Temple of Yesod. After this the way is made back concluding with a return through the doorway of the Trump.

There are now several books available giving texts of path workings for the Tree of Life and Tarot imagery which can be effectively utilised for solitary or group work or as suggestions for writing your own. These include Dolores Ashcroft-Nowicki's *The Shining Paths* (Aquarian, 1983) and *Inner Landscapes* (Aquarian, 1989) and Ted Andrews's *Imagick* (Llewellyn Publications, 1989). These books always contain, as does this one, warnings to approach these visualisations with common sense and discrimination, for it is possible to burn oneself out with an excess of esoteric work. Time is needed, often years, to truly assimilate the experiences of these pathworkings.

TAROT JOURNEY

If you are drawn to work with the Pillar as a focus for exploring the Tarot, you might try the following approach.

Place before you the Tarot card you wish to meditate upon or explore. Journey to the Temple of the Pillar to which that card is attributed. Make a connection with the Priestess of that Temple. She will then bring your attention to the image of the Tarot card you are working with as it exists in that place. This may take the form of a doorway where you can enter the symbolic world of the card. Alternatively you may find that the card becomes alive and the symbols and characters within come and speak with you. Be open to what happens and look to the Priestess to facilitate the experience. As always on your return to normal consciousness write up notes of your meditation.

After the following material on the correspondences, I will give some short examples of possible rituals which can be constructed using the Pillar as their focus. As with the pathworkings mentioned above, ritual can be an extremely powerful experience. When one is new to ritual working there is often a tendency to cram in as much experience of ritual as time allows. Difficulty arises when, without proper supervision or assimilation of the experience, the changes in consciousness that are experienced may have disruptive ramifications in the life of the participant. These are not, in themselves, negative, but can manifest as challenges which in the short term can be upsetting. When I have been working in group settings, one ritual a month is plenty. To really assimilate the material and experience of a ritual may take many months.

The pattern given of attribution of the shrines to the Quarters as given below and on the diagram is one which occurred to me intuitively when I worked out the system. However, feel free to change these as feels appropriate. This is not meant to become a fixed system but a map which may be altered by the individual user.

The Temple of Earth

To the Temple of Earth are attributed the Zodiacal Earth signs of Taurus, Virgo and Capricorn. Rituals worked here will invoke Goddesses and Gods of Earth and will have as their intention links to the experience of incarnation upon the earthly plane. Ritual themes may also include physical and planetary healing: prosperity, the consecration of a place of working or new home, rituals for physical protection and those which celebrate the bounty of the Earth.

I have attributed the Mysteries of the Labyrinth to the passage where we enter the tunnel leading to the Temple of the Earth. This refers to the Labyrinth through which candidates for initiation must first travel to gain the knowledge of their true selves and encounter their shadow selves which have been cut off and regulated to the underworld of the Labyrinth. The myth of Theseus and his encounter with the Minotaur of Crete may be used to illustrate this process. For the candidate the revelation of the shadow comes as a shock but the Thread of the Goddess is the shining cord that leads the candidate back to the entrance where their healing may begin.

Within the main area of the temple is located the Shrine of the Earth Mother which we have encountered previously. It is in the North of the Temple and is attributed to the element of Earth, the planet Saturn as well as the

Tarot Trump The World (The Universe). Key thought: Completion. The End and Beginning.

The shrine of Taurus is found in the Southern quarter of the Temple. The Tarot Trump is The Hierophant whose equivalent is the High Priest of the Mysteries. His key words are: education and spiritual authority. Ritual themes incorporating Taurus may include steady growth of physical skills, prosperity, stability, groundedness. Also rituals for animals, crop growth and fertility. Spring/ Summer rituals.

The shrine of Virgo is found in the Western Quarter and to it is attributed the Tarot Trump of the Hermit. Its key words: withdrawal, the inner search and contemplation. Themes for ritual may include the attainment of analytical and organisations skills, bringing a sense of order to any situation. Autumnal rituals.

Finally the shrine of Capricorn is found in the East. To it is attributed the Trump of The Devil/Horned God. This Trump in some modern decks is associated with the Green Man or Horned Consort of the Goddess. Key words: self-limitation and restriction. Ritual themes centred on Capricorn may include seeking practical achievement, self-confidence and independence. Winter rituals.

With respect to the Minor Arcana of the Tarot the suit of Pentacles/Discs is placed here as well as the four Princess Court cards (in some packs referred to as the Pages).

The Temple of the Moon

The entrance to the Temple of the Moon was decorated with the Mystery of Demeter and Persephone which has been discussed in Chapters 9 and 10.

The Moon Temple is associated with the Element of Water and to it are assigned the astrological Water signs of Cancer, Scorpio and Pisces. Goddesses and Gods of the Moon and Sea may be worshipped and connected with here. Ritual themes suggested are those linked to the acquisition and refinement of psychic and divinatory skills, protection from psychic forces, past life work and emotional health and healing. Healing work may also be linked to the cleansing of the bodily system as well as associations with water as the source of life. Rituals for the Sea and marine life are also appropriate.

Here you may wish to explore the story of the Celtic Goddess Ceridwen who owns the Cauldron of Inspiration and Wisdom and the tale of the boy Gwion Bach who accidentally drinks of the potion within the cauldron. After many transmutations pursued by Ceridwen, he is reborn from her womb as Taliesin, the Bard and Prophet.

In the West of the Temple is found the Shrine of Water. Rituals may be done for the cleansing of the waters – seas, rain, wells and springs as well as healing work suggested above. The Tarot Trump of The Hanged One (Man) is assigned here. Its key phrase is surrender and wisdom gained through hardship and voluntary sacrifice.

The astrological shrine in the North is that of Cancer to which is attributed the Tarot Trump of the Chariot which has esoteric associations with the search for the Holy Grail/Cauldron of the Goddess. Key words: Triumph/Victory. Rituals linked to emotional healing, calmness, forgiveness, childbirth and parenthood. Rituals for protection of women and children and from any type of psychic or magical interference. Rituals to assist healing where tumours or cancer have been diagnosed or surgically removed.

In the East is the shrine of Scorpio whose prime mystery is Change. It is often associated with strong emotions, sexuality and the secrets of life and death. The Tarot Trump attributed here is Death whose key words are: change and transmutation. Ritual themes may look towards the transmutative energies of the kundalini shakti and connection with the Scorpion goddess of magic, Selket of Egypt. Also assistance with moving through difficult times and coping with change, past life regressions and coming to terms with karmic problems.

In the South is Pisces and to this is attributed the Tarot Trump of the Moon. Its key words are: the laws of flux and reflux, illusion, dreams, feelings and intuition. Ritual themes can be linked to these preceding ideas as well as mystical awareness and devotions.

Also attributed to the Temple of the Moon are the Minor Arcana suit of Cups and the four Queens of the Court cards.

The Temple of the Sun

The Antechamber of the Sun which leads to the Temple of the Sun is dedicated to the Mystery of Isis and Osiris which has been discussed in Chapter 10. It indicates the awakening to new life by Isis herself as well as the further level of life in the mysteries where consciousness of the God is also gained.

The shrines of the Sun Temple link to the Zodiacal Fire signs of Aries, Leo and Sagittarius. Goddesses and Gods of the Sun and Fire may be worshipped and connected with here. Ritual themes may include healing linked to the immune system, recovery after invasive surgery or accident. Rituals for energy, creativity, fertility and growth based on the Sun's cycle. Generally vigorous, life-affirming rituals.

Within the Temple of the Sun to the South is found the Shrine of Fire. Attributed here is the Tarot Trump called The Last Judgement/The Aeon which has esoteric associations with the movement from the Age of Pisces to the Age of Aquarius. Its key words are: awakening to a higher state, evolution and renewal. Ritual themes of Fire as above may be explored as well as unlocking the life force of the kundalini as the Inner Sun.

The shrine in the East is linked to Aries wherein the Trump of the Emperor is assigned. Its key words are: temporal power and authority, kingship. A suggested theme is a purification ritual wherein we face the destructive and aggressive energies within and with the Goddess's help re-direct them towards constructive, life-affirming ends. Rituals themes may include those for self-confidence, to promote leadership qualities, initiative and to get things moving!

In the North is the shrine of Leo where is attributed the Tarot Trump of Strength. Its key words are: purity of heart, spiritual strength, love and courage. Ritual themes to connect with inner sovereignty, the seven gates of the chakras, to promote strength, courage and greatness of heart. Rituals honouring feline goddesses such as Sekhmet and Bast, animal welfare and healing rituals are very appropriate here.

In the West is the shrine of Sagittarius to which is

attributed the Tarot Trump of Temperance. Its key words are: transmutation of opposites, inner alchemy, combination. Ritual themes may explore the responsibility that comes with power as well as the acquisition of philosophical knowledge and how we may weave the Rainbow Bridge which links our world to that of the Deities. Rituals to protect animals in the wild and healing for horses. Goddesses associated with horses such as Epona, Rhiannon and Brunhild may be honoured here.

The suit of Wands is placed here along with the four King Court cards.

Antechamber of the Stars

To the Antechamber of the Stars is attributed the element of Air and therefore all of the Zodiacal signs attributed to Air – Gemini, Libra and Aquarius are found here. Goddesses and Gods of knowledge and wisdom as well as those who are winged in any way may be invoked and connected to here. Ritual themes may include healing linked to illness of confusion and to engage the mind of the patient in the healing process. Also, rituals to assist with learning difficulties, irrational fears and improving memory. Rituals linked to learning and to gain knowledge, also for inner peace, centredness and self-awareness. Weather magic and rituals in connection with birds and for safe travel.

The Shrine of the Air is found in the East and may be depicted by the figure of the Winged Isis. Attributed here is the Tarot Trump of The Fool. Its key words are: new beginnings, potential, expect the unexpected. In addition to ritual themes as above one suggestion is an invocation of Neith, the ancient Egyptian Goddess of Time, to become time travellers with her so that we may know both our past and future and, therefore, understand more of our appointed path.

In the South is the astrological shrine of Gemini. To this may be attributed Twin God/desses such as Apollo and Artemis, Diana and Lucifer and others where bi-polarity of Light/Dark are explored. Here is attributed the Tarot Trump of The Lovers. Its key words are: choice, partnerships and sharing on many levels. Ritual themes may explore the quest for Inner Truth and the recognition of the bi-polaritity of each soul whatever physical gender we now incarnate as.

To the shrine of Libra in the North you may attribute Goddesses such as Kwan Yin who incarnated as a Boddhisattva to bring enlightenment to humankind along with Goddesses of Justice and Truth such as Maat and Astraea. Its Tarot Trump is Justice with the key words of: equilibrium, cosmic law and divine justice. Rituals associated with legal matters are appropriate here as well as those to promote peace and harmony. As Libra is associated with beauty, love and the arts, rituals linked to romantic love and relationship, to encourage artistic skills and to heighten appreciation of beauty may be done here. It is a sign of balance so ritual aimed at correcting imbalances and to regain, with the Goddess's help, a sense of perspective are also very suitable.

In the West is the shrine of Aquarius to which is attributed the Tarot Trump The Star. Its key words are: hope, inspiration and the realisation of possibilities. Ritual themes here are linked to the healing brought by the establishment in our awareness of the Aquarian Grail which promises harmony for all beings, enlightenment and the opening of the doors of perception to higher levels. Rituals of communion, friendship and platonic love.

To this Temple is attributed the suit of Swords and the Court cards of the Knights.

The Temple of the Stars

The entrance to the Temple of the Stars is dedicated to the Nine Muses who each are attributed to a planetary sphere as discussed in Chapter 13. This charts the journey of the initiate through the spheres of the Underworld/Earth, Moon, Sun and into the realm of the Stars; indeed the journey taken by each of you who have worked through this manual.

The Temple of the Stars is attributed to the Element of Spirit. The shrine of the Spirit will be personal to each of you and has been indicated on the diagram by Pluto and the Holy of Holies. Each must discover the name of the Goddess whose image is contained upon their Holy of Holies. It is not for me or anyone else to determine.

The other shrines of the Temple of the Stars are associated with the seven planets explored in Chapter 13 along with attendant goddesses. Rituals for the planets may take many forms depending on your intention. In general they may pack more of a punch than rituals worked under the Zodiacal shrines. You may focus on the planetary shrines as various stages of your initiatory quest and to achieve ends linked to the planet's particular energies.

The first shrine is dedicated to Mars and to this is attributed the Tarot Trump of the Tower. Its key words are: drastic change and conflict, the shattering of structures. A possible ritual theme is learning to wield positively the weapons of magical power. These may be represented by the Elemental weapons of Wand, Sword (Athame), Cup and Pentacle or the Four Treasures of the Tuatha De Danann, the Spear which brings Victory and Healing, the Sword of Light, the Cauldron of Plenty and the Stone of Rulership.

The second shrine is dedicated to Venus and to this is attributed the Tarot Trump of The Empress. Its key words are: Queenship, fruitfulness, love and beauty. Rituals themes of love, sexuality, attraction and harmony may be placed here. A more abstract theme to be explored may be the connection with the Divine Anima/Animus of the seeker.

The third shrine is dedicated to Mercury. The Tarot Trump of the Magician is placed here. Its key words are: magical will and potential, intelligence and skill. Rituals for communication, intelligence and those linked to science (mundane or occult). An abstract theme for a ritual centring on Mercury might contain hermetic lore and symbolism along with an experience of the Goddess of Wisdom, Divine Sophia.

The fourth shrine is dedicated to Jupiter. Its Tarot Trump is The Wheel of Fortune whose key words are: life's natural cycles, fate and fortune – good or bad. Rituals linked to positive expansion, prosperity and success are well placed here. An abstract theme for a ritual could involve the gaining of the gifts of the planet Jupiter including sovereignty, nobility, friendship and success. In a ritual of Jupiter you may experience a deep sense of happiness and of the positive qualities of daily life as well as a sense of the family of the Deities.

The fifth shrine is dedicated to Saturn. The World/Universe may also be attributed here. Ritual themes can link to time (usually the past), the setting of limitations as well as bindings of all types. Rituals to access the Akashic Records and the development of mind and soul in perfect balance.

The sixth planetary shrine is dedicated to Uranus. There is no classical Tarot attribution for the Trans-Saturnian planets, for when the cards were designed these planets were unknown. Uranus is considered the higher octave of Mercury and to it may be attributed ritual themes linked to the acquisition of magical abilities, creativity, social reforms, invention, to gain insight and express freedom as well as future-oriented rituals. An abstract theme linked to Uranus can be the awareness of the Divine Language of symbols and the understanding of the lore of the cycles.

The seventh shrine is dedicated to Neptune. The planet is considered the higher octave of Venus and rules the Unconscious. Ritual themes for Neptune may include vision quests, the opening of mystical awareness, artistic inspiration and sea magic. The lost mysteries of Atlantis and Lemuria are attributed to Neptune and a ritual may be enacted to seek and to integrate these lost arts with our current consciousness.

The eighth shrine is dedicated to Pluto as the planet of inner changes. It is a planet of spiritual transformation, life, death and rebirth. Here is assigned the Shrine of the Spirit. Rituals here will be linked to Rites of Passage and inner initiations through the Spheres.

Beyond the Star Temple

Above the Pillar, where I have attributed the crown chakra and the Qabalistic Sphere of Kether, may be experienced Cosmic Consciousness. This is the initiation which is not, indeed cannot, be conferred by human hands but is received directly from the Goddess herself bestowing an awakening to full life and realisation of our destiny and true purpose.

I have also placed here the two streams of energy that exist in the human body associated with kundalini shakti that are called the Ida (Moon energy) and Pingala (Sun energy). To these I have attributed the Tarot Trumps of The High Priestess and The Sun respectively. For the High Priestess key words may be: the Goddess Within, Triple Goddess, Intuition and the Mysteries. For the Tarot Trump of the Sun, key words may be: positive energy and achievement, happiness and health.

Following are two rituals drawing on the material above which may serve as examples for your own rituals.

EXAMPLE A: RITUAL OF HEALING

Intention: Healing to be sent in absence to a friend who is suffering from kidney problems. Will be centred in Temple of Moon at the Shrine of Water and Goddesses Isis and Yemaja with attendant Gods Osiris and Obatala (Nigerian Sky/River/Father God).

Tools needed on shrine: candle (blue or white) and incense (choose one with Water/Moon associations). Bowl with spring water, bowl with sea salt. Images of Isis and Osiris may be utilised and between them placed a representational link, such as a photograph, with the one being sent healing.

Ritual may be done entirely 'astrally' – that is you may journey to the Temple of the Moon wherein you will do the ritual in its entirety or you may do the ritual physically and before its climax journey to the Temple of the Moon for a period of contemplation and meditation there.

Light candle and incense. Do preliminary creation of sacred space with Quarter Guardians, if you wish. Then following invocations carrying incense as you address quarters.

East: *Blessed Isis, Lady of the Moon and Waters, Mistress of All Magics and the Healing Arts, I would ask Your blessings and Inspiration that I may enact this rite of healing for . . . and be a channel for Your touch.* (Salute East)

South: *Obatala, Mighty Father, God of Purity and of the River Springs, I would ask Your blessing upon this Rite of Healing.* (Salute South)

West: *Yemaja, Goddess of the Seven Stars and Seven Seas, as Your Waters flow to the shores and sink into the waiting sands, I would* ask that Your blessings flow into me that I may enact this Rite of Healing. (Salute West)

North: *Osiris, Lord of Amenti and Consort of my Beloved Lady Isis, You who know of the powers of death and rebirth. I would ask for Your blessings and inspiration and also that You mediate these healing energies to . . . if this be in accordance to their destiny and True Will.* (Salute North)

Return incense to Altar/Shrine. Water in bowl is then purified and blessed in the name of Obatala: *Obatala, may these waters be as the waters of thy springs, pure and sweet and blessed.*

Salt is then blessed in the name of Yemaja: *Yemaja of the Sea, bless this salt that it may conjoin with the waters of the river's springs and thus embody the bittersweet essence of Your Seas.* (Mix together) *From the salty waters comes forth the essence of all life.* Bowl of water/salt is taken around the Circle and Elemental Quarters are saluted.

Return to Shrine and kneel before it, holding bowl between your hands. Meditation may be done here to link to energies of Moon Temple/Shrine of Water. Then concentrate, feeling the energies of the Goddesses Yemaja and Isis flowing through you and into the mixture.

As this energy flow peaks say: *I am the Daughter/Son of the Goddess. By the power of salt and water, this is true and this is real, this is the substance that shall heal!*

Sprinkle the water upon the images of Isis and Osiris (if present) and upon the representation of the one being healed with the words: *Great Isis, let these healing waters restore to health Thy chosen child . . ., just as You through Your art restored to health Your Consort and Brother, Osiris. May healing come to all who are in need, let joy touch the Earth again.*

Thanks is then given to the Goddesses and Gods and the Sacred Circle is disbursed as feels appropriate. Blessed water may be used to regularly anoint the photograph/representation of the one being healed or given to them (or sympathetic relative) to regularly anoint them.

(Note: Ritual of Healing inspired by 'An Isis Healing

Eucharist' written for Lyceum of Isis-Sophia by Rev Steve Wilson, Priest-Hierophant, 1988.)

EXAMPLE B: RITE OF AQUARIUS

Intention: To gain an experience of energies of Aquarius especially for inspiration. Will be centred at Shrine of Aquarius in the Antechamber of the Stars and also use Tarot Trump of the Star as meditational focus. Invocations to Aradia and the White Tara, both Goddesses who incarnated as Avatars to teach humankind.

Before Ritual: Study material on Aquarius and Tarot Trump The Star and write out a short meditational journey based on its imagery or use Tarot exercise given earlier in the Chapter as part of Ritual. Referring to an astronomy book draw diagram of constellation of Aquarius.

Tools needed: main candle (blue, peacock blue, green-blue); star-map of Aquarius and night-lights or birthday candles (and plasticine to make holders for same) to represent the light of the stars; 2 small glass pitchers (vinegar/oil cruets would be suitable) one containing spring water, the other white grape juice or wine; chalice, incense (pine or patchouli would be suitable), Tarot Trump of The Star.

Light main candle and incense. Create sacred space using ritual from Chapter 4 or your own adaptation. Holding incense aloft invoke at one side of your shrine:

Aradia, Aradia, Beloved Daughter of Diana, I seek Thy aid that I may gain the inspiration of the Aquarian Grail.

You may visualise the Goddess standing before you skyclad bearing the vessels of water and wine. Salute Goddess with incense and move to invoke at other side of your shrine holding incense aloft:

I give homage to Tara, compassionate Mother and Saviouress. I salute You who art the supreme and exalted Tara, keeper of the mysteries of the stars. I would ask for Your guidance that I may be inspired of the star-wisdom of Aquarius and know the truth of its glyph: as above, so below.

Visualise the Goddess seated upon a lotus throne over

which spreads a canopy of stars. She holds in her hands a sword as guardian and a chalice shaped like a lotus.

Lay out the star-map, placing upon it the candles or night-lights. Light these with words:

I honour the stars of the constellation of Aquarius and their divine Guardians that their path may be opened to my inner eyes.

Settle into meditation, journey to the Antechamber of the Stars and stand before the Shrine of Aquarius. Connect with the Priestess of the Antechamber and journey into the landscape of The Star utilising your written meditation or spontaneously as preferred. When experience is complete holding consciousness of the Antechamber. See the Goddess Tara come forth and place her chalice before you. See in your mind's eye this conjoin with your physical chalice on your Shrine. Say:

I honour the Goddess's gift of the Grail of Aquarius.

Then see the form of Aradia standing as the maiden of the Star Trump pour forth the water and wine into the chalice. Mirror the action by pouring the water and wine into your chalice with the words:

With the blessings of Aradia, do the waters of life and the fruit of the vine conjoin within the Grail of Aquarius to become the nectar of divine inspiration.

Drink of the Chalice and take a few moments in contemplation. Give thanks in your own words to the Goddesses for their gift to you. Connect back to the Antechamber and take your leave of it and the priestess, making your way back by your established route.

Return to normal consciousness and disperse your Circle. Offer the remainder of the wine/water as a libation to the Goddess by leaving it upon your shrine or pouring it onto the earth, perhaps by a special tree.

These two rituals may have given you some ideas. The following is a general outline for creating rituals and ritual meditations within the Pillar.

Ritual Guidelines

1 Decide on the goal of the Ritual.

2 Select the appropriate Temple and/or Shrine within the Pillar on which to base the inner aspects of the working and the Goddess/es (and God/s) you will connect to within the ritual.

3 Do some research and study of the symbolism of that Shrine, including the Tarot card attributed, as well as something of the attributes of the Goddess/es to be invoked.

4 Write your invocations and prayers with the intention of the ritual in mind, although you may prefer these to be spontaneous. You may want to include some simple blessings of the elements or other objects (maybe a crystal to be charged with the intention and carried or worn) and simple movements that carry through the theme of the ritual. Also write out details or an outline of the meditation journey within the inner landscape of the Tarot card or through the gateway of the Shrine. Transcribe the ritual in clear, large handwriting, especially if you intend to read sections by candlelight. This can also remain as a permanent record of the ritual.

5 Choose an appropriate time when you are free from distractions. Some may prefer to schedule the ritual on a day symbolically in tune with the working or to consult an ephemeris for an auspicious time (for example, Moon in the appropriate Zodiacal sign). The correspondences for the days of the week are as follows: Monday (Moon/Water), Tuesday (Mars/Fire), Wednesday (Mercury/Air), Thursday (Jupiter/Air/Fire), Friday (Venus/Earth/Water), Saturday (Saturn/Water/Earth), Sunday (Sun/Fire).

6 Gather any items you will need to enact the physical side of the ritual. These may include representations of the Elements: candle (Fire), incense (Air), water in bowl or chalice (Water), salt, a crystal or a bowl of earth (Earth). Some people may like to utilise a wand or Athame in order to more formally define the sacred space.

7 The Ritual:

a) Create sacred space including visualisation and if desired, Guardians. Ritual in Chapter 4 gives a quite formal definition but you may prefer to use personal totemic animals, plants or God/desses who are special to yourself.

b) Invocations and prayers to chosen Deities stating clearly your request for the ritual's intention.

c) Ritual with the meditational journey at its heart.

d) Earthing of the ritual's energy in object or in substance (such as charged water that is drunk and libated).

e) Thanks given to Goddess(es) and Guardians. Energies of the Circle dissipated in a way that the energies are shared as blessings to, for example 'all beings and existences'.

f) Ground yourself and write up notes of ritual for your diary-record. Especially noting dreams in the following days.

MEDITATION: THE TEMPLE OF ISIS

This final meditation work does not take place in the Pillar of Isis but introduces you to the main Temple complex. Do the journey as usual to the island; disembark, bathe and enter your own room. Wait there for your Temple Guide to come to you.

The Guide will lead you, not to the Gardens or the Pillar, but towards the main temple complex which contains formal temples to the Goddess and Gods of Egypt. You are led directly to the main temple which is the Temple of Isis of Ten Thousand Names. Your Guide leads you into an antechamber of the Temple of Isis. Here you are met by a woman and man clad in the ceremonial robes of High Priestess and High Priest of Isis.

They greet you and what happens from here will depend on the depth of contact you have made. It may be that you just talk with them or one, or both, may take you further within the Temple. Here is found the Holy of Holies. Or you may be escorted to another temple within the complex, perhaps the one which links to the statue you made earlier in the course.

SUGGESTED CORRESPONDENCES CHART

Shrine	Colour	Incense	Animal	Crystal/Gem	Tree	Other
Earth	Black/Green	Dittany/Myrrh	Stag/Bear	Rock Crystal	Oak	Gnomes/Winter
Taurus	Rich Brown	Sandalwood	Bull/Cow	Emerald/Jade	Birch	Venus/Spring
Virgo	Yellow-Green	Patchouli	Unicorn/Dove	Adventurine	Pine	Mercury/Autumn
Capricorn	Black/Brown	Benzoin	Goat/Ass	Onyx/Garnet	Beech	Saturn/Winter
Water	Blue/Green	Lotus	Dolphin/Fish	Aquamarine	Willow	Undines/Autumn
Cancer	Green/Silver	Jasmine/Lotus	Turtle/Crab	Moonstone	Yew	Moon/Summer
Scorpio	Red	Ginger/Pine	Eagle/Snake	Topaz	Cactus	Pluto/Autumn
Pisces	White/Green	Gardenia	Fish/Wolf	Amethyst	Water Lily	Neptune/Spring
Fire	Scarlet	Dragons Blood	Birds of Prey	Carnelian	Maple	Salamanders/Summer
Aries	Red/Flame	Cinnamon/Copal	Ram/Sheep	Ruby	Ash	Mars/Spring
Leo	Red-Gold	Frankincense	Lion/Cat	Tigers Eye	Sunflower	Sun/Summer
Sagittarius	Purple/Blue	Honeysuckle	Horse/Dog	Lapis Lazuli	Reed	Jupiter/Winter
Air	Yellow/Blue	Lemon/Lavender	Birds	Flourite	Spruce	Sylphs/Spring
Gemini	Orange	Mastic/Mint	Piebalds	Citrine	Hawthorn	Mercury/Summer
Libra	Emerald	Apple/Rose	Elephant/Dove	Opal	Hazel	Venus/Autumn
Aquarius	Sky-Blue	Sandalwood	Owl/Phoenix	Turquoise	Elder	Uranus/Winter
Spirit/Pluto	Black/Indigo	Frankincense & Myrrh/Kyphi	Spider/Phoenix	Diamond/Sugulite	Ash/Yew	Mistletoe
Mars	Red	Tobacco	Bear/Wolf	Bloodstone	Holly	Tuesday/Iron
Venus	Green/Amber	Rose/Violet	Swan/Dove	Amber/Emerald	Apple	Friday/Copper

SUGGESTED CORRESPONDENCES CHART

Shrine	Colour	Incense	Animal	Crystal/Gem	Tree	Other
Mercury	Yellow	Mastic	Monkey/Ibis	Alexandrite	Palm	Wednesday/Alloys
Jupiter	Purple/Blue	Cedar/Sage	Horse/Peacock	Amethyst/Lapis	Vine/Cedar	Thursday/Tin
Saturn	Black/Grey	Myrrh/Cypress	Raven/Crocodile	Obsidian	Oak/Yew	Saturday/Lead
Uranus	Crimson	Musk/Mastic	Dragon	Fire Agate	Beech	Hallucinogens
Neptune	Indigo/Blue	Lotus/Sandalwood	Dolphin/Fishes	Coral/Pearl	Elder	Opiates
Moon	Silver/White	Jasmine/Camphor	Hare/Camel/Cat	Moonstone	Alder	Monday/Silver
Sun	Gold/Orange	Frankincense	Lion/Bee/Hawk	Topaz	Bay	Sunday/Gold

This will be an individual experience for each of you. In a sense, from now on you are on your own, you may continue to work with the Pillar of Isis in some form or to connect in some other way to the Temple of the Neters, the Egyptian word meaning the gods and goddess. You may go on to seek ordination, formally or through intuitive connection with the Goddess. Some ideas as to where this might lead are explored in Chapter 16.

As always, once the meditation is complete, return completely to waking consciousness and write up your notes.

Chapter 15

The Year of the Goddess
Within the Pillar

This chapter is devoted to eight ritual meditations based on the cycle of the Goddess's year linked to the Pillar of Isis. These particular festivals are not universal, though they are very popular. With some research it is possible to work out a series of festivals linked to any pantheon one would wish to work with. Festivals may celebrate the mysteries of Goddess and God, as do these, or of the Goddess alone. It is also true that any day can be identified with an aspect of the Goddess and celebrated as her Festival.

Books which can assist with relevant dates of festivals and suggested rituals are Lawrence Durdin-Robertson's *The Year of the Goddess* and Diane Stein's *The Goddess Book of Days*, both of which are perpetual calenders for the Goddess and her Festivals.

The scientific, rational, patriarchal world-view is linear and sees life as a progression from birth through maturity to death, worshipping progressive oriented goals. The older way, the way of the Goddess, is represented by the carvings of circles and spirals found carved on stones throughout the world and illustrates the awareness of the circular nature of time and our experience. The celebration of some festivals marking the turning of the year have survived the influence of Christianity but have been incorporated into the mythology of that religion. This was the tactic of Rome even before the Christians came to the fore, to absorb local deities into their own pantheon. However, as successful as this might have seemed at the time, it has allowed the observance of these festivals to quietly continue in practice and in the consciousness of the people. Thus there remain in Western Europe remnants of the pagan festivals.

Those in the West who secretly followed the way of the Goddess – the witches and other magical groups and individuals – utilised as a focal point the yearly cycle of festivals which acknowledged the old ways. As these teachings have once more found an open expression, the eight-fold division of the year has become the pattern for groups and individuals to follow in their celebration of the mysteries.

The festivals fall into two groups, one solar and the other lunar. The four divisions of the solar year are determined by the earth's revolution around the sun and the length of the days and nights. This cycle begins with the Winter Solstice. At this point, where the hours of daylight are at their shortest, rituals are enacted to ensure the rebirth of the Sun. These rituals had the theme of the Sun's birth or the birth of a child of light, the 'sun' of the Goddess. Here are attributed many births of sons and daughters of the Goddess, including Demeter, Persephone, Apollo and Artemis, Mithras, Herne and Cernonnos, Frey and Freya, the Teutonic god and goddess of fertility, Adonis, Tammuz and Horus. The ending of the solar year and the beginning of the new is also marked on 2 January by the nativity of Inanna, the Sumerian Queen of Heaven and Earth. Many of the customs associated with the Solstice have been incorporated into Christmas celebrations of the birth of Jesus Christ, as the Son of the Judaeo-Christian God.

At the time of the Spring Equinox in March the days and nights are equal. Here the festival acknowledges the growing strength of the Sun. This has its height at the time of the Summer Solstice in June on the day of greatest daylight. At the Autumnal Equinox in September, the power of the Sun is on the wane. This festival is marked often by the death of the Goddess's child whether it be the departure of Persephone for her term in Hades, or the death of Tammuz and other fertility gods. In these festivals the harvest is also acknowledged. All of the above festivals fall roughly around the 21/22nd day of the month, as the solstices and equinoxes are astronomical events.

The other division is a uniquely Western European one which has been incorporated into pagan tradition throughout the world as have other exports such as the faerie and Arthurian traditions. As the solar festivals link to planting cycles, the lunar festivals were associated with the livestock cycles of the Celtic peoples. These are also known as fire festivals in recognition of the ritual bonfires which were lit during them. These are the four Celtic Lunar/Fire Festivals: Samhain, Imbolc/Candlemas, Beltaine, Lammas/Lughnasadh. Within the Wiccan tradition these are the major festivals, the Great Sabbats.

Samhain, which has been incorporated worldwide into Halloween and All Hallows Eve on 31 October, marks the Celtic New Year and is acknowledged by witches and druids as their new year. It marks the end of the harvest, indeed in olden times anything left unharvested by this time had to be abandoned, as it was believed that malicious spirits would destroy or contaminate anything unreaped. Livestock apart from breeding stock was slaughtered and the meat preserved for the coming winter. It marks a time of a thinning of the veil between this world and the Otherworld when the mounds of the Sidhe (or Faerie) were open and these folk and the Wild Hunt were abroad. It was a time of chaos and misrule when the natural order of society broke down. This aspect has been incorporated into the 'trick or treat' of modern Halloween celebrations. It was, and is, a time for honouring and feasting the dead, as the spirits of the departed are remembered and acknowledged as guardians of wisdom. Thus it is a time for divination and inner world journeys to the place of the ancestors.

The next festival, Imbolc, falls on 2 February, and is also known as Candlemas or Brighid's Day. It comes at the time when lambing begins and acknowledges the coming of spring and the growing light. It is the time of the Chinese New Year and Christian celebrations of the Virgin Mary. In the United States it has survived as that curious custom of Ground Hog Day, when the behaviour of an emerging ground hog from its hibernation is believed to determine the length of winter weather still to come.

The great fertility ritual of the Celtic year is marked by Beltaine which is celebrated between 30 April (May Eve) and 1 May (May Day). It was the time when livestock was purified by being driven between the Beltaine fires. The fire was also leapt over by those couples seeking to acknowledge their relationships and to ensure fertility.

Again, it is a time of great faerie activity and is marked by unashamed human sexuality, life and fertility. Survivals of this celebration have continued in the maypole dances and the custom of the May Queen who represents the living Goddess for a year and a day. It is believed the May Queen is given the power to bless and to heal, to name children and empower those of her tribe or community. In England, the legends of Robin Hood, Maid Marion and the Greenwood link to May Day celebrations as does the custom of staying up all night to see the May Day sun rise. Children born as a result of May Eve/Day celebrations were considered to be extremely lucky and were given special surnames which acknowledged they were children of the greenwood.

The final fire festival is Lughnasadh, also called Lammas, named for the Celtic Sun and Corn God, Lugh, who dies with the waning year. It marks the time of harvest for both human food and animal fodder. It is a festival which especially honours the God as consort of the Goddess who, as the grain, undergoes the process of death and rebirth. In some ancient traditions the sacred king was actually sacrificed at this time. Held at the point of high summer it was a time for clans to gather together and to hold horse races as well as to trade goods and feast together. It was traditionally a time for people to form attachments and enter into a period of trial marriage which would last a year and a day. If after that time things were not going well the couple would part and not take more lasting vows.

This completes the cycle of the year. The meditations that follow utilise the eight-fold year and the Pillar of Isis. These were circulated throughout 1991 to my current and former students as well as other colleagues in the mysteries. They were done as a linked meditation where we 'met up' at the Pillar, though living in separate cities and, in some cases, countries. The meditations focused upon the inner processes and tides in our life experience marked by these yearly festivals. The ongoing work of the Lyceum of Isis-Sophia of the Stars is concerned with Earth healing projects. This was part of the connection for those joining in. The meditations emphasised this work and were utilised to focus and enhance these projects. They can be done solo or in a group. They can be supplemented with ritual, with journeys to the Pillar of Isis contained within as a meditation period.

The meditations are, in some cases, quite lengthy and complex. You may like to read them out onto audio cassette.

WINTER SOLSTICE

Using the usual meditation text make your way through the Temple of the Earth and Moon to the Temple of the Sun. Stand facing East before a vessel within the centre of the temple containing the sacred flame. Before the Eastern window is an altar upon which stands a cup of clear honey-mead and a golden equal-armed cross with a red rose at its centre. This cross is symbolic of the four Elements in equal balance and the rose of your awakened Spirit. The Priestess of the Sun stands with you there.

Through the arched window be aware of the sun in the Eastern sky. We are here at the time of the Winter Solstice – when the sun is re-born and the time for celebrating the birth of the Child of Light.

Spend a few minutes contemplating the meaning of the Solstice. Also consider your life over the past year and that part of your life which has linked to a concern for the healing of the Earth. This might have been expressed in many ways, inner and outer, perhaps in the form of ritual work, meditation, financial support to various projects or an active concern for the environment through awareness or activity.

As you do this, a shaft of sunlight suddenly streams through the archway and strikes the cross causing the gold to shine and the rose at its centre to blaze with light. Open your heart centre and allow this image of the red rose upon the cross of gold to be present in your heart centre. As you hold this symbol consider the coming year and how you can further this work of mediating healing to the Earth and your connection to the Goddess.

Be aware of others who are with you as part of this work, those known and unknown to you. From the Temple of the Sun send out from your heart, which is filled with the light of the rose-cross, rays of healing and love to all beings and existences. If there is a special project close to your heart, allow it to come into your consciousness and perhaps state it aloud. Allow energy from your heart to reach out for this specific cause and perhaps you might receive some form of insight into how you might further aid that project.

Finally be aware of the energy of the reborn sun bathing the entire Earth in its essence. The priestess steps forth and holds up the cup of mead and the light of the sun imbues the mead with its radiance. She brings it to you and you drink from it and then hold the cup as she takes from it. She gives you the cup to take down to the Temple of the Earth where you place it reverently on the altar before the figure of the Earth Goddess.

Make your way back to the entrance where the ancient guardian sits and be aware that upon her lap lies a small child. You part from her in peace, complete the meditation sequence and return to everyday consciousness. It would be a good idea to write down specific tasks that you felt drawn to work with so that you can note how, in the coming months, you might be able to further this project.

CANDLEMAS/IMBOLC

This time of the year is marked by two celebrations. In ancient Greece it was the time of the Lesser Eleusinian Mysteries which celebrated the return of Persephone (the Kore) from the Underworld. It is also the time of Candlemas, one of the four Fire Festivals within the Native Tradition of Britain, which is sacred to the Goddess Brighid and to the Christian equivalent, St Brighid, the patroness saint of Ireland.

Using the main meditation text make your way first to the Temple of the Earth and collect from there a crystal (you may also like to have a crystal of your own physically present before you).

Ascend to the Temple of the Moon and cleanse the crystal in the pool of clear water there. Then carry on to the Temple of the Sun. With the Priestess of the Sun, stand before the vessel containing Brighid's sacred flame. Upon the altar before the Eastern window stands a cup of wine and the golden equal-armed cross with a living red rose at its centre. Brighid's cross is there also (see Figure 16).

Step forward and place your crystal upon the altar. Be aware, as you do so, that the scene you see beyond the

The Cross of Brighid

tower is that of a winter landscape and that the sun is visible in the South-Eastern sky. Reflect upon what Imbolc means to you both on a personal level and for the world around you. It traditionally marks the conclusion of the Tide of Cleansing and the time when the first flowers of spring begin to show themselves.

Holding these thoughts in your mind, move towards the alcove containing the stairwell leading to the Antechamber of the Stars. Ascend the stairway and sit in a chair placed along the wall of the Antechamber. Become aware of the doorway which leads to the Temple of the Stars. This door opens and there the Priestess of the Stars enters the Antechamber. Standing before you she whispers a word, phrase or gives you a small token gift which relates to the thoughts that you had brought to this place linked to Imbolc. Remember this message clearly so that you can return with it to your waking consciousness.

She, who is a living representative of the mysteries of

Stars and the Stars within the Earth, bids us to depart from the Antechamber. We do so and return to our places around the vessel of perpetual flame in the Temple of the Sun.

The Priestess of the Sun picks up the Bridget's cross and passes it to you. Rotate it in your hands and contemplate its significance. Link to the season and affirm the hope and sense of future that this festival indicates. Place the cross back upon the altar and receive a sip of the cup of wine.

A shaft of sunlight strikes the golden equal-armed cross with its living red rose and as it is so illuminated the light falls upon your crystal. Be aware that the crystal has been consecrated by the sunlight as it was purified by the waters of the Moon. Again visualise the Rose-Cross as existing within your heart centre.

Send out from your heart centre rays of healing and love to all beings and existences. Be aware of any special project linked to healing the earth that may be of special significance to you which you might like to mention at this point. If it feels appropriate speak it aloud.

Be aware of the relationship of the Sun to the Earth, of the fine balance and harmony that there is in this. Before departing the Temple of the Sun retrieve your crystal from the altar and place it in your pouch. The priestess hands you the Cross of Brighid and this is carried through to the Temples of the Moon and the Earth. As you pass the Guardian, hand it to her. As she takes it, you notice that although her face is still veiled the Guardian has herself changed as the Tide has turned and that beneath the veil is a young woman radiant with love, vitality and mirth. The Spring Maiden is still clothed in Winter's robes but that the time of her return is near.

Complete the meditation sequence and return to your everyday consciousness. Again it would help you to make a brief note of your experience, especially of what the priestess said to you.

SPRING EQUINOX

You come in darkness to the Pillar of Isis bearing a torch and passing the black-robed Guardian who extinguishes your light. You come to the Temple of the Earth by the Earth light and travel upwards by the radiance of the upper

Temples. Ascend to the Antechamber of the Stars where you are met by the white-robed Priestess of the Star Temple.

After a period of quiet contemplation she leads you into the Temple of the Stars. Be aware of the constellations above you and especially of the stars whose rising marks the coming of the dawn of the Equinox. Allow the energy of the stars to enter you and be receptive to their healing radiance.

Descend to the Temple of the Sun. The altar to the East and the Temple are decorated with spring flowers and greenery. A chalice of fresh spring water gathered from the Earth Temple stands upon the altar.

Meditate upon the meaning of the Vernal Equinox both within your life and for the Earth. It is the time for sowing seeds, for beginning projects. As the dawn breaks in the clear morning sky, the Priestess of the Sun Temple begins to hum and you join in. The hum becomes a word which is 'Kore'. Other words may come to you calling back the Kore from the Underworld. The sun's rays stream in through the portal illuminating the Temple and those within it.

Allow the Sun to penetrate your heart centre and listen to its voice within you. Take a minute or so to focus on this and feel the return of Spring within your depths. The priestess brings you the chalice and you share the water as companions. She indicates that you should take a flower or some greenery from the altar and she takes up a crown of flowers which she holds before her. Together you journey to the Temple of Earth where you place the greenery upon the altar of the Earth Mother.

You become aware of a young woman robed and veiled in black, wearing a serpent crown, standing before the statue, her arms held up in adoration. She turns and regards you with smiling eyes. The priestess steps forward and assists her to set aside her veil and crown. She places the flower crown upon her head. She also sets aside her sombre garb and stands revealed in robes of green and gold embroidered with leaves, flowers and fruit. The priestess takes the maiden by the hand and leads her before you up the passageway into the spring morning. At the entrance you gather before the Guardian who exclaims with delight that the Kore has returned to the Upper Earth. There is a great sense of celebration and hope for this new cycle of life upon the Earth.

The priestess leaves you as you walk with the Maiden to a place where there is an outpouring of the underground springs. A well has been placed here. Stand before it and listen to the voice of the well through which all wells speak to us. The Kore speaks to you and you share with her your love for the Earth and the Goddess, your hopes and dreams for the future. Together you mediate the vital energy to these and indeed to the whole Earth at this time.

You are keenly aware of the devas of the natural world as they are engaged upon their work in the world. Remaining aware of the new life all about you, return to your normal time and place, bringing from this place and meeting a sense of joy and abundance.

BELTAINE

Go to the well which you encountered at the conclusion of the Spring Equinox meditation and be aware of a great profusion of flowers and greenery all about. You are met there by the Kore who draws water from the well and bids you to bathe your face and hands. She gives you a garland of spring flowers to wear in your hair. At her bidding you gather flowers to bring into the Temple.

She leads you to the entrance-way of the Pillar of Isis through to the Temple of the Earth. There you place lovingly the flowers and greenery you have brought before the image of the Mother. Be aware of the vibrant springtime energy of the Earth. You are led by the Kore to the Temple of the Moon and then up into the Temple of the Sun which is already bright with spring flowers.

Before the Eastern archway is suspended a clear white quartz crystal which refracts the sunlight so that all about the walls of the Temple shine tiny rainbows. Stand before the altar upon which is placed a flowering branch of hawthorn.

Your gaze is directed by the Kore to the land beyond the Pillar and as you do this you seem to leave your body behind and together with the Maiden fly high above the land in the shape of birds. Your visionary eyes are aware of pathways of energy and light running throughout the landscape. Especially be aware of Gaia as a living being renewing herself through the vibrant energies of the springtide.

You are drawn to the sea and there become aware of the energies of the Inner Realms which hold a perfect, pollution-free pattern for the Earth, seas and air. Through holding that pattern in our consciousness and bringing it, through creative thought, back to the outer world, so do we each assist in the manifestation of the healing process of the Earth.

The soft winds assist you in journeying back to the Pillar of Isis where you join again with your body. There in the Temple of the Sun send out love and healing to all beings and all existences. If you wish to direct the energy of your meditation towards any special project or issue linked to Earth healing, then do so. Leave the Temple of the Sun by the usual route and receive of the bounty of this inner place to assist you in your work in the world.

SUMMER SOLSTICE

This Solstice is rich in symbolism of the time when the powers of the Sun are at their height. Midsummer's Eve and Day is another time of the year when the gates to the realms of Faerie stand open. In Brazil, the beautiful Candalaria ceremony is held where the sea-goddess Iamanja, a derivative of Yemaya, the Holy Mother of the Sea of the Afro-Caribbean traditions, is honoured by offerings of flowers and gifts being set adrift in sacred boats. Roses, which feature in this meditation, are especially linked to festivals in June and July honouring Rosa Mundi, the Rose of the World.

You may wish to further earth this meditation by enacting its final section. For this you will need to place before you one or more roses and some form of representation (a map, picture or photograph) of the Earth or part of it. This represents a local area, country, continent, etc, to which you would wish to send the healing energies of the Goddess in her aspect of Summer Queen.

Make your preparations and after relaxing begin your visualisation by making your way to the Pillar of Isis. As you do so, be aware of the lushness of the trees and vegetation and the profusion of summer flowers. Also be aware of the abundant animal and insect life as well as the heat of the summer sun upon your face and body.

As you approach the gateway, greet the Guardian and proceed to the Temple of the Earth. Pause there and be aware of the Earth in her totality, not only of the surface where we make our home but of the energies held within the depths. Journey on to the Temple of the Sun where you are greeted by the Priestess of the Sun. The altar has upon it a wooden disc tablet divided into eight sections representing the 8-fold wheel of the year and also is adorned with summer greenery and red roses. A chalice of honey-mead is present.

Be aware of the sun outside the Pillar as it rises towards noon and the apex of the year's cycle. The Priestess steps forward, takes up the disc and passes it to you, asking that you consider the significance of the Solstice tide. When this is done the circle is replaced on the altar and the priestess then makes invocation to the Sun. You also may salute the sun as feels appropriate.

As the invocation is complete, as if in response, a shaft of golden sunlight falls within the Temple and in it is seen the form of a large golden honeybee. As it buzzes about the altar become aware of a resonate buzzing within your aura. As the bee ascends the shaft of sunlight, follow in your spirit-body. Rise through the atmosphere of the Earth and still higher so that the Earth is viewed as from space as a bright jewel suspended in the indigo, star-studded heavens.

Your attention is drawn to the Sun and to the planet Venus and you perceive that from Venus rays of green and golden energy are streaming towards Earth. Enter this beam and feel within it a sense of great love, healing and compassion for the Earth and all that lives upon it. As this energy nears the Earth it is transformed into a mystic dew of honey and rose petals which transmit the energies of Venus to our home. See with your visionary eyes that deep within the Earth is a living, fiery rose which is the Rosa Mundi, the Heart Rose of the World, and this opens to receive and be nourished and healed by the energies of the sphere of Venus.

The bee which has accompanied you now leads you back

to the Earth and the Sun Temple. Re-orient yourself and receive from the Priestess a drink from the goblet of mead. As always the fruits of the meditation are sent forth as feels appropriate and thanks given to the Summer Goddess for her bounty.

Leave the Pillar and return to waking consciousness. If you have chosen to do this, then as you open your eyes take the rose and place it with intention upon the map or picture you have chosen, making a link with the meditation's energies. Let it remain upon your shrine for the duration of this festival.

LAMMAS/LUGHNASADH

This is the time of the year when the abundance of the harvest is celebrated in various traditions. Aside from the Celtic Fire Festival in the Graeco-Roman mysteries it marks the beginning of the late summer festivals of Demeter and Ceres which celebrate the Goddess as the Source of all life. This is also the time for the Corn Dances within some Native American tribes.

The period of 19 July to 3 August is very significant within the Egyptian tradition as it marks the Festival of Opet, the celebration of the Sacred Marriage of the God and Goddess. It is also the time when Sirius, the Star of Isis, has its heliacal rising which marks the time of the inundation of the Nile and the beginning of the Egyptian New Year.

The theme of this time when the Gods and Goddesses of Egypt were available through ritual and ceremony to the people provides the inspiration for this meditation. Also incorporated are received teachings that during this period the cosmic influences of Sirius, as the Star-Gate, are at their height, making possible contact with stellar influences and beings.

You may wish to have with you the crystal dedicated to this work and a vessel containing spring water. Relax and centre. Make your way as usual to the Pillar of Isis and ascend through the Temple of the Earth and Moon first to the Temple of the Sun. The Priestess of the Sun stands before the altar before the Eastern gate. She gives thanks for the abundance of the harvest and speaks of the meaning of this time of year. In your heart consider the turning of the year and what harvests you are now gathering unto yourself. Connect to how this will be shared with others – your loved ones, special causes that have meaning for you, the inner and outer realms.

The Priestess comes with a bowl containing water she has gathered from the underground spring and anoints your brow with a symbol saying 'may you receive true vision'. As this is done within the meditation you may, if you wish, physically anoint your brow thus. After this is done you ascend to the Antechamber of the Stars and then to the Temple of the Stars. There be seated in a chair placed to one side of the temple and prepare to go even deeper in your journey. You are joined there by the Priestess of the Stars.

A low hum is heard and for a few minutes with the Priestess of the Stars leading, intone the names of Isis and Osiris, Mut and Amon-Ra (or others as you choose). This may be also done aloud. As the chant ends be aware that above your head are the stars, the body of Nuit, Our Lady of the Stars. Be especially aware of quite a number of shooting stars in the sky, the meteor shower of the Perseids which appear during the time of Leo.

You find the far wall of the Temple of the Stars is adorned with a painting of the Black Isis, her winged arms outstretched and her body surrounded by stars. With the priestess as guide you rise in your spirit-body and approach the painting. Your attention is drawn to the constellation of Canis Major depicted above Isis's head and particularly to the binary stars of the Sirius system. You are aware that this painting is a portal to the stars. As you watch, the painting becomes translucent and you see a passageway stretching before you, flanked by seven sets of columns. Step forward into the passageway and become aware of the figure of the Priestess of the Stars beside you. She guides you towards the light at the end of the passageway, passing the columns which are marked with murals depicting gods and goddess. At the end of the passageway you find a beautiful crystalline boat which you board, the priestess guiding it as it glides into a river of stars.

You journey thus and the Priestess gently touches your brow and heart. You now find yourself standing within a landscape of surpassing beauty and you are guided to where you are able to meet with the Goddess who is relevant to your path at this time. Be open to this without preconceptions. It may even be that you are guided to a God whose energies you need to integrate at this time. Through this encounter gain through words, symbol or mind-to-mind contact a sense of your path and part in the unfolding Divine Plan of the Goddess. Do not judge what you are given, it may seem quite insignificant but still have implications beyond what is first apparent. Awareness of the meaning may not come during the meditation but may be as a seed thought which will come to consciousness in the days to come or within a dream.

After you have had this encounter, give thanks for what you have received, withdraw and be led back to the boat and sail the river of stars until you find yourself by the passageway leading back to the Temple of the Stars. Disembark and pass once more the seven gateway pylons and return to the Temple of the Stars.

In the temple merge with your seated form – the painting of the Black Isis once more becomes solid as the Stargate closes. Yet you are aware of the stars above your head and their energies streaming down. Be aware of any messages carried in the starlight.

Now leave the Temple of the Stars carrying the experience you have had back to the world. Pass through the Antechamber of the Stars, the Temples of the Sun and Moon and gather in the Temple of the Earth where the priestess offers a libation and a prayer to the Earth. At this time you may wish to think of any special project close to your heart. Find a way to express your love for the Earth. Be aware that although we are able to soar within the starry realms we each have a sacred trust to this planet and all of its life as stewards holding a unique position individually and collectively. Give thanks and send out the fruits of the meditation.

Journey back as usual and become fully aware of your physical body closing each chakra and properly earthing yourself.

AUTUMN EQUINOX

The Autumn Equinox marks the time when the length of daylight is once again equal to that of night and is the completion of the tide of harvesting when the nights begin to draw noticeably in. Summer is over and we begin to prepare ourselves in various ways for the coming winter. With this equalising of day and night, you stand at a pivotal point in your inner life where new projects may be commenced – usually associated with personal rather than transpersonal aspirations.

Within the Greek tradition the period of the Equinox was the time for the celebration of the Greater Eleusinian Mysteries when Persephone, the Kore, returned to the Underworld and her Mother, Demeter, began her time of mourning while the Earth entered a period of decay and slumber.

In the last few meditations you have been 'flying high' and now is the time for connecting back more fully to the Earth and the inward spiral of contemplation. You may wish to display autumnal flowers and some barley, corn or some other grain upon your shrine along with a candle, a glass of apple juice (or something stronger), some fruit and a small bowl of water.

Take a few minutes before doing the meditation sequence to reflect on your own harvests and what seeds you will be carrying within that will germinate during the winter months. After this light your candle and anoint your brow with water.

Proceed as usual, although as you move towards the opening to the Temple of the Earth you are aware of the changes even here in response to this new season. Move as usual past the statue of the Mother taking whatever time you need to connect with her. You note that autumnal fruits and seeds are placed before this image. You may wish to add to these gifts.

You proceed to the Temple of the Moon where you are greeted by the Priestess of the Moon Temple. She speaks of the significance of this tide and season. Search your heart on these themes. She draws you to look within the pool of crystalline water, the moon-pool at the centre of the Temple. Be aware that within this you see a vision of the Goddess (or God) who has been calling to you in recent times. For a few minutes, although you are in one sense sitting by the Moon Pool with the priestess, your soul goes forth. However, rather than receiving advice or a symbolic gift on this occasion the one whom you encounter in this vision, goddess or god, asks you a question. This is not something to be answered here and now – it is for you to find the an answer in the time that is to come between now and Samhain. It is a form of quest for you on various levels.

If you do not get a direct sense of the question ask for it to be given in a slightly different way – in a dream or through a meaningful coincidence. If need be, physically write it down before proceeding with the meditation sequence.

After this has been done and you have reconnected to the Temple of the Moon, give thanks and proceed to the Temple of the Sun where you join with its priestess to mark the Equinox through a simple ritual of sharing in an atmosphere of goodwill. Fruit, flowers, bread and wine are offered as gifts.

Be aware of the special projects linked to Earth healing that you have been involved with throughout this cycle of meditations (and beyond) and send out, as usual, the energy of this meditation. While in this special inner place make one definite commitment to follow this through in the world whether that be through practical action or supporting with time and/or money a particular charity/ organisation. However small this will serve as a talisman and allow you practically to channel the energies of this and other meditations into the collective. The catchphrase of Friends of the Earth seems particularly apt here – 'Think globally, act locally'.

After this the priestess places her hand over your eyes and you see before you the enactment of a solemn ritual. The Kore, accompanied by the queenly figure of her Mother, Demeter, who has in her hands a sheaf of wheat, approaches the dark entrance to the cave which leads to Hades. There sits Hecate robed in black, red and white. Persephone sets aside her bright crown of flowers and takes from the hands of Hecate the sombre serpent crown and star-strewn black robes which denote her station as the Queen of the Underworld. Demeter wails in mourning as her beloved child departs once more. The grains of wheat fall freely upon the Earth which has already grown barren with her grief.

The priestess once more touches your eyes and the scene

fades. She hands to you some seeds of various kinds and asks that you keep these throughout the wintertide until the time is right for their planting. Take your leave and return by the usual route to the entrance and return to normal waking consciousness, enjoy the glass of juice/wine you have upon your altar, making a libation to the Earth afterwards and the same with the fruit. Do remember to write up the experience and especially your question.

SAMHAIN

As this is both the ending and beginning of the year as marked by the inner tides you might wish to take some time to reflect upon your work with the Goddess over the past twelve months, whether in this or any other context. You may wish to have your crystal present upon your shrine as well as some wine or mead and a small cake or roll. Decorate your shrine for the New Year and have a new white candle present to burn as a remembrance for both your physical ancestors and your spiritual ancestors who have passed into the Otherworld during this year's cycle or previously. Before beginning the meditation light the candle with this intent and spend a few minutes in contemplation of your dead. Remember that as day follows night and spring follows winter, so rebirth follows death and there is no need for sorrow in this remembrance.

Open the meditation and journey to the Pillar of Isis. You are aware that the day is drawing to a close and as you approach the entrance you are aware of two figures. The Maiden who has been the Guardian since the springtide hands the key of her office to the ancient figure of the Wise One who was our first Guardian. You are aware of their gaze and exchange greetings. The Crone takes up her position once more and the Maiden now assumes the role of Priestess of Persephone and guides you into the passageway holding aloft the Lamp of the Mysteries. She takes your hand saying that on this occasion she will be your guide into the Underworld Kingdom of the Earth.

Within the Temple of the Earth she gives invocation to Gaia and suggests you say whatever feels appropriate. She then asks that you take the crystal you have consecrated to this work and place it as an offering to the Earth Mother. Do this.

She then takes from about her neck a symbol upon a chain and places this about your neck. Look on it for this is a special gift from the Dark Maiden who is both guide and initiatrix and this symbol will allow you to connect to her whether in waking life, meditation or the dream state. She leads you to the Moon Temple and then to the Temple of the Sun and remains with you throughout the meditation sequence, standing slightly behind you. The Sun temple is quite sombre in the dying light of the setting sun.

The Priestess of the Sun greets you and invites you to make any declarations of intent as you may wish for Samhain. She councils you that this is the beginning of the cleansing tide when all that is unnecessary and outworn must be put aside or the energies of the time will take them. Before you speak be aware that anything said here is as an oath and will be binding. The priestess will then give an oracle to you which will give you some indication of the path that lies before you. As this is complete she turns to the altar and lights a candle.

You are aware that this act marks the passing of the tide as the New Year begins. The priestess blesses the wine and cake and gives this to you as well as sharing with the Priestess of Persephone. Together you give thanks to the Goddess of the Year for all she has brought you. You may now ask to be led to any part of the Pillar of Isis that feels appropriate and to have there an experience linked to your review of the past year as well as looking forward to that which lies ahead.

When this is complete you return to the Temple of the Earth and your crystal is returned to you. Upon it has been delicately carved a spiral symbolic of the year. Although this pattern is a circle it is also a spiral wherein we return to the same place and yet move onwards upon our journey. The Priestess of Persephone walks with you to the entrance and there takes her leave for until the Spring dawns she will remain here with the one she serves, Persephone. Return to normal waking consciousness and partake of the wine and cake to close you down and write up your experiences.

Chapter 16

Beyond the Pillar

Having completed this series of meditations and exercises you may well be wondering how your work with the Goddess can proceed from here. You may have found, as did many of my original students, that working with these meditations has opened you in such a way that a path has been made clear. Through this you may have been drawn to further express your love for the Goddess either solitarily or in the context of a group or organisation such as the Fellowship of Isis.

You may have already joined with friends or had some experience of working in a group context. Certainly having the opportunity to study together, sharing ideas as well as meditation and worship can be an extremely rich source of growth and possibilities.

We in the West live in a time when a great number of journals and organisations offer opportunities for contact between like-minded individuals and networking that extends a sense of community over large geographical areas. Many towns and cities have shops selling 'New Age' books and products and the proprietors of such places will often have knowledge of local groups and individuals who share an interest in esoteric matters. Larger establishments will often have a national profile and again are usually willing to direct a seeker. It certainly is true that if you wish for contact with others this is usually possible, if not in person, then through correspondence.

I have provided at the end of this chapter a short address list of some national and international organisations working with the mysteries of the Goddess which can be contacted for further information.

Everyone who seeks the Goddess is looking to make

some form of connection with her yet some are drawn by an inner vocational calling to express this relationship as her Priestess or Priest. When we speak of the function of a Priestess or Priest of the Goddess it is a very different role to that of the priesthood of the Judaeo-Christian tradition where the priesthood stands between the worshipper and the God and serves as the only direct contact with Deity.

In the modern mysteries of the Goddess we are not speaking of a hierarchical priesthood but one which acts, when appropriate, as a living channel or mediator of the Goddess and assists those under their guidance to find their own direct connection to the Goddess. The Great Goddess does not demand anything of her children or the sort of obeisance as the patriarchal 'Father God' does. Therefore all life is precious to her and all are honoured whether or not they respect her. To many of us brought up on a diet of 'thou shalts' and 'thou shalt nots' this may be a difficult concept to come to terms with.

To serve the Goddess as a member of her priesthood does not confer a 'higher' or more special relationship with the Goddess. It does, however, denote a commitment. Some groups working with the mysteries of the Goddess prefer to dispense with any formal recognition of priesthood because of this previous patriarchal conditioning.

However, for example, the majority of mixed Wiccan groups will designate every initiate 'priestess and witch' or 'priest and witch' and while covens may have a High Priestess (and Priest) her function is as a facilitator and guide for the group. In many covens this position is held as an elected office. In the context of the Fellowship of Isis, it is usual that an Iseum of the Fellowship will be founded by someone who is either already ordained as priestess or priest or who is seeking ordination. Their experience of running the group will form part of their informal training.

However, while group work can be extremely rewarding, it is only fair to say that no group is immune to the possibility of power politics or game playing of some type. Sometimes this will take the form of those in a position of leadership expecting other members to treat them as if they were the Goddess (or God) incarnate. There is always likely to be those who seek 'groupies' to pander to their fantasies rather than colleagues and co-workers and they usually find them, at least for a time. Sometimes group dynamics will manifest in dependency, scapegoating or take-over bids. For some the dispensing of formal leadership is a solution for this type of syndrome and for others the answer is shunning groups in general.

This is not the only sort of behaviour that can make a group an uncomfortable place to work within, for whenever people gather together, 'group dynamics' will tend to come into operation. What I would hope is that, having worked through the various exercises aimed at self-awareness, you will have gained a clearer understanding of others and your relationships. Also that you will deal with other people with this sense of discrimination and understanding.

I would always advise that you check out any group that you are drawn to. Established groups will always in some way vet those that seek to join it and this should be a two-way process for you should seek to gain 'a reference' on the leader and the ethos of the group. This may seem a cold way of approaching the situation but remember that in opening up to worship and meditation with other people you will be sharing on a very deep level. You need to feel good about that. Through your contact with your Inner Guide and those of the Temple of Isis, it is also a good idea to gain an inner 'reference' on any person or group you wish to align with. Trust your self and your Guide in this for it is much better to remain a solitary worker than to have a negative experience.

There is also the possibility that you might wish to form your own group with friends or to place some form of notice in a journal or local shop. Again it is important to formulate in the early stages both the aims of the group and the format within which it will function for this will provide you with a template to build upon.

I have, over the years, worked in quite a number of groups and experienced the ways in which people relate. It has been at times a difficult experience but I feel that, on the whole, I have grown through it. I have been part of some appalling groups and others which have been positive milestone experiences on my path. I speak of these dynamics not to put you off from ever working in a group context, but simply to inform. Wherever human beings gather, whether in a work or social situation, there will be group dynamics. Unless you completely cut yourself off from contact, you will relate to others in accordance to these sort of dynamics. Whether these are positive or negative will depend on many things.

Group dynamics is a subject often ignored by esoteric writers as it is an uncomfortable one. The American writer, Starhawk, has, in her books *Dreaming the Dark: Magic, Sex and Politics* and *Truth or Dare: Encounters with Power, Authority and Mystery*, written lucidly on group dynamics and the creation of workable group structures. These should be required reading for anyone considering running their own group. It is a good idea for anybody who is interested in, or profoundly affected by these kind of dynamics, to study such practical methods to harmonise the more negative patternings when and if they develop. Being conscious on a group level of such dynamics can be a powerful growth experience for all concerned.

While a group may choose not to have a recognised leader, there are usually people whose innate talents will put them in a position of being the facilitators of the group's activities. That may be the person or persons who have founded the group or the person who functions as the group's administrator.

I would like to share with you a natural cycle corresponding to all tasks which can assist in a group's healthy functioning. The cycle is called the 'Creative Orgasmic Cycle' and is once again based on the pioneering work of Wilhelm Reich expounded by John Southgate and Rosemary Randle in their studies of cooperatives and group dynamics in the 1970s (*Co-operative and Community Group Dynamics – or Your Meetings Needn't Be So Appalling*).

The Creative Orgasmic cycle looks at the sexual cycle in its ideal stages and then applies this to all creative situations, in this case the task of a group. These phases are Nurturing, Energising, Orgasm/Fulfilment and finally Relaxation. In the sexual act this relates to the gentle touching and stroking of initial foreplay which 'heats up' to passionate foreplay resulting in orgasm and then the gentle touches and caresses after orgasm.

In a group situation the Nurturing phase will be the initial period where people arrive at a meeting and there will be greetings and a general catching up amongst people. This will proceed to the Energising phase as the group approaches and engages the task at hand whether this be discussion, meditation, or ritual.

At some point the main task will 'peak', resulting in a sense of union between the participants. This comes when the 'work' of the meeting is fulfilled: task completed, resolutions made, discussion wound up, meditation or ritual reaching its climax. Sometimes this is gentle and at other times, such as with the conclusion of a ritual, quite intense energy is experienced.

The final phase, Relaxation, comes after the work and can take the form of a sharing of food and drink, informal discussion of the working and leave-taking from the group situation. It does occur that some individuals in a group, or indeed an entire group, will get 'stuck' at one phase or be unable to function through the complete cycle. For example, the person who cannot disengage from the Nurturing phase and resists work or those who want to proceed immediately to the Relaxation! In a group situation where there is a flexible sense of 'leadership', it will be obvious that there will be some people who function best as nurturers, able to put people at ease and welcome them into the group situation. Others who function as energisers are able to get people moving into the work of the session. Leadership then passes to those individuals who have the ability to bring the energies of the group together and direct them to the climax and finally to people who are excellent at facilitating the relaxation phase.

Thus, in a healthy group, true leadership does rotate no matter what the designation or title of anyone in the group. If you can observe the way in which members function it is obvious that within any group there will be a variety of talents. Whether a role is formally designated or not, it is important to recognise and acknowledge the gifts brought by each member to the whole.

Also, it is important to keep in mind that the totality of anyone's life and experience will be greater than their involvement in a group, as important as this work may become. The bonding within a group will often become very close, taking on the function of a family or clan for its members; but it should be kept in mind that there will remain other important relationships with families and other friends that need to be honoured.

This may seem an overstatement, but the bonding is often very intense in an esoteric group and can result in some individuals having difficulty expressing themselves in a non-esoteric context. As one of my close colleagues is known to quip: 'Honour the Lady, but please not fairies and unicorns 24 hours a day!'

Training for the Priesthood

Certainly, to become a Priestess or Priest of the Goddess does involve at least a lifetime's dedication to that task. Often it is found that women and men drawn to this as a vocation have already undergone some form of initiation and training in the mysteries in previous lives. While this may be so, memories are usually very sketchy or will manifest in instinctive ability.

It is not necessary to be formally ordained though for those who wish to do so organisations such as the Fellowship of Isis and others offer a way in which the desire to be priestess or priest can be ratified through a formal ceremony. In this an already ordained priestess/priest will consecrate the candidate through their own mediation of the Goddess.

Training is a very personal thing. With the people I have trained and ordained as both Priestess and Priests of the Goddess I have found that no two people are the same in the way that their preparation proceeds. There is no doubt that whatever happens, it will involve a period of testing often in the candidate's 'mundane' life. This is neither a game nor an empty honour but a living and practical vocation.

The testing comes from one's own stellar self and from the Goddess herself and again this is unique to each candidate whether formally ordained or when ordination is conferred by direct experience of her. This latter approach is possible and usually will happen in an out-of-body or powerful dream experience which leaves no doubt that something important has happened.

A woman functioning as priestess takes on the mantle of

the Goddess, becomes for a time her 'garment', and for that time she is the Goddess. This is not a matter of ego and a great deal of the training focuses on being able to deal with the altered state of consciousness without succumbing to inflation.

The path to priesthood is chronicled in such works as *The Golden Ass* but there is little contemporary literature on the subject, though this may change as more men gain confidence in speaking forth of their relationship with the Goddess. In speaking with men who are functioning as Priests of the Goddess, there is no doubt that their relationship is intense in a different way to that of a Priestess, but none the less valid for that.

I have spoken in the chapter on the Moon Goddess of how a man may also relate to her through connecting to his Muse. Also there is a teaching which has been spoken of by Dolores Ashcroft-Nowicki and hinted at by Dion Fortune that a priest is essentially made through his relationship with an already initiated priestess and that this is his only route to the Goddess. Certainly this concept has been observed by me many times over the years.

However, I also believe that a man who is truly devoted to the Goddess will find her answering his call. In speaking with a number of men functioning as Priests of the Goddess in various traditions, they have usually come to her mysteries with a relative freedom from patriarchal values and a sense of their own internal feminine nature. Many of these men have more difficulty in relating to the Divine Masculine and in recent years have been seeking to reaffirm male mysteries in a way which compliments their relationship to their sisters and the Goddess without accessing old masculine stereotypes.

Self-training – Guidelines

The question of what is necessary to train towards her priesthood again is likely to depend on the background of each seeker. Most important is their dedication to the Goddess and the wish to express that relationship. When asked by people how to embark upon training, I usually advise that they initially set their own period of preparation: nine months being an optimum time period to symbolise gestation and to address the Goddess that they wish to serve as priestess or priest with a simple request that she prepare them. This deceptively simple act sets into motion a process which indeed will prepare the candidate, which will have little or nothing to do with my work with them. It is more often than not a period of intense testing and I often see my task during this time as being the person to help the candidate to understand the process rather than to be a comforter.

On the more concrete side I have, over the years, identified a number of general guidelines which I have followed with respect to advising others on their preparation for the priesthood.

1 Service and the role of the priesthood. Gaining an understanding of this aspect of the priesthood especially in relation to the community whether this be an actual community, or a 'tribal' community of friends, relatives or others one comes into contact with. Being prepared and able to give advice, healing and, when asked, to be able to conduct rites of passage. This should include an appreciation of the historical and contemporary ideas of priesthood.

  If not already a healer you should try, in some respect, to familiarise yourself with various areas of alternative medicine and psychological therapies so that you are able to direct people to appropriate practitioners. The ability to network and also to deal with compassion and detachment towards those who come to you.

2 Ethics. Within any process of training there is a great deal of emphasis upon ethics. The ethics of any priesthood also involves the just use of the powers contacted. Within Wicca this is partially represented by the Law of Three-Fold Return in that whatever sort of energy sent out will be received back three-fold. As it is likely that a priest/ess will be asked formally or casually to give advice to others relating to their mundane or spiritual lives, strict confidence is a cardinal rule. Whereas in the world at large it may be socially acceptable to share such information with others, once the mantle of the priesthood has fallen on someone's shoulders there is an

association with the position of a 'wise one' and this needs to be respected as a sacred trust.

3 The ability to enter altered states of consciousness and to induce these in others. This can only be gained by direct experience and having the confidence in yourself to control the situation. In my training of others I have utilised the material incorporated into this book to teach the skills of entering altered states of consciousness. The next step was to encourage my students to write their own guided meditations which can be used with others, incorporating soothing images such as sea-shores, meadows and woodland walks to aid in deep relaxation. Books on creative visualisation and hypnotherapy can give many useful ideas. With hypnotherapy I would also usually advise interested students to seek some form of training in order to understand its complicities and to gain practical oral instruction.

4 Competence in one or more methods of divination. It is obviously helpful to have the ability and confidence to consult some form of oracle in order to assist others and where necessary gain one's own sense of direction from an impartial source. There are many systems of divination, from the ability to cast and interpret a horoscope to working with the Tarot, I Ching or Runes. Each system will have its own demands regarding study and training, whether in some form of class, or working with books on the subject. As with learning a foreign language, once one system has been mastered, it is often far easier to gain proficiency in another.

5 Healing and Magical Work. While I do not feel that these are as necessary as some other skills for the priesthood, it is often so that many drawn to the Goddess will also be drawn to express their love for her in some form of healing and magical work. However, any form of magic or healing are skills which are highly specialist tasks and lack of skill in these areas is not something I would consider a barrier to ordination as Priestess or Priest of the Goddess.

6 Devotion to the Goddess. This is undoubtedly the most important of all the aspects of training and this will be covered in depth below.

7 Appreciation of mythology. To approach the Goddess through gaining an understanding of how she manifests in different traditions can be done by simply reading the stories and myths associated with her. Various pantheons or aspects of the Goddess will appeal to different people. There is no hard or fast rule how this takes place. For some it may be the tradition associated with their background or one of a completely different culture. There are many books on Greek, Celtic, American Indian, Teutonic and Egyptian mythology. Other pantheons may be less accessible at first but given a little research there are, in the rich atmosphere of publishing that exists today, likely to be books available.

The Pillar of Isis, structured as it is upon elemental and planetary attributions, can be altered in order to work with your chosen pantheon. All that is necessary is a little imagination and creativity. At the moment there is such a wealth of information and practical material available that there is more danger of being swamped by choices than being starved.

8 The Unwritten Training. There are aspects of the priesthood which of course cannot be conveyed through the written word and which can only be gained through life experience or direct oral teachings. Secret teachings may also be received in dream form or during meditations. Such contacts are possible from working through this course of training.

Devotion to the Goddess

The devotional method which concludes this book is an adaptation of the technique I utilised initially to come into an active relationship with the Goddess. It is a guaranteed technique, which I have never known to fail to have a life-transforming effect. Dion Fortune's classic novel *The Goat-Foot God* is a fictionalised account of a similar working.

1 Time. Choose the Goddess with whom you wish to work in this way. Decide at the outset on the length of time you will take. The minimum period suggested is nine weeks. The idea is to focus intensely on the chosen Goddess so

that every moment of the day is centred on her. Write up your intention in your diary-record as a pledge so that the time is fixed by this.

2 Shrine. Create a special shrine to your chosen Goddess, either in a room set aside for this purpose or in a portion of a room which can remain private. It is best that this working be kept secret so as not to dissipate the energy you are building (although someone with whom you share intimate living space may need to know what you are doing!). The shrine represents the heart of the devotee and should contain an image of the Goddess as a focus and repository for the energies invoked. The decorations and symbols on the shrine should be appropriate to the Goddess worked with as well as any incense, flowers, food and wine offered in the course of your devotions.

3 Ritual. An invocationary ritual is written by the devotee. It is best written in several parts, each reflecting an aspect of the love experienced. For example, that of a lover, a child to a parent, a friend, a sister/brother, a servant, a priest/ess. Once written it is advisable for the ritual to be performed one to three times a day with supplemental meditations in between. Because of time restrictions once a day may be all that is possible but other meditations and guided journeys can be done at other times of the day. Whatever timetable is set up it is a good idea to break one's sleep to do at least one practice in the middle of the night. The purpose of this is to stimulate one's dreamlife. When I undertook such a working I found that these early morning rituals often produced the most powerful effects on my consciousness.

Within the ritual ceremony you can incorporate singing, music and dance (if appropriate to your chosen Goddess). Investigation into the way in which this Goddess has been worshipped as well as incorporating where possible the original language of her invocations. This attention to detail will add to the overall ambiance you create with your rite.

4 A Way of Life. It is very important that your lifestyle during the period of your devotion be pleasing to the

nature of your chosen Goddess. While it is not necessary to go into seclusion for this period of time, you should allow the entirety of your life to reflect your love and devotion to her.

While out in the world a piece of jewellry can serve as a portable image of the Goddess and your invocations can be done mentally when the occasion presents itself. It is essential that you transmute every action, thought and deed into one of devotion. So, as you eat, keep in mind you do this in honour of her; sleeping, working, relaxing likewise. Gratitude and an attitude of thankfulness are also important spiritual exercises.

5 Additional Practices. One valuable technique is to visualise the image of the Goddess within your heart centre, burning like a living flame therein. You can construct visualised journeys to her Inner Temple. Two examples of this technique were mentioned in Chapter 11. By experiencing the Goddess within your heart and your inner journeys to her temple you are internalising the shrine. You become the temple wherein the Goddess dwells.

You can also utilise a mantra, a short phrase which is repeated over and over again aloud or in the mind. This can be a traditional one, such as a title of the Goddess, her name or one created by yourself. You may wish to read and meditate on the great love stories of history, myth and legend using this as impetus to inspire your love for her. Read these, placing yourself in the position of the lover and the Goddess as your beloved.

6 Resistances. Expect to encounter all manner of these! Both outer and inner distractions will tempt you to drop the devotions. Remember that there is no such thing as coincidence and although hard to overcome, overcome them you must and continue the operation as you have pledged. You will also pass through a period of intense 'dryness', the Aphosis stage referred to back in Chapter 1. This is a good sign as it is the death that precedes your rebirth into the Goddess.

7 Ending. You may wish to complete the operation by a few days of retreat where you simply focus on the Goddess

of people I have known to do this operation have chosen one of the Festival Days as the end marker and combined their completion with the Festival celebrations. Others have used the completion day for their formal ordination or to acknowledge in some other way the union they have experienced.

However, once your pledged time is over, do not continue with the rituals and devotions. If necessary, close or cover the shrine for a lunar cycle and busy yourself with other tasks. Return to it once you have re-entered your normal life and integrated the experience. The point here is to avoid the devotion becoming an obsession.

The seed will have been planted; you will know when the germination occurs. Look for the green shoots of new ideas, new creativity: a new awareness. The Goddess will then become an integral and living presence within your life. She will bestow her blessings upon you and while you walk with her, you shall be clothed in her radiance. This is a tangible quality and the sign of a True Priestess or Priest who serves in her Name.

Resource List

When writing to individuals and organisations, please enclose a stamped, self-addressed envelope or, if overseas, an international reply paid coupon.

The Fellowship of Isis, Foundation Centre, Clonegal Castle, Enniscorthy, Co Wexford, Eire.

Welcoming all who venerate the Goddess in her many forms. Worldwide organisation with active priesthood, centres, temples and shrines. Publishing quarterly newsletter for members as well as many other publications.

The Lyceum of Isis-Sophia of the Stars, BM STARGATE, London WC1N 3XX England.

Details available of training workshops given by the author in collaboration with others of the College of Isis. A new correspondence course exploring the 'mysteries of the Goddess of the Dragon and the Dove' is being developed by Vivienne and Crys O'Regan.

The House of Net, BCM Box 6812, London WC1N 3XX England.

Offering a priestess-training programme combining correspondence course with workshops.

The Pagan Federation, PO Box 7097, London WC1N 3XX, England.

Long established pagan organisation. Offers regional contact among members.

Matriarchy Newsletter, 114 Hill Crest, Sevenoaks, Kent, England.

Feminist newsletter about the Goddess and Goddess groups in Britain.

Arcania, 17 Union Passage, Bath, Avon BA1 1RE, England.

Regularly offers courses with respect to women's and men's mysteries, Celtic and Western Magical Tradition. Write for catalogue.

The Covenant of the Goddess, P.O. Box 1226, Berkeley, CA 94704, USA.

A national organisation of cross-traditional Wiccan and other Goddess-worshipping groups.

Circle Network News, PO Box 219, Mt. Horeb, WI 53572, USA.

Long-running Wiccan and Pagan journal which contains notices of gatherings and training workshops.

Bibliography and
Books of Interest

Anderson, Marianne and Savary, Louis *Passages: A Guide for Pilgrims of the Mind* (Turnstone Press 1974)

Andrews, Ted *Imagick: The Magick of Images, Paths and Dance* (Llewellyn 1989)

Apuleius *The Golden Ass* (translated by Robert Graves) (Penguin Classics 1976)

Ashcroft-Nowicki, Dolores *Highways of the Mind: The Art and History of Pathworking* (Aquarian Press 1987)

—— *Inner Landscapes: A Journey Into Awareness by Pathworking* (Aquarian Press 1989)

—— *The Shining Paths: An Experiential Journey through the Tree of Life* (Aquarian Press 1983)

Ashe, Geoffrey *The Virgin* (Paladin 1977)

Assagioli, Roberto *Psychosynthesis: A Manual of Principles and Techniques* (Penguin Books 1980)

—— *Psychosynthesis Typology* (Psychosynthesis Monographs 1983)

Austin, Hallie Inglehart *The Heart of the Goddess: Art, Myth and Meditations of the World's Sacred Feminine* (Wingbow Press 1990)

Baring, Anne and Cashford, Jules *The Myth of the Goddess: Evolution of an Image* (Viking Arkana 1991)

Berger, Pamela *The Goddess Obscured: Transformation of the Grain Protectoress from Goddess to Saint* (Robert Hale 1988)

Berne, Eric *A Layman's Guide to Psychiatry and Psychoanalysis* (Penguin 1986)

Boadella, David *Lifestreams: An Introduction to Biosynthesis* (Routledge & Kegan Paul 1987)

Bolon, Jean Shinoda *Goddesses in Everywoman* (Harper & Row 1984)

Bonowitz, Ra *Cosmic Crystals* (Aquarian Press, 1983)

—— *The Crystal Heart* (Aquarian Press, 1989)

Bradley, Marion Zimmer *The Firebrand* (Michael Joseph 1988)

—— *The House Between the Worlds* (Ballantine Books 1980)

—— *The Mists of Avalon* (Alfred Knopf Inc 1982)

Brennon, J.H. *Astral Doorways* (Samuel Weiser Inc 1971)

Branston, Brian *The Lost Gods of England* (Thames & Hudson 1974)

Budapest, Z. *The Grandmother of Time: A Women's Book of Celebrating Spells and Sacred Objects for Every Month of the Year* (Harper & Row 1989)

Budge, E.A. Wallis *The Gods of the Egyptians* Vols 1 & 2 (Dover Press 1969)

Butler, E. *The Magician, His Training and Work* (Aquarian Press 1972)

Campbell, Joseph *The Power of Myth* (Doubleday 1988)

Carr-Gom, Philip *The Elements of Druid Tradition* (Element Books 1991)

Cox, David *How Your Mind Works: An Introduction to the Psychology of C.G. Jung* (Teach Yourself Books, Hodder & Stoughton 1973)

Crowley, Aleister *Magick* (Samuel Weiser 1973)

—— *Magical and Philosophical Commentaries on the Books of the Law* (93 Publishing, 1974)

Cunningham, Scott *Encyclopedia of Crystal, Gem and Metal Magic* (Llewellyn Publications 1988)

—— *Encyclopedia of Magical Herbs* (Llewellyn 1988)

—— *Magic of Incense, Oils and Brews* (Llewellyn 1986)

D'Alviella, Goblet *The Mysteries of Eleusis* (Aquarian Press 1981)

Denning, Melita and Phillips, Osborne *The Magical Philosophy: Vol 1 Robe and Ring* (Llewellyn Publications 1974)

Downing, Christine *The Goddess: Mythological Images of the Feminine* (Crossroad Publishing 1988)

Durdin-Robertson, Lawrence *The Year of the Goddess: A Perpetual Calendar of Festivals* (Aquarian Press 1990)

—— *Idols, Images and Symbols of the Goddesses: Egypt Parts I–III* (Cesara Publications 1979)

Faraday, Ann *The Dream Game* (Temple Smith 1975)

—— *Dream Power* (Berkeley Books 1980)

Farrar, Janet and Stewart *The Witches' Goddess: The Feminine*

Principle of Divinity (Robert Hale 1987)

—— *Eight Sabbats for Witches* (Robert Hale 1989)

Ferrucci, Piero *What We May Be: The Visions and Techniques of Psychosynthesis* (Turnstone Press 1982)

Fortune, Dion *Applied Magic* and *Aspects of Occultism* (Aquarian Press 1987)

—— *The Goat Foot God* (Aquarian 1989)

—— *Moon Magic* (Aquarian Press 1989)

—— *The Mystical Qabalah* (Aquarian Press 1987)

—— *Sane Occultism* and *Practical Occultism in Daily Life* (Aquarian Press 1987)

—— *The Sea Priestess* (Aquarian Press 1989)

Freud, Sigmund *The Interpretation of Dreams* (Allen & Unwin 1967)

—— *An Outline of Psychoanalysis* (Norton Press 1949)

Gadon, Elinor *The Once and Future Goddess* (Harper & Row 1989)

Garfield, Patricia *Creative Dreaming* (Simon & Schuster 1974)

Gilchrist, Cherry *The Circle of Nine: Understanding the Feminine Psyche* (Dryad Press 1988)

Greene, Liz *Relating: an Astrological Guide to Living With Others on a Small Planet* (Coventure Ltd 1977)

Grian, Sinead Sula *Brighde Goddess of Fire* (Brighde's Fire 1985)

Grof, Stanislav *The Adventure of Self-Discovery* (State University of New York State Press 1988)

Grof, Stanislav and Halifax, Joan *The Human Encounter with Death* (E P Dutton, 1977)

Gunther, Bernard *Energy Ecstasy and Your Seven Vital Chakras* (The Guild of Tutors Press, USA)

Hall, Manley Palmer *The Secret Teachings of All Ages* (The Philosophical Research Society Inc 1962)

Hall, Nora *The Moon and the Virgin* (Harper & Row 1980)

Hampden-Turner, Charles *Maps of the Mind* (Mitchell Beazley, 1981)

Harding, M. Ester *Women's Mysteries: Ancient and Modern* (Rider & Co 1982)

Hardy, Jean *A Psychology With a Soul: Pyschosynthesis in Evolutionary Context* (Routledge & Kegan Paul 1987)

Hart, George *Egyptian Gods and Goddess* (Routledge, Kegan & Paul)

Hoffman, Enid *Huna: A Beginners Guide* (Para Research, USA 1976)

Hope, Murry *Ancient Egypt: The Sirius Connection* (Element 1990)

—— *The Psychology of Healing* (Element 1989)

—— *The Psychology of Ritual* (Element 1988)

—— *Practical Atlantean Magic* (Aquarian 1992)

—— *Practical Celtic Magic* (Aquarian Press, 1987)

—— *Practical Egyptian Magic* (Aquarian Press, 1984)

—— *Practical Greek Magic* (Aquarian 1985)

Humphrey, Naomi *Meditation: The Inner Way* (Aquarian Press 1987)

Ions, Veronica *Egyptian Mythology* (Newnes Books 1972)

Johnson, Buffie *Lady of the Beasts: Ancient Images of the Goddess and Her Sacred Animals* (HarperCollins 1988)

Jones, Kathy *The Ancient British Goddess* (Ariadne Publications 1991)

Kaplan-Williams, Strephon *The Dreamwork Manual* (Aquarian Press 1984)

—— *The Elements of Dreamwork* (Element Books 1990)

King, Francis *Tantra for Westerners* (Aquarian Press 1986)

Knight, Gareth *The Magical World of the Inklings* (Element Books 1990)

—— *The Rose Cross and the Goddess* (Aquarian Press 1985)

Le Shan, Lawrence *How to Meditate* (Turnstone Press Ltd 1983)

Leland, Charles *Aradia: the Gospel of the Witches* (Gates of Annwn 1991)

Lemesurier, Peter *Healing of the Gods: the Magic of Symbols and Practice of Theotherapy* (Element Books, 1988)

Long, Asphodel 'The Goddess in Judaism' from *The Absent Mother: Restoring the Goddess to Judaism and Christianity* (ed Pirani, Alix) (Mandala 1991)

Mairowitz, David Zane and Gonzales, German *Reich For Beginners* (Writers & Readers Documentary Comic Book in assoc. with Unwin Paperbacks 1986)

Masters, Robert and Houston, Jean *Mind Games: The Guide to Inner Space* (Turnstone Books 1973)

—— *The Varieties of Psychedelic Experience* (Turnstone Books 1966)

Masters, Robert *The Goddess Sekhmet: The Way of Five Bodies* (Amity House 1986)

Matthews, Caitlín *The Elements of the Goddess* (Element Books, 1989)
—— *The Elements of Celtic Tradition* (Element Books 1990)
—— *Sophia, Goddess of Wisdom* (Mandala 1991)
—— *Voices of the Goddess: A Chorus of Sibyls* (Aquarian Press 1990)
Matthews, John and Caitlín *Hallowquest: Tarot Magic and the Arthurian Mysteries* (Aquarian Press 1990)
—— *The Western Way* Vols 1 & 2 (Arkana 1987)
McCrickard, Janet *Eclipse of the Sun Gothic* (Image Publications, 1990)
McLean, Adam *The Triple Goddess* (Hermetic Research Series No 1 1983)
Mookerjee, Ajit *Kali: The Feminine Force* (Thames & Hudson 1988)
Monagham, Patricia *Women in Myth and Legend* (Junction Books 1981)
Mountainwater, Shekinah *Ariadne's Thread: A Workbook of Goddess Magic* (The Crossing Press 1991)
Ozaniec, Naomi *The Elements of the Chakras* (Element Books 1990)
Parfitt, Will *The Elements of Psychosynthesis* (Element Books, 1990)
—— *The Elements of the Qabalah* (Element Books 1991)
—— *The Living Qabalah* (Element Books 1988)
Pennick, Nigel *Practical Magic in the Northern Tradition* (Aquarian 1989)
Perrera, Sylvia Brinton *Descent to the Goddess* (Inner City Books 1981)
Rainwater, Janette *You're In Charge* (Turnstone Press, 1981); reissued as *Self-Therapy: A Guide to Becoming Your Own Therapist* (Crucible 1989)
Regardie, F.I. 'The Art of True Healing' within *Foundations of Practical Magic* (Aquarian Press 1979)
Reed, Ellen Cannon *The Goddess and the Tree: The Witches Qabala* (Llewellyn 1990)
Richardson, Alan *Dancers to the Gods* (Aquarian Press 1985)
—— *Introduction to the Mystical Qabalah* (Pathways to Inner Power Series, Aquarian Press).
—— *Priestess: The Life and Magic of Dion Fortune* (Aquarian Press 1987)
Robertson, Olivia *DEA: Rites and Mysteries of the Goddess*

(Cesara Publications, 3rd Impression 1988)
—— *Gaea: Initiations of the Earth* (Cesara Publications 1991)
—— *Ordination of Priestess and Priests* (Cesara Publications)
—— *Pantheia: Initiations and Festivals of the Goddess* (Cesara Publications 1988)
—— *Rite of Rebirth* (Cesara Publications)
—— *Sophia: Cosmic Consciousness of the Goddess* (Cesara Publiscations, 1986)
—— *Sybil: Oracles of the Goddess* (Cesara Publications 1989)
—— *Urania: Ceremonial Magic of the Goddess* (Cesara Publications, 1983)
Rowling, J. Thompson 'The Rise and Decline of Surgery in Dynastic Egypt' (*Antiquity* Magazine No 63, 1989)
St. George, E.A. *Cat Worship Ancient and Modern* (Spook Enterprises 1981)
—— *Under Regulus: A Handbook of the Magic of Sekhmet* (Spook Enterprises 1985)
Scott, Mary *Kundalini in the Physical World* (Routledge & Kegan Paul 1983)
Shuttle, Penelope and Redgrove, Peter *The Wise Wound: Menstruation and Everywoman* (Paladin 1978, revised edition 1986)
Sjöö, Monica and Mor, Barbara *The Great Cosmic Mother: Rediscovering the Religion of the Earth* (Harper & Row 1987)
Starhawk *Dreaming the Dark* (Beacon Press, 1982; new edition Mandala 1990)
—— *The Spiral Dance: A Rebirth of the Ancient Religion of the Great Goddess* (Harper & Row 1979)
—— *Truth or Dare* (Harper & Row, 1987)
Stein, Diane *The Goddess Book of Days* (Llewellyn 1988)
—— *The Women's Book of Healing* (Llewellyn 1987)
—— *The Women's Spirituality Book* (llewellyn 1987)
Steinbrecher, Edwin C. *The Inner Guide Meditation* 6th Edition (Aquarian Press 1988)
Stepanich, Kisma *The Gaia Tradition: Celebrating the Earth in Her Seasons* (Llewellyn 1991)
Stewart, R.J. *Robert Kirk: Walker Between the Worlds* (Element Books 1990)
—— *The Underworld Initiation* (Aquarian 1985)
—— *The Waters of the Gap* (Arcania 1989)
Stone, Merlin *Ancient Mirrors of Womanhood: Our Goddess and Heroine Heritage* Vols 1 & 2 (New Sibylline Books 1979)

—— *When God Was a Woman* (Harcourt Brace Jovanovich 1976); also known as *The Paradise Papers* (Virago Press)

Sunflower 'The Path of the Solar Priestess' from *Voices of the Goddess* edited by Caitlín Matthews (Aquarian 1990)

Taylor, Jeremy *Dream Work: Techniques for Discovering the Creative Power in Dreams* (Paulist Press 1983)

Tolkien, J.R.R. *The Silmarillion* (George Allen & Unwin 1977)

Vernon-Jones, Vivienne 'A Search for the Beloved' from *Voices of the Goddess* (Aquarian Press 1990)

Vernon-Jones, Vivienne *The Way of the Star* Papers 1–19 (Lyceum of Isis-Sophia of the Stars 1986–90)

Versluis, Arthur *The Egyptian Mysteries* (Arkana 1988)

Walker, Barabra *The Book of Sacred Stones* (Harper & Row 1989)

—— *The Crone: Woman of Age, Wisdom and Power* (HarperCollins 1985)

—— *The Women's Encyclopedia of Myths and Secrets* (HarperCollins 1983)

Whitmont, Edward C. *Return of the Goddess* (Routledge & Kegan Paul 1983)

Wilber, Ken *Up from Eden: A Transpersonal View of Human Evolution* (Routledge & Kegan Paul 1981)

Witt, R.E. *Isis in the Graeco-Roman World* (Thames & Hudson 1971)

Wolkstein, Diane, and Kramer, Samuel Noah *Inanna: Queen of Heaven and Earth* (Harper & Row 1983)

Wombwell, Felicity *The Goddess Changes* (Mandala 1991)

Index